autobiography of a
BABY BOOMER

robert schultz, md

www.lightmessages.com

Copyright© 2012, by Robert Schultz, MD

Robert Schultz, MD
rschultz@lightmessages.com
rschultz.lightmessages.com

Published 2013 by Light Messages Publishing
Printed in the United States of America
ISBN: 978-1-61153-049-0

To Mom, Dad, Helaine;
my first family, the one into which I was born
and
To Debbie, Eric, Stephanie, Morgan;
the family I was blessed to help create.

Contents

Acknowledgments

Without the encouragement of family and friends like Carol Stanziale, Carl Waldman, Marta Leipzig, Elliott Brown, and Peter Peuler who knew of and showed fascination with my personal odyssey, I might have gone silently to my grave, never disclosing those special memories of the very sexy '60s and '70s. Despite my wife Debbie's dissimulation of my formative years, Eric, Stephanie, and Morgan would not let such tales disappear. "Hippies", "India", "Jail" were words that could not be forgotten. One story at bedtime led to another and pleas for just one more. The probing finally frenzied into my belief that I had a worthy (okay, freaky) story to tell.

How to present it, however, was not easily forthcoming. Toying with the idea of a novel based on truth seemed more like a cop-out based on fear that a memoir would be too narcissistic. Lacking celebrity status could well mean that no one other than family and a few friends would have any interest. But, then it dawned on me that *Autobiography of a*

Baby Boomer is about an era and a (medical) profession that are filled with nostalgia and entertainment.

All of us post-war Baby Boomers deserve credit for being so massive in number and so resilient in spirit that we have, by our very nature, exciting stories to tell. *Autobiography of a Baby Boomer* is just one of them.

If not for Pat (Paladino) Tanis introducing me to Tom Dust (Dusty Roads Media) this work might never have made it into eBook form and subsequently come to the attention of Elizabeth Turnbull, Senior Editor of Light Messages who recognized its worth and brought *Autobiography of a Baby Boomer* to life in print.

Thanks to Scott and Jill Sample and again to Pat Tanis and Carol Stanziale for their Beta testing, and to Light Messages for preventing me from looking like a rank amateur.

Preface

The Great War is over. Economic prosperity begins. The transistor is born along with more babies than our nation has ever seen. One of them is me, fresh out of the Blizzard of '47, and ready to jump into the perfect life of the 1950's: TV, bobby sox, and the birth of Rock 'n Roll. *The Life of Riley* until the '60's warps it all into revolution and psychedelic euphoria.

Somerset Maugham's *The Razor's Edge* becomes reality as I leave the confines of Cornell University Medical School to explore the first half of the 1970's across four continents. I am not alone. Many of my fellow Westerners, from North America and Europe, join the "Road People" seeking mysteries only the East can reveal.

Though totally vulnerable I am blinded by the enchantment of youth and immortality. Miracles occur that carry me around the world physically and evolve me spiritually so that when I land back in the safe haven of Fair Lawn, New Jersey I am no longer the naïve pilgrim or cynical egotist (with $100 in his pocket) that left his parents at the airport, refusing their desperate plea to accept their monetary assistance.

Through no simple logic (rarely a trait of us post-war Baby Boomers) I resume my medical training (for all the wrong reasons) and actually become a Harvard trained orthopaedic surgeon, eventually settling down to career and family in the 1980's and 90's.

But the spirit lives on though the outward accomplishments of stature and wealth seemingly mask its fiery flame. My approach to life's vicissitudes is deeply flavored by an acceptance and welcoming of the ebb and flow that each new decade brings. I yearn to pass this discovery on to my children, but know that they must make their own journey and, hopefully, survive in a much more complex world.

The new millennium brings forth a barrage of information that leaves little time for existential thinking. Because of this we Boomers have much more work to do than did our parents. Pick-up games and drive-ins are now organized sports and interactive warfare. TVs that stopped broadcasting at 9:00 PM are now computers with a 24/7/365 blitzkrieg including hard-core porn. The quiet sanctuary of the library is replaced by Google/Bing (anywhere; anytime).

Is this the way our parents saw *our* generation? Perhaps?

Some accuse us Boomers of being spoiled brats; that the Greatest Generation (before us) provided too much security and pampering. But I am part of a hardy lot, living longer and stronger, embellished by sixty years of remarkable change.

Excited to keep up the vigil, I look forward to what each

new decade brings. Come along with me on a journey back through our era and see if my life to date is not a lot like yours.

Part One

CHAPTER 1

Twelve Days in Hell and the Sanctuary of my Mind

Germany was one thing; Turkey another; but this absolutely freaks me out. The 9x12 foot cell (I have plenty of time to get exact measurements) is entirely empty with the exception of two emaciated Afghan prisoners sitting comfortably on their haunches, obnoxiously amused at my inability to assume their pose. The slime all over the floor and walls of this putrid box prohibits sitting or leaning like the Westerner I am. A faucet, no more than a foot off the ground near a hole for defecating, is encrusted with mold and is the only structure, besides the hole and door, which change the monotonous rectangular dimensions of this shithole. My fellow cellmates most certainly do not speak English and are unnervingly content to communicate their excitement through constant eye gaze. I am their new entertainment and am thoroughly screwed!

How I got through the night is unclear, but my right side

is slippery and my matted clothes smell of methane. The only way I know it is daytime is because the well-armed, wretched prison guard just led me out past the heavy wood door (with a hole in the center, no larger than a baseball catcher's mask complete with iron bars for further security— as if someone could actually squeeze through the frickin' opening) for twenty minutes of exercise in the courtyard. In order to see the sky I had to look straight up, *a la* New York City but without a sole around except for the malodorous goon who obviously enjoys his work. Problem is, when I got back to my cell the overpowering smell of stale urine brought me to my knees. Guess I got used to the stench a few hours after being locked up. If my olfactory system can cope, maybe the rest of my brain can, too. But at this point, I'm not really sure.

Now, all I have is plenty of time to think…that's all I have…time to think.

Damn! Damn! Damn it! My parents were right. I'm a stupid naive punk; in over my head. Nirvana? You can't be serious, Bob. What were you thinking? That the world was out there for the taking? That your ridiculous questions about other dimensions and the spirit world would simply be answered by venturing out? Be honest. It was as much about having a good time: drugs, free love and adventure as it was about God. And now this might be the end; right here in this piece of shit jail in a God-forsaken country. Dad knew I threw my medical career away. I can't imagine his disappointment and Mom's devastation when they hear about my pitiful death in an Afghan prison.

***

The walls are closing in. I can hardly breathe. I was being choked by my own thoughts as I lay in my studio apartment in Olin Hall, the medical school dormitory on 70th Street and York Avenue across from The New York Hospital in New York City (home of Cornell University Medical College). Gimillie, my cat, sensed my terror and forced her way under my arm as I lay on the bed in a sweat. *Is she supersensitive? Are all animals this way? Or is she just anxious to be stroked?* She was, nevertheless, my savior; as she had been every time I got down like this. If it weren't for her and the basketball court downstairs in the basement I'd have gone nuts! The nightly pick-up games gave me an endorphin rush that got me through to morning. But for the most part, I was just plain miserable being locked away in medical school after being free; truly free for the first time in my life that summer of '69.

***

Robert Buchanan, dean of Cornell Medical School, was a tall, debonair leonine figure who drove a De Lorean DMC-12. Our first session was abbreviated when his secretary interrupted to remind him of his very important meeting with the school chancellor. I could, nevertheless, see that my cry for help registered concern enough for him to schedule another opportunity for us to meet. That time he made sure we were not disturbed.

"There is something more out there than just this. There has to be. I am sure of it." My words must have sounded so foolish and naïve to this man of science, but, thank God, Dr. Buchanan's face spoke otherwise. With a gentle smile he walked over to the bookshelf and handed me *The Razor's*

Edge by Somerset Maugham. "Here son, read this; but don't let it interfere with your studies. We'll meet again next month."

The story is of a young man, Larry Darrell, who rejects conventional life in search for more meaningful experience, taking him to India and back. He eventually thrives while other, more materialistic characters in the book suffer from the berating vicissitudes of life. Not a particularly fast reader, I devoured the book in a couple of days. *Why, on earth, would my dean give me this to read? It doesn't make sense. Isn't his job to keep me on the straight and narrow? As a man of science, shouldn't he be contemptuous of the mystical?*

My parents, of course, were constantly in touch with school authorities pleading for help for their misguided, but "brilliant" son who had so much going for him and was about to throw it all away! "Speak with the dean. Get counseling. The first year is always the hardest." Their pleas tore me apart and kept me away from home in Jersey to avoid confrontation with them. Mom handed me an unopened (luckily) envelope from the German government containing a letter summarizing my mishap in Lorrach the previous August and the fact that I was no longer welcome back to their country. Had she known her Bobby was in jail (though even for one night) she most certainly would have been impossible to deal with.

My next meeting with Dr. Buchanan was a shocker. He unequivocally admitted that he admired my curiosity and, most of all, my opportunity to explore the world. "I am dean of this medical school, married with three children, and bound with endless responsibilities." I could see the earnestness in his eyes. "You are inquisitive and adventurous.

Most importantly, this is your time. I envy you." I was at a loss for words. All at once he had unburdened me and given me permission to follow my heart. "But," he added sternly, "if you ever tell anyone what I have said, including your parents, I will deny every word of it." I managed a joyful, teary-eyed "Thank you" as I left his office.

The game plan became: finish out the year in good stead as were the wishes of my parents and the dean. A year's leave-of-absence would be granted me even though I had no intention of using the time as a sabbatical. No indeed, I was hell-bent on making a clean break. I wanted no safety net. I was giving up the prospect of becoming a conventional medical doctor for the possibility of finding some real answers. This might well take the rest of my life; not simply one year.

Once the decision was made and my parents were on board (though "silently" kicking and screaming) I was able to get through the next several months without those damn choking attacks. I still made weekend visits up to Boston to see Marta, and she and my local friends from college visited me in the City. It was a mob scene at the Ziegfeld Theater waiting in line to see the documentary *Woodstock*. At the ticket counter Marta and I were shocked to hear that the charge was $5.00. I handed over the five bucks and the cat behind the window smugly said, "Aren't you bringing your chick?" I almost dropped a load when I got his drift that **each** ticket was $5.00! Being a real sport, I came up with another five despite the fact that sweet Marta offered to pay her own way. She was always like that. The movie was awe-inspiring. Completely different from what I had heard while on the island of Formentera. Billed as a wash-out of the worst magnitude my friends Billy, "California" Jim, and I were happy to have missed the disaster.

After seeing *Woodstock* I couldn't help telling Marta, again, about the full moon party on Formentera that took place at the same time the festival at Yazger's farm was happening. And, again, she seemed terribly bummed-out because it was something we hadn't shared together. My big *faux pas*; so we got stoned on some sensemilia and I decided to give her a special treat. I took her over to the cadaver lab to meet Hitchcock. "Breath through your mouth," I said in response to her complaints about the smell. The morgue-like presence of all the draped bodies freaked her out a bit, but not half as much as when I pulled the sheet off of Hitchcock. We had been working on his digestive system the whole week and I guess the exposed abdominal contents just took the legs right out from under her. I managed to sit her down with her head bent low between her knees. "I'm okay. I'm okay," she whispered through her hyperventilation. Always the good sport, she eventually struggled to her feet, as I sensed that we had better cut short the anatomy lesson.

***

Christ! What are you looking at? I don't belong here with you mindless Afghani scum! I'm a clean, good person. I did nothing wrong. Say something, you animals! Tell me to go to hell! Damn it.

It is two days before J.G. manages to find out my location and gets permission to come see me. Making no attempt to keep my cool, I press my face painfully up against the bars as I hear him approach. His inappropriate grin and lame joke about my "looking like Yogi Berra taking one off the face mask" are totally annoying.

"Get me the hell out of here! I'm going nuts!"

He seems to reel back as he gets close to the cell door; no doubt the penetrating smell of rancid piss is the cause. In his unshakable laid-back style, he tells me that the boy I hit ("That punk ran into me!" I yell through the catcher's mask) happens to be the little brother of the Commandant. His leg is broken and I am to remain in jail until it heals.

"You've got to be kidding!" I rant. "Where the hell is the U.S. Ambassador or Consul? I'm a United States citizen!"

J.G. calmly tries to explain that he found me through the U.S. Embassy and they are working on getting me freed. "How can you stand that smell?" he has the nerve to ask.

Looking around curiously, he then passes me a folded piece of paper through the catcher's mask. "I'll be back tomorrow and every day you're in here until this thing is over. Don't worry, I'm working on it." The sadness is gut wrenchingly painful as the guard pulls him away and all I see is the back of J.G.'s long curly hair. I am emotionally eviscerated; my guts ripped out by the thought of an impotent state department that cares little for a foolish hippy who got himself thrown into a snake pit instead of safely remaining at home.

***

J.G. and I met at a Hamilton College house party in '67. Jimmy (aka, J.G.) and Mitch both grew up in Glen Cove, Long Island. Mitch came to Hamilton in '65 while J.G. went to Harvard on a baseball scholarship. Being left-handed, with an 85 mph fastball (and one of the rare financially challenged kids from Glen Cove) he was warmly accepted to our country's most prestigious academic institution. He continued to get "full ride" academic aid even after his arm gave out in the spring of his sophomore year.

Having lost the love of his life when his two young sons were not quite teenagers, J.G.'s father never remarried and struggled with depression. How on earth J.G. got his perpetual smile and easy nature is a testimony to his old man's fortitude and inner strength. Whatever the case, "Lefty" and I were instant friends. By the next year I was making regular road trips up to Boston to visit Marta (who had just entered her freshman year at Simmons College) and crashing at J.G.'s dorm room in Dunster House at Harvard. Al and Tommy, J.G.'s roommates, had no problem with me staying in their pad. After an afternoon of Ultimate Frisbee along the Charles, we would bring in Chinese or pizza, get stoned, play albums, and philosophize all night long. J.G. was always the last to crash and the first up in the morning, often with coffee and bagels for us lazy schleps.

More solo than not, J.G. never had apprehension about hanging with Marta and me. The concerts at the Filmore East in New York City (Richie Havens, The Chamber Brothers, Sly and the Family Stone); those at the Capitol Theater in Passaic, New Jersey (The Band, Buffalo Springfield, Steve Miller Band); the unforgettable summer at the Newport Folk Festival (Janis Joplin and Big Brother), and our trip to Billy's Island were dynamite.

Billy's parents owned a small, but magnificent island in Upper Saranac Lake. It was a beatific spot that God reserves for the lucky few. This time the lucky ones were Billy and Jeannine, Carl and Molly, Marta and me, Peter, Og, and J.G. (these guys were simply solo, not gay). We spent several unforgettable days canoeing, water skiing, doing group yoga, getting wrecked and watching the sun set. Aside from a bruise I suffered on my hip from getting accidentally knocked out of a stall shower by Marta, it was totally far-out! Unencumbered by responsibility and inhibited only by our own innate sense of morality we talked of love and peace and hope. We were flower children living in the now—at least for a few fantastic days.

***

Temporarily stupefied with nostalgia, and full of self-pity, I suddenly remember the folded paper J.G. managed to slip me when the guard wasn't looking. An escape plan, maybe? Some word of encouragement that this nightmare is coming to an end? No; not a note at all. Instead, I find that it contains about a gram of Raymond's white powder. When put to the test, this stuff absolutely makes a dope out of me. Magic up my nose instantly changes my hell into heaven; a testimony to the ultimate inherent danger of this junk. Far better than any opium dream I can imagine.

***

"Wow" is what I remember shouting at that stellar moment ("awesome" had not yet come into vogue) when I caught sight of the field at Yankee Stadium in the spring of 1952. The image is indelibly blazoned on that part of my cerebral cortex reserved for the spectacular: my first childhood memory. (Although I do recall being told to blow the ether soaked gauze away, and feeling absolutely terrified that I could not, just before they fixed my inguinal hernia)! I was five years old.

(The discussion of our earliest memories comes up every year or two at the dinner table. My family's recollections change as often as the menus, but mine is fixed on the vastness of the rich green grass of the outfield and the sharp contrast of the perfect diamond cradled like a jewel in the apex of the bleach-white foul lines that seem to stretch forever out to the foul poles rising majestically toward the sky.)

Mickey Mantle, every boy's hero, roamed center field after taking over for recently retired "Joltin" Joe DiMaggio. The hot dogs and mustard tasted better than anywhere else—even better than Toby's Grill in Paterson. Being with my dad—both of us with baseball mitts, in hope of catching a home run ball—was special, particularly because he was usually at the office or hospital. Doctoring was his life, and when he came home he was so tired that he'd fall asleep on the couch.

Unfortunately, a nine-inning baseball game was far too boring for a five year old kid who didn't get to play catch or at least run the bases. With no sign of my friends from Ferry Heights in Fair Lawn, whose dad, Gene "Rock" Woodling, just happened to play left field for the New York Yankees, I soon tired and fell asleep by the fourth inning. Having paid good money for the tickets, Dad was not about to miss the rest of the game. He padded my head with a "pillow" made out of my glove wrapped in my Yankees jacket (which I insisted on wearing despite the warm weather that day) and made do. Of course, the Yankees beat the Washington Senators, and it was I who got to tell Mom the score when we arrived home. Dad swore he wouldn't mention that I fell asleep.

I have always been proud that I did not simply jump on the winning Yankees' bandwagon, but became a Yankee fan for the right reason: my playmates' dad wore pinstripes! He actually gave me an autographed ball, fully signed by all the players on the 1952 club. Unfortunately, I played with that ball, as I would woefully regret nearly twenty years later when I found it in my parents' basement.

The rest of 1952 was not very vivid except, of course, for the excitement of a new toy, Mr. Potato Head, which allowed me to play with food and not get yelled at. Oh yeah, and that permeating smell of the ether soaked gauze that the hernia doctor held over my nose and told me to blow away: I tried; I really did, but the terror of not being able to make it go away still haunts me. I remember Mom telling me that I got the scar in my groin from that surgery when I was three. That would make it 1950. Weird; so maybe my first memory wasn't Yankee Stadium at all. I guess profound fear trumps ecstasy (though both share indelible data ports in my brainy cortex).

I certainly do not remember that in 1952 Queen Elizabeth II was proclaimed Queen of the United Kingdom upon the death of her father George VI; that *The Diary of Anne Frank* was published; that the B-52 Stratofortress made its first flight; or that 1952 was the year traffic lights were installed in New York City.

The blazing mushroom that lit up our Dumont TV (a huge box with a tiny screen) in 1952 and the sound that shook our den is not forgettable despite the lack of color or surround sound. It was the detonation of the first hydrogen bomb, by the United States at Enewetok Atoll in the Marshall Islands of the Pacific Ocean. Pride (that we were the most powerful nation on earth) and fear (that my family and I might die in a nuclear war) filled my entire day. There was no reassurance when, at St. Anne's Nursery School on Broadway in Fair Lawn, "milk and cookies time" was interrupted by an air-raid drill. Filing down to the basement and putting our heads between our legs was scary at first, but eventually morphed into a session of ponytail pulling and girl teasing. Movies that showed how to set up and stock a bomb shelter made me wonder what I would find outside after the explosion. Would everything be sizzling? Would there be any people? Would I have to learn Russian?

General Dwight D. Eisenhower, who led the Allies to victory over Germany and the Axis powers, was running for President of the United States. The newsreels and TV documentaries of the five star general, in combat gear, liberating Europe were really cool. So when I came home sporting a big "I Like Ike" badge, I was surprised when Mom sat me down, unpinned the badge and explained to me why Governor Adlai E. Stevenson (the Democratic nominee and "true intellectual") was the better man for the job. Although Dad sat there, totally noncommittal, he was anxious to hear how the Democratic Governor would help him keep more money in his pocket than the Republican General.

Mom was a Democrat all the way. This clearly dated back to her undying devotion to Franklin D. Roosevelt, whose New Deal policy Mom attributed to ending the Great Depression. The fact that FDR was a womanizer might well have aborted her loyalty, but "back in the day" reporting on such personal escapades was considered taboo. The fact that my very traditional mother was able to overlook Kennedy's indiscretions cements, for me, her legacy as a die-hard

Democrat, despite her claim that she "votes for the man, not the Party." *Forgive me, Mom, if you somehow snuck in a vote for a Republican along the way.* In any event, General Eisenhower won the election (as well as the next in 1956) and for the next eight years we listened to Mom rant about how "he should be running the country instead of playing so much golf."

My Cousin Edna (Mom's first cousin and the sister of Cousin Bob, an FBI agent who told exciting spy stories and brought over very cool detective gadgets) was a hunchback polio victim with a cane and braces on her legs. She told me how lucky my sister and I were that we would never get polio now that Dr. Jonas Salk, at the University of Pittsburgh had developed a polio vaccine to protect us. It would soon be available to the public and Cousin Edna urged Mom to get us vaccinated as soon as possible. She pointed out that nearly 58,000 new cases of polio had been reported in the U.S. that year, with 3,142 deaths and 21,269 left with some form of paralysis. She was extremely bright and well read. A career woman, despite her severe physical handicap (which she called a "limitation"); she helped pioneer wheelchair access to government and commercial buildings. She proudly showed us her car outfitted with hand controls for delivering gas, braking, and facilitated steering. "No way is this quirky body going to inhibit my independence," she trumpeted.

I am grateful to Cousin Edna because she made it natural for me to look at the lame without bias, fear, or pity. Always willing to discuss her infirmities as if they were matter-of-fact attributes, I saw my aunt as a strong, self-reliant role model. As a little kid who was not that much shorter than she, I enjoyed her visits because she was that unique adult who showed a genuine interest in my point of view and opinions. I was really sad when her mom and constant companion, Aunt Mary, passed away. It signaled the end of those spirited off-the-cuff concerts when she used to play Gilbert and Sullivan on the piano and sing for my sister Helaine and me. Aunt Edna got old fast (and shorter) after that, but her eyes were always bright when she saw me. Her not-so-secret one-sided love affair with Dave Garroway, the host of the new *The Today Show* on NBC was legendary.

Cousin Bob, Edna's younger brother, was exciting because he was an FBI agent. But when I heard that he lied about being Jewish to get the job, I lost a lot of respect for him. Seems he worked in a post office during the war (WWII) and was brought to the attention of J. Edgar Hoover because of an idea he put in a suggestion box to make the department run more efficiently. Given the opportunity to join the Bureau (by first becoming an accountant or lawyer) Bob readily jumped at the chance. Whether he flat out denied or simply did not mention his Jewish background is unclear. In any event, he not only served in the FBI for decades, he went on to become a top executive in ITT (eventually its president) and later head of U.S. Customs under Secretary of State Blumenthal. While I am not a deeply religious Jew in the ritual sense, Bob's story of denial was never more poignant for me than in 1969 when my ethnicity was questioned by a prison guard in Germany.

***

We were making the trip back up the Costa Brava, through the south of France and into Switzerland on our way up to Holland to meet my girlfriend Marta in Amsterdam. There was only one hitch: as we crossed from Basel, Switzerland into Lorrach, Germany we were told to get out of our vehicle for a search by the border guards. Not surprisingly, they found a couple of pipes and some hashish. What was surprising was that they confiscated my van and threw us in jail! "California" Jim (who came along in anticipation of a high time in Amsterdam) told me that he heard that these European border towns were notorious for busting hippies in order to be paid off for their release.

Sure enough, after spending several hours in a rather comfortable cell (with a cot, sink and toilet) a guard came to interview me and mentioned that I could get out of prison by posting bail. While reviewing my passport, he asked me my religion. Without hesitation, I told him that I was Jewish. No way was I going to wimp out like my illustrious Cousin Bob. Suddenly the guard's grasp of the English language failed. "Hebrew," I said angrily, drawing the six pointed Star of David on a piece of paper. Incredulously, he still claimed not to understand. At this point I was livid (partly because I knew we were being detained for money and partly because this guy was playing with me). "Jewish, I am Jewish!" I shouted. "You killed six million of us, *kappish*? You know exactly what I mean!" Somehow my ranting got the attention of his superior who decided to let me, and only me, out in the morning with the stipulation that I obtain $1,000 per person for the release of my companions (Billy, Jim, Hannuke and Evoud) and my vehicle. That was a total of $5,000. Hannuke and Evoud, a beatific Dutch couple we picked up somewhere along the way, deserved better. Somehow, the fact that I was the most vocal of the inmates and the owner of the van made the German guards believe that I would accomplish the task and not simply run off, abandoning my comrades.

The next day I am ecstatic to have my freedom back. I mean, ecstatic! After some wild jumping around in the streets, and swearing that I would always remember how good it is to be free, I set out for the American Express office to contact Billy's parents, Jim's girlfriend back in the States, and Evoud's dad in Holland. Somehow, I managed to get $3,000 wired within a week. I had $500 from the Moroccan goods I had sent to Marta (who supposedly sold them to college friends of hers in Boston). I knew those crooked guards would settle for $3,500 to get rid of us. *Damn, I probably could have kept the $500...those pigs would have been happy with three grand.*

***

Prior to my first memory, my life was what my parents told me it was.

The storm was brutal with snow drifts up to the roof. The Northeast was paralyzed and Fair Lawn, New Jersey was buried that winter of '47. My mother, Edna, had not planned to breast feed me, but given the fact that no sane milkman would even think of working under these conditions she really had no choice. So much for the old saying: "March comes in like a lion and out like a lamb." This lamb showed its teeth clear into April!

We lived in the back of my dad's office. He was the only doctor in town and most of his colleagues wondered why he chose to practice out in the sticks instead of three miles west in the booming textile city of Paterson. The waterfalls from the Passaic River powered the mills and had made Paterson the richest city in North Jersey. Fair Lawn, located between it and New York City (twelve miles to the east), would not get a paved road or traffic light for several more years.

Mom took to watching *A Woman to Remember*, a soap opera (the first in the U.S.) that began that year. My dad had bought her a Dumont TV as a surprise when I finally came home from the hospital a couple of weeks after the delivery. I had developed erythroblastosis fetalis, a disease in which my red blood cells were being attacked and destroyed by my own mother's antibodies because of the unique difference in our blood types. I turned yellow almost immediately, but survived only because of a new technique called an exchange transfusion where my tainted blood was completely replaced with fresh donor blood. It was the first such procedure performed on the East coast and was filmed by *Life Magazine*; but Mom never let them publish this very personal and near tragic event.

I remember Dad telling me years later that the reason Mom was always so forgiving of every nasty thing I did was because she almost lost me at birth. My older sister, Helaine, had every right to resent such inequity, but for the most part, took it like a trooper. Although my parents planned on having a *Father Knows Best* sized family (three children with both sexes represented), they were warned not to have another child because of the blood type incompatibility. This, of course, gave even more impetus toward sparing the rod and spoiling the child. Being the baby, I received most of the spoils.

Television really "came into its own" in 1947. The opening session of Congress was televised and, along with the soap opera, the TV dinner was born. *Meet the Press* and *The Howdy Doody Show* debuted on NBC. Bell Laboratories developed a solid-state electronic component that they called the transistor. It would eventually make it possible for me and my friends to sneak into the boys' room at school and listen to the World Series on a tiny (transistor) radio. Rin Tin Tin (the German Sheppard wonder dog from the '20s and '30s) made a comeback in *The Return of Rin Tin Tin* starring alongside the very young Robert Blake. (*The Adventures of Rin Tin Tin* aired on TV from 1954 through 1959 and competed with *Lassie* for all of our dog lovers' hea rts.)

It was the year that Dad finally began to build a house on the property he had purchased in town a few years earlier. Since the family had grown to four, it was time to move out of the office and keep business separate from home. Not all of his doctor friends felt like that. It was certainly much less expensive to have one building instead of two (not to mention the tax benefits of working out of one's home), but Dad was particular, despite growing up during the Great Depression.

The house was to be our castle, his sanctuary. Over the nearly year and a half of construction, he monitored each shovel of dirt moved and the laying of every brick. The property on Berdan Avenue, 2.2 miles from the office, was on the high side of the street—high enough to be able to see the New York City skyline from the front stoop on a clear day.

This was also the year that Jackie Robinson joined the Brooklyn Dodgers and broke baseball's color barrier. The New York Yankees won another World Series; Notre Dame won another College Football National Championship (the Heisman Trophy went to its star John Lujack). The Chicago Cardinals were the Pro Football Champions, and the Toronto Maple Leafs won the Stanley Cup. Holy Cross secured its only NCAA Basketball Championship with the help of its slick point guard Bob Cousy. Race cars at the Indianapolis 500 were clocked at over 110 miles per hour!

Harry S. Truman was President of the United States, but he had no Vice President. Because of this, the Presidential Succession Act (which placed the Speaker of the House next in line of succession after the Vice President) was signed into law.

On the other side of the world, the British finally pulled out of India under pressure from the peaceful resistance of Mahatma Gandhi and his followers. Jawaharlal Nehru became the Prime Minister, and although he abhorred the division of his country on the basis of religious differences, Pakistan (Muslim) soon declared its independence from India (Hindu). Meanwhile, the Marshall Plan (for the reconstruction of post-war Europe) and the Truman Doctrine (proclaimed to help stem the spread of Communism) were instituted by the United States.

Back in New York City, Edwin Land demonstrated his "instant camera" to The Optical Society of America. The Polaroid Land Camera made a huge hit. Dad got one a few years later when the price came down and loved the novelty of seeing the picture right away, but hated the messy application of the preserving goo. Up in the sky, Chuck Yeager, flying the X-1, was the first to break the sound barrier. Soon we kids were marveling at the sonic boom (just like thunder) that the jets overhead routinely produced.

After office hours, Dad would make house calls (charging $1.50 per visit) until dark when he could no longer read the street address numbers. Eventually, he got a search light fixed to the driver's side of his car so he could stay out even later. If there were forty-eight hours in a day he would see patients for forty of them.

A stamp cost 3 cents; gasoline 15 cents per gallon; a movie ticket 55 cents; tuition at Harvard was $420 per year. Although the average family income in the U.S. was only $2,854, you could buy a new car for $1,290 and a new house for $6,650.

In 1947 the average life expectancy was only 62.9 years (freaky now, since Dad is already 60 and shows no sign of slowing down).

Mom's favorite male singer was Bing Crosby and Dinah Shore her favorite female vocalist. Dad was always partial to Perry Como and Frank Sinatra. Both loved the movie *Miracle on 34th Street* and were disappointed that it did not beat out *Gentleman's Agreement* for Best Picture at the Academy Awards.

In 1953 first grade was a huge step up for me with big responsibilities, like explaining to the class that Santa Clause didn't exist. I knew because I found Christmas and Chanukah presents (we celebrated both holidays when I was little) in my parents' closet. Miss Davis' reaction to my discovery and attempt at peer enlightenment was extremely hostile! She sprinted right over to my desk, ripped the pencil case (that I was using for emphasis) right out of my hands and broke it in two. While I burst out in tears, she refuted the obvious by shouting "Santa lives!" I loved that pencil case (that looked like an oversized pencil itself) and was demoralized at being called a liar. Miss O'Neil, my kindergarten teacher never would have done that to me… and she was a lot prettier than big-bottomed Miss Davis.

Of course, Mom got involved. Nobody was going to treat her boy that way; the child she almost lost at birth! No way! The very next morning I was sitting in the principal's office with Mom insisting that my first grade teacher apologize to me. Oh, the embarrassment flavored with sweet revenge. All three adults agreeing that I should not interfere with the harmless fantasies of others further diminished the backhanded apology I received. *Aha! They admit that there is no Santa Clause!* Miss Davis promised to get me a new pencil case, which turned out to be pink! @#!

"Unfortunately," she told me the next day, "they were all out of blue so pink will have to do." It took me most of the morning to fully cover up the pink with blue marker because the surface was so shiny that the ink barely stuck.

When I complained about the color of the new pencil case at home during dinner, my sister told me to quit whining; that the whole school knew the story and that I acted like a brat. So much for telling the truth; at this point I was totally confused, about what I should and should not say. Like the day my dad took me over to Paramus Lanes to watch a big time professional bowling tournament. All the stars were there: Don Carter, Joe Joseph, Lou Campi, Dick Webber, Ray Bluth, Buzz Fazio, Andy Varipapa, Ed Lubanski, Tom Hennessey, you name it.

As I worked my way through the crowd, trying to act grown up. I kept saying, "Excuse me. Pardon me." So some big guy turns, looks over his shoulder down at me and says, "Why, kid? Did you fart?" I was so embarrassed that it took me years to figure out that he was just some clown picking on a little kid, and that it is indeed proper to say "Excuse me" when trying to get by someone.

As smart as Helaine was (straight A's all through grammar school), I was glad that she kept messing up the Pledge of Allegiance because she would forget the words "under God." She said, "That part was just snuck in there this year (1954) by President Eisenhower to screw me up." It was really funny because, being nearly five years younger, I learned it the new way from the start.

The '54 brand new Ford coup that Dad got Mom was a creamy tangerine color with white walls that took up most of the side of each tire. Mom thought it looked like a dream. To me it looked like some huge custard dessert. Helaine used the word "pimp," but Dad wouldn't let her explain what she meant by that. This was around the time when my sister was acting like an entitled teenager, listening to records all day. The 78 rpm was losing some of its play to the new 45s. A little plastic disc had to go over the center peg to hold the 45 in place because it had such a large hole in the center. Soon the little disc was replaced with a cylinder that fit over the central peg and allowed the 45s to drop down automatically. *Technology is really something!*

April 12th was a special day. Decca Records came out with a song called *Rock Around the Clock* by Bill Haley and His Comets. It wasn't Blues or Swing. They called it "Rock and Roll." Helaine and her annoying friends (all in ponytails, bobby sox and crinoline) flipped over it. I liked it a lot also, but wasn't sure if it was for kids who weren't teenagers yet. Later in the summer, Dewey Phillips, a DJ at WHBQ in Memphis, Tennessee aired a record called *That's All Right*

(Mama) by a local singer named Elvis Presley. I prayed that Rock and Roll would last long enough to be around when I officially became a teenager.

Soon Helaine was practicing her jitterbug steps in the basement in front of a mirrored wall (complete with a ballet bar) that Dad had fixed up with Helaine's ballet career in mind. She was quite an accomplished dancer, so much so that at age fifteen she drew the attention of Igor Yuskavich of the Ballet Russe. When he and his entourage came to our house, I was freaked-out by the make-up worn by the men and the over-the-top flamboyance of the visitors. Apparently, my mother was as well since she quickly rerouted my sister towards college rather than joining a French dance troupe.

Every Sunday night each of us would drift into the den about an hour after supper to watch TV together. Dad would slowly get up from his nap on the couch and sit in the chair nearest the lamp so he could do the crossword puzzle and then count his money. He arranged each bill so that every President was facing the same way. The older bills were placed on top, the newer ones on the bottom, so that when he folded them in half like a book the new ones were on the outside. The wad felt better that way, he would say. Then a rubber band was secured around them; later, when he took off the rubber band and opened the book of money he could peal off the old bills first and save the crisp new ones. (Aside from the rubber band part, I do the same today.)

The real reason Dad always got up from the couch was so that I could lay down there directly in front of the television. Long ago Mom encouraged him to relinquish the most comfortable spot in the den for her baby (the one born with erythroblastosis fetalis; the one she almost lost at birth). Dad's gentle nature and kindness made that request hardly an imposition. He always had plenty to do over by the lamp in the corner.

Helaine would dance into the den and assume her usual seat on the carpeted floor at the foot of the couch. It was only four feet from the TV which was elevated about three feet off the ground in its cabinet. This created a severe upward angle which required that she cock her head backwards for viewing. She never complained.

Meanwhile, Mom would be rushing about; cleaning up from dinner and doing her last minute laundry. There was no way she was going to miss watching *The Ed Sullivan Show* with us.

It was September 9, 1956. Charles Laughton was guest hosting for Ed who was recuperating from a near fatal car accident. This was a *really big show*; being watched by sixty million people (more than 82% of the United States TV audience). Elvis Presley was about to make his first appearance on the nation's most popular variety show. I was not usually allowed to stay up passed 9:30 PM (the only time I ever got to see a TV sign-off pattern was on a Friday or Saturday night) so it was frustrating to watch Charles Laughton read poetry and the like before getting to Elvis. Minutes seemed like hours as I prayed that Mom would not send me to bed. But finally they sent the broadcast from New York out to Hollywood where The King was shooting *Love Me Tender*. With the Jordanaires behind him Elvis sang *Don't Be Cruel* and then *Love Me Tender*. I knew that Mom was smitten by the ballad because she let me stay up, past commercial, for the second set to hear *Hound Dog* and *Ready Teddy*. At that point the camera came in close (I later found out) in order not to show Elvis' gyrations and wild dancing. It was a time of innocence; and Elvis was there to shake things up a bit.

It was tough to get to sleep that night. I kept hoping that Rock and Roll would still be around when I became a teenager. For the next two Elvis appearances on the *Ed Sullivan Show*, Helaine and I taped a plastic multicolored transparent sheet over the TV screen so we could watch The King in color! What a blast!

What wasn't fun was a sixth grader named Ralph who was a fat old bully. He preyed on smaller kids like me and loved to scare the crap out of us. I guess I didn't do such a good job at hiding my fear of him because, sure enough one day, on my way home from school he started making fun of me. So I crossed over to the other side of Philips Street, hoping to make it home without getting pounded. That, of course, sent up the "coward signal" that drew Ralph to me like a magnet. As he made his way over to my side of the road I decided not to run. It wouldn't do any good anyway because sixth graders are always faster than fourth graders. His mocking that I "killed Christ" didn't even register because I had never been discriminated against before for being Jewish. Besides, I really didn't understand what the heck he was talking about. His shove on my back, on the other hand, triggered my tears; the one thing I didn't want to do was cry. A couple of my friends tried to save me by talking Ralph down from his fury, but they didn't really have to because all Ralph wanted was for me to cry so he could call me a crybaby and enjoy the triumph (without even having to get his hands dirty).

So home I went; the chicken who got out of a fight

because he cried. It was absolutely gut-wrenching and I simply despised myself for it. The only saving grace was that Bobbie, my little fourth grade girlfriend, wasn't around to see my humiliation. No doubt, she'd hear about it later.

When I got home Mom, of course, coddled me and wanted to know what the tears were all about. I told her that there was this bully and I was in a fight (I only wished I had had the guts). More codling. She asked if I was hit anywhere and I started crying again so she stopped asking. I never mentioned the part about being accused of killing Jesus Christ since it still didn't make sense to me anyway and the real problem was that I cried. At bedtime she told me that she was going to walk me to school tomorrow. I told her that I was never going to school again.

In the morning I realized that the bully thing was not a dream and Mom was actually walking me to school. The next thing I remember: I'm standing on Philips Street with my mother accusing Ralph of picking on me. Bathed in overwhelming embarrassment, I cried out something incoherent and lunged at the stupefied sixth grader. The fist in my mouth tasted so much sweeter than huddling like a coward in the shelter of my mother's shadow. I don't really remember much after that. The fight was broken up quickly and the pain and swelling of my hand gave me pride that I landed at least one good punch. I wore my swollen lip as a badge of courage, milking it for days until it was no longer there. Best of all, I do not recall Ralph being a problem for me anymore after that.

Oh how I wanted to be like Audie Murphy and John Wayne; bigger than life (although Murphy, an actual Medal of Honor winner, stood only 5'5") tough guys that took no prisoners. A steady diet of westerns and WWII movies will do that to you. Hollywood even made a skinny runt like Frank Sinatra seem like a war hero. The truth was I grew up in a *Leave it to Beaver*, summer camp world where good grades and not striking out were all I had to worry about. Occasionally a punk like Ralph or a humorless teacher like Miss Davis (or getting covered in poison ivy from head to toe on a two day canoe trip down the Delaware River) would muddy the waters; but for the most part it was a charmed childhood.

For a while the Russians were raining on my parade when, in 1957, they seemed to be winning the race for space. On October 4th the Soviet Union launched the first satellite to orbit the earth. About the size of a bowling ball with two pair of antennae, Sputnik took us all by surprise. On November 3rd they sent up Sputnik II which made us look really bad.

But on December 6th we were excited to watch the United States launch Vanguard TV3 at Cape Canaveral.

Our entire class huddled together around the television with all the excitement of the seventh game of the World Series. The rocket was huge and majestic in front of a clear blue sky, dwarfing the launching pad below. The count down took forever; not the simple 10, 9, 8, 7, 6…that everyone expected. Finally, the booster engines fired; the smoke beneath billowed; and ever so slowly the rocket lifted off the launching pad to deafening cheers. Up about four lousy feet, the cheers suddenly dissolved into sickening silence as the massive rocket lost its thrust and settled back down, like a tall balloon loosing air, into an explosive heap on the ground. It's always hard to watch your team lose; but when your team is your country and all year long you have been drawing and cutting out pictures of USA rockets with expectations of showing up the Russians, it really hurt. And it was scary, too.

Not the kind of scary that we looked forward to on "Goosy (Mischief) Night." That was different because getting frightened was fun, without any bad consequences. It was way better than Halloween; like the time one of the older kids put a paper bag full of poop at the doorstep of a nasty neighbor, lit it and rang the bell. That old prank was never supposed to work, but it actually did that night. The look on that guy's face as he stomped out the fire made me laugh so hard I pissed in my pants; which was probably instant karma for the open milk bottle filled with piss that I carefully leaned up against the front door so that it would fall into the foyer when he opened the inside door. Throwing rolls of toilet paper up into trees and spraying cars with shaving cream was far more benign than pelting cars and front doors with raw eggs. Though organic, the yolk starts to smell after awhile and the enzymes can eat away the paint if left too long. We didn't think of ourselves as hooligans, but more like "little rascals" on one very special night of the year.

All of us were pretty good kids. It was a time of innocence, growing up in the suburbs. Doors of cars and houses were left unlocked. Residential security systems had no market. Even my own overly-protective mother allowed me to go down to "the field" at T.J. (Thomas Jefferson Junior High School) with just a few friends who were also about ten or eleven years old to play ball until the street lights went on which meant we had to head home.

When I came home one night, dribbling a basketball

with my right hand and squeezing a baseball in my Al Dark baseball mitt on my left hand, Mom annoyingly greeted me at the garage door.

"Where's your bike, Bobby?" she asked knowing the answer well before my big grin melted away.

"Oh no! Rats! I left it at the field."

"All right. Come on in. We'll get it in the morning," she said comfortingly. "But next time think. Be more responsible."

In the morning, my new Schwinn bicycle with gears and double foot and hand brakes, was right where I left it, in the bike rack despite no chain or lock securing it. No one ever locked anything in Fair Lawn, in the '50s. I really miss that freedom.

***

BAM! Just like that my freedom was stolen from me while driving down from the hills of Pagman with J.G. to check our mail at the American Express office in Kabul. Knowing full well about the wisdom of "keep right on driving if you hit something or someone on the road in the East; they will ask no questions as they throw you in jail," I still carefully put that idiot kid, who slammed into *me* on his bicycle, in my van and took him to the hospital. With God on my side, I thought I was pretty clever to bring along a cop who saw the whole thing—just in case! Unfortunately, he was looking out for his own skin, not mine. So I got stuck with these two emaciated zombies gawking at my every move. I don't belong here with these bastards, probably thieves or rapists who earned their way into this hell. Okay, maybe not; Sharia law would have them stoned and mutilated for such crimes. Christ! What will they do to me if they find out I am Jewish? The ultimate infidel! No way will I pull my Lorrach, Germany stunt here. Cousin Bob was not facing life or death back in his postal days when asked his religion. It's all about survival now. Hopefully, J.G. or the embassy won't give me away. My passport! What about that? Does it have my religion on it? Holy shit!

I'm freaking out! Bergen Record headlines: *Local Boy Rots in Afghan Prison!* Prominent Fair Lawn obstetrician and wife mourn son's foolish decision to run off and see the world. A warning to all good children: Listen to your parents!

Sweet saving grace: Raymond's white powder…ah… My two Afghan mates understand. We're in this together, and it's not so bad. Kind of like *Life of Riley* when Chester (William Bendix) would find himself in a mess and utter, "What a revoltin' development this is!" Ha. What a great show. Must have come up with that line from Oliver Hardy's "That's another fine mess you've gotten us into!" Poor Stan Laurel. My Uncle Joe just loved Laurel and Hardy.

I remember him always asking me how I got my crew cut so perfectly flat on top; the flattest top in seventh grade (except for maybe Stuey Schutsmann). Sure, a lot of guys had the big Elvis Presley pompadours with the D.A. (duck's ass) in the back. But keeping it in place was a lot of work; like Ed "Kookie" Burns in *77 Sunset Strip* constantly with the comb. I tried it in sixth grade, but not for me. A little stick wax in the morning to form a T.C. (Tony Curtis) in the front and you're good all day. The key is a good Italian barber like Joe or his brother Frank on Broadway in Fair Lawn. They were absolutely the best, with the brightest barber pole in town. Fifty cents for the cut; some dirty jokes (too nasty to reveal to my folks), and a dime tip at the end made my flat top even sweeter.

Tight black pants, with a good three inches of white sox showing above the penny loafers, and a fitted, collared short sleeve shirt with the sleeves rolled up over the biceps was the look I went for; somewhere between a rah-rah and a greaser. The pure greaser guys wore the tailored slacks with lace up narrow wing-tip shoes. They were more into smoking cigarettes than playing sports and somehow got the slutty chicks...hmmm. I didn't pay much attention to what most girls wore, except for Caryn who was absolutely beautiful. She was in most of my classes except language. She took Russian, which was offered by the Fair Lawn Public School System because the Soviet Union was the other super power and I guess they thought that if we lost the Cold War at least some of us would be able to speak their language. I stuck with French. At least I didn't have to learn a whole new alphabet.

Somehow my attention paid off and Caryn became my girlfriend. We wrote each other's names on our notebooks and won marathon kissing contests at parties. Our lips were locked (no real tonguing went on) "The Day the Music Died." It was the winter of '59 when we heard about a chartered plane carrying Buddy Holly, Ritchie Valens and The Big Bopper (Jiles Perry Richardson, Jr.) going down in an Iowa snowstorm killing all four aboard.

Caryn was very down about the tragedy, and all too vulnerable. I probably could have taken advantage and gotten to second base, but hey, I was only twelve and couldn't get up the guts to try. That dream ended when we each wound up running for class president. She won, and since I came in second I got to be vice president. That wasn't good at all. Weeks later we broke up, but remained friends—sort of.

That was the year that Alaska became the forty-ninth state. It was hard to look at the flag or a map of the United States and accept a new non-attached state; but no sooner did I make the adjustment than the number jumped to fifty with Hawaii, way out there in the Pacific Ocean, becoming part of the Union.

Yeah, life was simple back then; until Alice Eberhardt was murdered in Dunkerhook Park. All of a sudden my parents no longer permitted me to go play there or even walk through the park. The stream I used to catch frogs in was now off limits and, since the killer was never caught, Dunkerhook became a haunted hallows for those of us who grew up with Alice.

Less than a year later the story of Georgia W., a girl my age, getting accosted and nearly raped on Sunnyside Drive near her home reinforced the neighborhood fear. The death of one of my sister's classmates from a drug overdose closed out the 1950s in shocking fashion for those of us growing up in "Father Knows Best" Fair Lawn, New Jersey. Boom! The '60s were closing in fast!

On top of losing the decade of innocence, I was becoming a man according to Jewish tradition even though I was just turning thirteen. The good news was that Bar Mitzvah meant that I was done with Hebrew School which was always a bummer to have to attend after regular school was out. Three days a week I simply had no time to play.

After the Bar Mitzvah ceremony at the Fair Lawn Jewish

Center, the celebration was grandiose with a ten piece band, a master of ceremonies, and all the trimmings. After all, The Schultz Family was in competition with the Levy Family for the most outrageous ("memorable" as Mom put it) affair of the year. It was part of the culture. Who cared if Mom wanted Dad to spend his money any way she saw fit? It turned out to be very successful as was evident by the fact that for years afterward Mom would mention how someone she ran into at the grocery store just had to tell her how marvelous Bobby's Bar Mitzvah was. The fact that Dad screwed up the Hebrew blessing and had to be rescued by the Rabbi was incidental to everyone but him. I knew he was going to choke because his hands (resting on my shoulders) made my Bar Mitzvah suit shake like a jackhammer.

By the time I was fourteen I got my first summer job, so to speak. As a camper/waiter at Camp Indian Trails in Milford, Pennsylvania I waited on tables during meals, three times per day. I didn't actually get paid a salary, but got to go to camp for "free" (enjoying all the activities I did for the two prior summers when my folks were paying for it). It felt really good to practically be a grown-up and pay my own way. I even got a social security card with my own number; and, at the end of the season, I received tips from the campers at my tables and got to keep the money. Best of all, it was obvious that the senior girl campers were really into us stud waiters as we strutted around the mess hall while they sat and drooled. Got to second base a couple of times that summer, but still not sure I would have known what to do at third.

But wait. It gets better. One of the counselors arranged for two of us young bulls to serve as bar waiters at

Tammamint Lodge in the Poconos for a week after camp was over. Although both underage, we were hired anyway. Even more miraculously, I managed to convince my parents to let me do it. Talk about growing up; I followed my friend's lead and took sips from the drinks we were serving. Of course, we both got sloshed, but kept from getting fired by consenting to our manager's underhanded plan (for hiring us in the first place) of being farmed out to the "single" older ladies who frequented the night club.

My friend and I swapped stories about our conquests, but the truth was that I could not go through with it and somehow managed to talk my way out of several encounters with women my mother's age! When I came home from camp that year I felt worldly and matured beyond my years. I had gotten drunk and had the opportunity to slide into third base.

My mother the artist had that same bohemian streak in her; but it was Dad who stepped outside the box that summer and surprised us all with the "new" car he had just picked up.

The '59 Cadillac El Dorado convertible with sky-blue exterior, white top, red and white leather interior, and bleach white side wall tires was accentuated by the high fins in the back that made it look like an American flag rocket ship to me. Of course, Helaine thought it looked like a pimp-mobile. The whole display was way out of character for Dad, but he seemed so excited and kept showing us the little button on the floor next to the brake pedal that allowed him to change the radio station without removing his hands from the steering wheel. Later, when Helaine and I joked that our conservative dad actually bought such a car, Mom took offense and insisted that we really didn't know about our father's wild side. She seemed really turned-on as she vigorously defended her man. Helaine and I thought that was very cute.

So Dad had a wild side and Mom was an artist. Maybe I had "bust-out" genes after all? But on my fifteenth birthday my swagger stepped on a landmine of brutal reality that blew my self-esteem to bits. The disturbing thing about my upcoming birthday was that my parents didn't seem to have any plans for the special day—no party or family day trip or special present. In fact, I was downright outraged that on the big day no one seemed to care other than Dad who took me to Radburn Sporting Goods to buy a new basketball and sneakers. But when we got home I heard music in the basement and was ecstatic to hear everyone yell, "Surprise!" as I hit the lower landing.

Good thing we had a large basement because just about my whole grade was there. The decorations and presents made me feel so happy to be liked and in the spotlight. Everyone was dancing and having a great time. Then came time for the birthday cake: It was a big one with *mucho* candles on it—many more than just fifteen. In fact, there was twice that number of candles and written across the cake in bold blue letters were the words **Happy Birthday Bob and Norman.** What the ?#@!!

Norman was, of course, there. He was a very popular guy. Everybody liked Norman. He was a decent athlete, not bad looking, and smart. But most of all, he was a really good guy and fun to be around; actually he was a riot to be with. So when wiseass Larry G. explained to me that Norman's birthday was only a few days after mine I accepted (though reluctantly) the gesture to celebrate Norm's birthday along with mine. It was not until later in the evening when loud-mouth Larry could hold back no longer and obnoxiously informed me that there would have been no surprise party at all had Norman not been included as an honoree.

"No one would have shown up for just you Schultz." Oh how I wanted to punch out Larry right then and there, but I didn't for two reasons: he was twice my size and would easily have ripped me apart, and—most sadly—I believed him. Kids may be cruel, but they are painfully honest (about some things). I tried hard to be self-critical, but unfortunately found it terribly difficult to laugh at myself and compliment others; unlike Norm who did it so naturally.

***

But enough of my teenage bullshit; I need another snort.

Ahhh… So my skinny Afghan friends, you probably know nothing about dating or going out with girls. How do you let those crazy mullahs get away with covering chicks up in those ghastly burkhas? Are you nuts?! Ever see a cheerleader? Ha! Of course, not.

***

Joan was a cheerleader; cute and very athletic. We were going steady, even though at that age it meant only some light petting. Actually, the "respect" thing was an excuse for having no guts.

Anyway, we did a lot of talking, especially after parties on the long walks up Radburn Road to her home. (I wasn't old enough to drive yet.) Somehow things just spilled out of Joan; like her confusion over her religion or lack thereof.

You see, Joan's father was Jewish and her mother Catholic, but neither was very religious, so they never brought her or her older brother to temple or church. She used to say she wanted to have a faith, like everybody else, but didn't know who to worship. Not having experienced such a void I really didn't understand her frustration and tears over being free from inconvenient non-secular obligations. She actually punched me one night for telling her how good she had it because she didn't have to learn Hebrew or Latin. Girls! They always want what they don't have. Sports, at least, made sense.

Coach Sharman really liked me and I worked really hard on my game; making the Junior Cutters All-star Team in the summer. It was my year to be a starter on the T.J. varsity basketball team. As an eighth grader I got to play off the bench in each game, but was the third guard behind Marty and Les. So in the first game of the '61-'62 season, I was really pumped to line up for the opening tip off. My folks were in the bleachers and Joan was cheerleading. I was psyched! I hit my first two shots from my favorite spot, the top of the key. Sensing I had a hot hand, Coach called for me to get the ball. In the third quarter we were up by double digits and I had contributed twelve of those points. I was feeling good, really good and got in there with the "bigs" to grab a rebound when I came down on someone's foot. My ankle turned and popped. The pain was almost as bad as the fact that I knew I was done. Dad came to the sidelines after they helped me off the court, examined me and then tried to cheer me up. But it was the end of the world because I knew the injury was serious enough to keep me out of the line up. I got taped and bought a pair of high-top Keds sneakers, but my ankle just wouldn't let me move side to side quickly enough to save my job as a starter. "Bummed" doesn't cover it; "devastated" comes close.

Despite Mom and Dad's best efforts to get me to see things in the proper perspective by reminding me of Tommy Strax who was confined to a wheelchair with cerebral palsy, or ghetto kids who have to dodge bullets just to get to the basketball court, I just could not get past my own disappointment. I was especially annoyed when Helaine pointed out that my self-pity made her want to puke. "Worry about whether we're all going to get blown up by Soviet missiles from Cuba, instead of your dopy sports," she said disgustedly.

But President Kennedy took care of that crisis, all right. He was amazing.

I was in tenth grade health class when it happened. It was a beautiful fall day and the leaves were swirling outside in front of Fair Lawn High school on Berdan Avenue. I barely heard Mr. Rosenthal talking up front by the blackboard because it was an easy course and my mind was wandering. Suddenly, there was commotion in the hall; maybe a fight? Then the door flew open and someone yelled, "The President's been shot! President Kennedy's been shot!"

The sickening feeling was immediate, though the thought of JFK actually dying from his wounds was impossible. I found myself in front of a TV with countless others while the entire school remained deadly quiet in a surreal atmosphere. The footage of the motorcade in Dallas and the talking heads describing the shooting of the President and Texas Governor John B. Connelly being rushed to Parkland Hospital with possible mortal wounds were numbing. And then the words, "President Kennedy is dead." The reality of it did not strike home until the visual impact of Vice President Lyndon B. Johnson being sworn in as the thirty-sixth President of the United States (right there on Air Force One by Federal Judge Sara T. Hughes), flanked by Lady Bird and Jackie Kennedy, left no room for doubt.

Stores and businesses were shut down for the entire weekend. The nation was comatose until Sunday the 24th when we witnessed, live on television, the shooting of the alleged assassin, Lee Harvey Oswald, by Jack Ruby in Dallas. Monday we had no school. We simply watched tearfully as John-John and Caroline bid their father farewell as he was laid to rest in Arlington National Cemetery.

It was about this time that I realized that I had no black friends (other than Ozzie who was really my friend Eddie's friend at Eastside High School in Paterson) with whom to discuss the raging Civil Rights Movement. I remember Eddie joking about Ozzie sleeping over his house one night and checking the sheets in the morning to see if any color wiped off. It made me wonder if any had. Fair Lawn was 99% white and there was not one black student in our entire class. We also had no black teachers.

Ida, who used to work for my parents as our nanny and housekeeper, never discussed things from a black person's perspective with me. I just remember Mom firing her over the telephone when Ida called me a spoiled brat; I happened to pick up another phone in the house and overheard the whole conversation. It made me cry because I thought Ida liked me and because part of me felt she was right. Estelle, on the other hand, was a young black woman, just a year or two older than Helaine. She used to sing with the Shirelles before they became famous, but had to quit the group because she was committed to raising a child she had out of wedlock. She had a way of conveying the deprivation in which she lived—a hardship that was partly because of poverty and partly because of her skin color. This was all the firsthand information I had on the subject of race. But I surely noticed how wonderfully my mom treated her—literally like a second daughter. So I tried to think of Estelle as my second sister. It made me feel funny when she asked me if I ever kissed a black woman. I assumed she had kissed a white guy, but who knows?

I liked Estelle because she never smoked and hated the fact that my folks did. She'd clean the ashtrays really well and get rid of the stale smoke smell. Right around that time U.S. Surgeon General Luther Leonides Terry reported that smoking may be hazardous to one's health. Just about every adult, including movie stars and athletes, smoked cigarettes. Even some of Helaine's friends would light up when the folks weren't around. It was always uncomfortable for me, especially in a car. Years ago we took a family trip to Williamsburg, Virginia. Helaine and I sat in the back seat playing the license plate game with the rear windows open mainly because of the smoke (although it was helpful, at times, to spot the proper lettered license plate by sticking our heads out the window). Mom, of course, was afraid that we would fall out or something so she kept asking us to roll up the windows. I'll never forget how nasty the smoke was.

But once the Surgeon General declared that smoking was bad (or at least *may* be hazardous to your health) Dad, also a doctor, decided to read the medical report. The next thing I knew, he started holding an unlit Chesterfield between his long and middle fingers, but never lighting it. He did this for a month or two and then was totally free of the habit. He never bought another pack. Mom, on the other hand, switched to filtered cigarettes reasoning that she was now safe. Keeping weight off was more important than keeping her lungs clear, or the house free of that smell.

The only time I thought it looked cool to have a cigarette was when George Harrison used to play with one sticking out of the strings of his guitar. Of course, The Beatles were new and just about everything they did was cool. They came over from England that year, same year that Cassius Clay "shocked the world" by knocking out big bad Sonny Listen. But '64 was a golden year for me, too. I pulled off the biggest coup of my life: Beth, the prettiest girl in high school, and one grade below me. I wish I could say that I orchestrated the relationship, but I did not. She did.

It began with some dancing at a party we both "happened" to attend. During the slow dances she wore my jacket, and at the end she gave me a goodnight kiss. Soon after that we started double-dating with Lee and Maryann (her best friend). While sitting in the movie theater between Beth and Maryann one night, Beth began leaning across me to whisper things to Maryann. She kept rubbing her jugs on my lap. Right then and there I knew that something really big was going to happen—soon. It was perfect timing, too, because I was going through Driver's Ed. at school and would soon get my license. Some solo drive-in movies (just the two of us) and it wasn't long before the humping in the back seat started. A month or so later we both entered adulthood. A magical moment filled with excitement, uncertainty, and triumph! There is a song that describes the feeling perfectly; I just can't remember the name.

We used to make trips to the Red Apple Rest on Route 17 just across the border in upstate New York. It started the day I turned 18, or there about—that was the legal drinking age in that state back then. I thought I was real sophisticated until I got to college later that year and learned what was really going on. The pub at Hamilton was an eye-opener, not that I was so into beer. It was more the independence, being away from home and the crazy things fraternity life brought. Beth was still in high school and absolutely turned on by the wildness. It was all I could do to drag her away from the parties so we could run back to the empty dorm room for a "quickie" before my roommates returned.

Life was so very simple then. Sure the whole Vietnam thing was going on, but I had a high draft number (the Hackensack draft board had plenty of non-college kids to pick from) and never really felt vulnerable. Besides, being pre-med gave me some deferment status in the early days of the war. Mom, of course, had Dad look into ways of getting me a 4F on medical grounds if need be. She spoke of my becoming a conscientious objector or evening running off to Canada; no way was her Bobby going off to the jungles of Southeast Asia!

We were quite isolated on the small, conservative all men's liberal arts college campus way up in Clinton, NY. Protests and civil rights rallies were things we read about or saw on TV. While things were heating up at Michigan and Kent State, we were debating whose turn it was to drive on rolls to Skids (Skidmore) or Caz (Cassanovia Junior College) to find chicks. The northeast blackout of '65 provided perfect opportunity for us to protect the innocent coeds from the darkness. Candlelight, incense, and intoxicants made it thirteen hours of bliss before power was restored.

Making it back to the campus just before tryouts began for the freshman basketball team was exhausting. Through glassy eyes I met Carl, a lanky corner shooter with a good move to the basket. He was impressive, not only because he was a longhair raised in Greenwich Village, but also was obviously secure enough within himself to have no desire to rush a fraternity. Instead, he remained quietly satisfied to be an Indy (independent, unaffiliated with any Greek house). He ate in the Commons with all the other Indies and never bothered worrying about which house wanted him or what the "brothers" were thinking. Despite my admiration of his attitude, I pulled strings to get DKE to take me in their rushing class of '69. That meant going through it all: the humiliation; the DKE Run (downing whiskey shots at each strategic station around the house until you puked); chauffeuring "brothers" at my expense; being blindfolded and abandoned in the woods; begging for more humiliation, etc. The house parties were worth it though... especially with Beth.

CHAPTER 2

Boom!

When the whole psychedelic thing began exploding the next year, I became fascinated with the first Acid Test at the Filmore in San Francisco (the original entertainment center run by impresario Bill Graham who would open the Filmore East in NYC. in '68) The Warlocks (later known as The Grateful Dead) with their black lights, florescent paint and strobe lights sure sounded groovy. Author Ken Kesey and his Merry Pranksters apparently put LSD in the Kool-aid and watched the entire place levitate.

As a sophomore, no longer under the watchful eye of the resident assistants in Dunham, the freshman dorm, my buds and I had our own space. The smell of pot and incense pervaded the night air, but I remained disciplined, getting stoned on weekends only. I was zeroed in on getting good grades so I could get into medical school (my original purpose for going to Hamilton). I watched "Cakes," "Flipper," Billy and a few others make getting wasted a nightly ritual.

Of course, two Harvard professors of psychology, Timothy Leary and his associate Richard Alpert, were busy becoming celebrities on college campuses as proponents of psychedelics. Both had actually been terminated by Harvard University in 1963 for sharing their research drugs with undergraduate students. Apparently, Leary had gone down to Mexico in 1960 with an experienced friend to try the psychedelic mushroom *Psilocybe mexicana*. He concluded that he learned more about his brain and its possibilities in the five hours after taking the mushrooms than in his previous fifteen years of doing research in psychology. Unlike Ken Kesey and his Merry Pranksters who used drugs to "get off" and goof on the "straight" world, Leary and Alpert seemed to give some kind of legitimacy to the stuff.

I was struck by an epiphany while walking back to Carnegie Hall (my dorm) one peaceful fall evening from the library. The sensation overwhelmed me all at once as I was looking up at the full moon on a perfectly clear night. *I am young; I am healthy; I am not in Vietnam; and despite having broken up with Beth, I am having the time of my life! From here on I will use that full moon as a constant against the changing chapters in my life. It will be my specter and reference that reminds me of this special night; a time for reflection and appreciation of my life as it speeds along.* A eureka moment! And I was not high on anything but life.

My roommates in Carnegie, Carl (basketball player and "indy" from the Village), Bennie (a white Jewish lead singer in a "soul" band and pre-med drop-out), and Og (an underclassman who was just naturally freaky) were perfect. We had a bedroom with two separate bunk beds, our own bathroom (unlike most other dormitories that had communal bathrooms down the hall), and a huge common room that we set up to serve a myriad of purposes (which my future girlfriend, Marta, called *bizarre*). Between the four of us our record collection was more than six cardboard cartons deep. Life was good—real good—until Thanksgiving break when I met up with my buds from high school and we went looking for chicks at Maxwell's Plumb in New York City.

As usual, we came up empty handed; though we got at least a phone number each (or so the story went). I was the first to yell out "shot-gun," so I jumped in the front passenger seat for the drive home. Jeff was driving (it was finally his turn); Mike and Bob were sitting in the back. As we left the parking garage and came to the first red traffic light, I turned to the guys in the back seat. Then I heard that awful screech! As I whipped around to the front to see what happened I was met squarely by the windshield. The high-pitched "PING" that filled my face and head before I blacked out was unforgettable (along with the memory of my teeth not fitting together right).

After being rushed to Jacobi Hospital emergency room in the Bronx, I was transferred to NYU to be under the care of John Marquis Converse (renowned reconstructive plastic surgeon) at the urgent request of my father. My multiple facial traumas (a pyramidal fracture of the maxilla and comminuted fractures of the nasal bones) included a blow-out fracture of the right orbit, so severe that it allowed my eye to drop down into the maxillary sinus below. The importance of this was immense because Dr. Converse had theorized a new method for the reconstruction of blow-out fractures and he was anxious to try it out. I thus became his first patient to receive the "Open Sky" procedure and even made it into the *Journal of Plastic and Reconstructive Surgery*. Of course my dad, to this day, thought that his plea as a fellow physician was the sole reason that Dr. Converse and Dr. Byron Smith, the ophthalmologist, took on my case.

Upon awakening in my hospital bed after hours of surgery I found that I was unable to see out of my right eye, and the only way I could breathe was by parting my lips. In a panic I yelled out for help, but the sound was muffled by my teeth. The private duty nurse hired by my folks tried gently to explain to me that my jaw was wired together, my nose was packed with gauze, and there was a patch over my right eye. *Oh fine. That explains it. Well how the hell am I going to talk or eat?!*

The plastics resident doctor was called in to calm me down and explained that I should write things down on a piece of paper if I could not make myself understood and that I needed to squirt milkshakes in the back of my mouth with a bulb syringe for nourishment. Oh yes, and if a mucous plug started building up behind my front teeth it could be somewhat dissolved by squirting hydrogen peroxide solution between my front teeth with a needle syringe. In just six to eight weeks the wires in my mouth would be removed and talking and eating could resume. The good news: The eye patch will come off in a few days, but there may well be diplopia (double vision) for several months.

ARE YOU SHITTING ME?!

I was told to stay on bed rest for a few days, but that night I had to take a crap and refused to use the bedpan. While the nurse was off doing whatever, I slid out of bed and made it to the bathroom. My mistake was turning on the light and looking in the mirror. The horrific thing staring back at me brought me to my knees weeping. I managed to crawl back into bed (crap and all). The only thing more difficult than trying to talk with my mouth wired shut was crying. My whole face hurt and swelled, and I knew I would look like a monster forever. This was my Vietnam!

Ten days later I was released from the hospital. Fortunately, I had the days between Thanksgiving break and Christmas break to recover before having to go back to school. Of course, I would have to study with a hand or patch over my right eye until the double vision (hopefully) resolved. At any rate, by that time I was able to look in the mirror without passing out. I sort of recognized myself, but my self-esteem was rock bottom. I guess looks really mattered after all.

But then Beth came over. My old girlfriend, the prettiest girl in Fair Lawn High, paid me a visit while I was held up at my parents' afraid to venture out, looking like a monster, into the nasty world. As I opened the front door I was not only shocked to see her standing there, I detected absolutely no horror or even surprise in her eyes at my broken face. She kissed me right on the lips and asked if I was going to let her in. While I fought back the tears, she told me how the news of my accident made her worry for my life; just the way she felt when her dad told her that her mother had brain cancer. That moment gave me the resolve to get better and deal with it. I thought *her new boyfriend is one lucky guy.*

I watched a lot of TV because reading was difficult. The "Human Be-Ins" at Golden Gate Park in San Francisco were captivating. Words like "happening," "counterculture," "higher consciousness," "communal mind," and "hippies" sounded far-out. Timothy Leary urged all to, "Turn on, tune in, drop out." On Easter Sunday, ten thousand gathered in the Sheep Meadow for a Central Park Be-In. There was no stage, no MC, and no entertainers. They spontaneously gathered there to simply celebrate spring.

Spring House Parties at Hamilton rocked. The college entertainment committee was deified for getting acts like Simon and Garfunkel, Smokey Robinson and the Miracles, The Four Tops, The Box Tops, and Patty La Belle. This time we had Chuck Berry. Of course, after the concert each frat house had its own party that lasted well into Sunday. Benny's band was playing at the DKE house.

Because Benny was a local celebrity and my roommate, we got special seats just off the stage for the concert. Right from the start we were blown away, not by Chuck Berry but by the back-up guitarist with the funky clothes, big afro, and upside down guitar. At intermission we asked the cat if he wanted to do a doobie with us back at the dorm. "I'd like that, man," he said softly. So back we went, rolled a "J" and lit up. He was cool, very cool. He told us that his name was Jimi Hendrix and this was just a part-time gig. Soon he was heading across the pond to England to cut a record. "I'm gonna be famous like you never seen before," he said with bravado. *Right*, we thought. *Must be the pot talking; but he* is *damn good*. On August 23rd *Are You Experienced* was released by The Jimi Hendrix Experience. We pretty much wore out the album that fall, that and *Sgt. Pepper's Lonely Hearts Club Band.*

Before I got back to campus in '68 Mom's dear friend Ruth Pocatillo, who did custom alterations for all the Jappy girls in Passaic, NJ, fulfilled her biggest passion by playing match-maker. It was right out of *Fiddler on the Roof.* I was the centerpiece of a blind date of which I wanted no part, especially when I heard that the chick was only seventeen and her name was Marta. When my folks started talking of a new Pontiac Firebird convertible for my birthday in the spring, however, I began to soften. My Mustang had a bent A-frame from a skid into the curb after sliding down an icy College Hill Road several months before. Despite the repairs Dad felt that the front end alignment was off and it was no longer safe for me to drive that car three and a half hours back and forth between upstate New York and Jersey. I was certainly not about to argue. One miserable date was a small price to pay for keeping The Folks on track. With my face pretty much back to normal (except for the numbness around my nose and right eye, and a few crooked teeth from the ligation wires that held my jaw shut), I had my swagger back in full gear. I figured I'd hold my nose and get through the evening. An action movie would make the chore tolerable.

As the front door to her house opened I found myself face to face with a gorgeous, slim, blue-eyed blond with long legs and a very short mini-skirt. My first thought was, *How is she going to sit in a skirt like that, and can I position myself directly in front of her when she does sit down?* My second thought was, *Why the hell did I not come more prepared with a better plan than just going to a movie?... and I could have spent more time on my personal grooming.* Then it happened. She spoke in absolutely the most delightful way: easy, relaxed, and apparently interested in me. She brought me into the living room to meet her parents, Libby and Fred, who were also lovely and apparently very trusting. And so began a wonderful relationship that was nothing short of a blessing.

House parties at college were perfect for me to impress my young high school sweetheart; just like I did with Beth. Despite her saying that my dorm room was "bizarre" I knew she really dug it because it was "freaky" and the times dictated "freaky." Pot and psychedelics were all part of that. The concerts at the Filmore East in The City, the Capitol Theater in Passaic, New Jersey; and that unforgettable summer at the Newport Folk Festival were dynamite!

In the spring Marta knew that I was planning a weeklong trip out to California. Fred and Libby forbade their daughter from going (not so trusting, after all) so it was just the boys (Cakes and Billy) and me. When she heard we were planning to visit Telegraph Avenue in Berkeley she said, "I know you are going to try acid." "No way," was my very transparent lie.

The trip was an eye-opener. All the way from the beach scene at Laguna to the rampant drug scene at Berkeley, I was exposed to the freakiest people I had ever met. Though some were college students like myself, many more were simply hard core drop-outs selling lids, snow, and even smack, right there on the street with little or no regard to the local "pigs" (who seemed overwhelmed and paralyzed as to which battle to pick).

My lie to Marta began at about 6:00 PM on Telegraph when Cakes handed me a rather large white capsule, which he said, with an unforgettably silly grin, was called "White Lightning." About forty-five minutes later Telegraph Avenue was bathed in day-glow and reminiscent of Bourbon Street—although I had never even been to New Orleans. The carnival lasted all night and was filled with revelations about everything, from the meaning of hair to the ecstasy that only a snow cone can provide. I believed that everyone, even the cops, was aware of the wonderland I saw, and that Berkeley was a very special place. I couldn't wait to tell Marta all about the experience and to share a trip with her.

Back at college I discovered that LSD had already made it to the campus. Now that I had lost my drug "virginity" it seemed that the substance, along with psilocybin was everywhere. As alluring as the epiphany of a trip could be, the mental toll was exacting and the time it took for physical recovery made me loath to do it except on special occasions (when I was with the right people and had the weekend to recuperate). For me, there was always a sense that the psychedelic experience was more entertainment than real.

The classic example was my New Year's Eve party of '68: My folks were already struggling with their baby getting a little "off track." The longish hair, the funky clothes, the hip language, and the constant philosophizing were foreign to them and unanticipated from their pre-med student son. Helaine (half a generation ahead of me) never posed any problems. By this time, she was married to a doctor and preparing to raise a family. In an attempt to keep me happy and "on board," they consented to allowing me to have a New Year's Eve party at the house. In fact, they actually took a motel room for the night to stay out of my hair.

The most memorable part of the night was J.G. making me a cup of coffee (which I had never tried before) with cream and sugar to wash down the Purple Owsley acid. Outside, a clean snow was falling and our trip around the neighborhood was like traveling inside a giant snow globe.

The softness of sound and texture went uninterrupted, probably because the neighbors were all off at parties of their own and the Fair Lawn Police Department had better things to do than patrol the yet unplowed roads. Remarkably there were no incidents aside from some mild "bummers," mainly from a couple of chicks who had never tripped before.

Despite the numerous political bummers that year: assassinations (King and Kennedy), the Tet Offensive, My Lai, the Chicago riots at the DNC, the Chicago Eight, and Nixon's return, it was a very good year for me. By the grace of God, co-education was taking the nation by storm and in the fall of '68 some one-hundred-fifty teenage girls were miraculously shipped up to Clinton, NY in order to start Kirkland College, Hamilton's new sister school. With my spot already secured for next year at Cornell University Medical College, I had abundant free time to help the chicks get acclimated to college life. With the help of my bros Carl and Elliott, we spent endless hours at McIntosh, Major, and Minor dorms making certain that the young ladies were properly educated. The new NBC comedy show *Rowan and Martin's Laugh-In* (replacing *The Man From U.N.C.L.E.* in the Monday 8:00 PM time slot) became a ritual for us over at Kirkland. The only thing that compared was getting stoned and listening to the Beatles' new *White Album*, over and over and over and over...

***

And now it's just me with my own wheels spinning 'round and 'round. No music, no friends, no one to talk to. Two emaciated statues hugging their territory, protecting me from pissing on it. Huh, like I care. I'll piss anywhere

I please. It already smells like a urinal in here, anyhow. It's shameful and disgusting. I've done nothing to deserve this... except being trusting and frickin' stupid. Idiot! You damn idiot!

My arms are getting skinny. Skinny is in, but not my guns! And my chest!... all ribs and sternum. Push-ups are particularly hard and disgusting; my hands slide apart on the slime and that shit gets all over me. Damn you assholes for laughing! You think I'm pathetic? Look at *you!*

Last little bit... hmph... hmph... ah, there. Now, that's better. A lot better.

***

It's dream-like; my last year in college was dream-like. With a spot in the class of '73 at Cornell Medical School already secured (choosing Cornell over Columbia was an ego trip because Hamilton had an "in" to Columbia and getting into an Ivy League med school "without help" was delicious) I thoroughly immersed myself in "senioritis." Spending just about every weekend off campus, taking road trips to Boston to visit Marta at Simmons College and crashing in J.G.'s room in Dunster House at Harvard, was a beautiful thing.

J.G.'s roommates, Al and Tommy, were regular guys who had no problem with me finding a spot on the floor or empty couch for the night, whenever. In fact, things got downright social after awhile. Tommy was a bit of a thespian who usually hung out with another crowd, but Al and Tipper, Chris and Mary (a couple who's origin in this party scene was unclear), Marta and I, J.G. (sometimes solo and sometimes not), and a mix of others found a sort of mellow excitement in our own little "be-ins."

It was all perfect for me right up to graduation day—not so for my folks. They were visibly sickened by my lack of a proper haircut, my goatee, and my gown flopping open, exposing my cut-off tee shirt as I received my diploma. *What is trivial to some is monumental to others* I thought at the time, despite such a special moment when giving parents deserved to be proud. *Oi vey*, what I have wrought?!

Despite my embarrassing display at graduation, Mom and Dad agreed to fund my summer trip to Europe. After all, I was going to a top-notch medical school in the fall and needed a break between studies, a reward, if you will. Reminds me of the old Jewish joke whose punch line is "life begins when your son gets into medical school." Well I got in and I intended to take full advantage of the triumph.

Billy, Elliott and I flew across the pond together; landed at Heathrow Airport in London and then made our way to Koln, Germany to stay with friends of Billy's parents. After that we figured we would play it by ear for a month or so and then hook up with Marta who planned on meeting me in Amsterdam—a very cool itinerary.

Germany was a bit stuffy, but we were wined and dined by the old man and his hot young wife. We had the run of the place for several days until Katrin took us aside and abruptly suggested that we leave. Obviously dismayed at this sudden turn of events, Billy asked what it was we had done to offend her. It turned out that she had seen one of us take something from a store without paying for it and she was worried that we would steal from her as well.

"No. No, we would never do that," Billy passionately explained. "Don't you see? That was a store. You are our friends. We would never steal from you!" Simple enough; but far too presumptuous for Katrin, who was kind enough not to mention any of this to her husband, thus sparing Billy and his parents big-time embarrassment.

Next morning we were dropped off at a used car dealership and bought a red Volkswagen van with a broken odometer for $200. Our destination became the Black Forest to taste some Bavarian cheesecake and check out the scene in Schwaben. The Greenwich Village of Bavaria, highlighted by its proximity to an amazingly dense population of perfectly aligned pine trees, was billed as hippy heaven with an old world look. An apt description.

We were welcomed by thin, long-haired, multi-lingual freaks with abundant curiosity and weed to spare. The food was rich, the accommodations a bit crowded, but the kindred spirit abounded. No question, we could have enjoyed the entire summer right there, but the word was that the real scene was in the Balearic Islands off the coast of Spain. So after a few spaced-out days we mapped our route and headed south.

Switzerland was pristine; the magnificently groomed landscapes and flower trimmed monuments were awesome. Playing Frisbee on Lake Geneva made the same activity on the filthy, dirty Charles River in Boston seem like sewer saucer. Lausanne and Geneva were hard to leave, but the countryside of southern France ripe with firm, sweet, succulent peaches the size of softballs made the journey delicious. In Avignon and Arles I practiced my high school and college French. It was absolutely exhausting. Somehow the Bs (and occasional A-) I got did not translate into the ability to communicate with real live French people. By the time we passed through the Pyrenees into Spain though, it really didn't matter much. I got by on "dose heuvos con fritos y café con leche."

Barcelona was quaint, but at the same time quite cosmopolitan with lots of piazzas and action. We actually got hold of some dated New York Times newspapers from May and early June and learned about the Apollo launchings as a dress-rehearsal for landing a man on the moon. The notion was just way too spacey to believe or take seriously. It was kind of like the crazy "Bed-In" that John Lennon and Yoko Ono were conducting for days on end at the Queen Elizabeth Hotel in Montreal, Canada. Unreal stuff; it was just that kind of world at the time. But the record *Give Peace a Chance* (the first solo recording by a Beatle and released under the goofy name *Plastic Ono Band*) was pretty groovy. We managed to get it on tape along with an album called *Led Zeppelin I* by a new group of the same name (which, from an oxymoron standpoint was also groovy). Every night our van was filled with freaks that just couldn't get enough of our sounds.

Just about all of our new friends were European. They talked of Ibiza and Formentera (two of the smaller of the Balearic Islands to the south in the Mediterranean Sea) as wild beach scenes and the place to be in the summer. So we headed down the Costa Brava towards Valencia in order to catch the overnight ferry that would take us to paradise. The trip down the coast was magnificent. Tarragona, Tortosa, and Calstellon were all right on the rich blue Mediterranean. I never saw water so clear except in a glass. As anxious as we were to get to our destination, the public beaches all along the way were irresistible. We had the entire summer so WTF!

Arriving in Valencia was all about finding the ferry that would take our van and us to Ibiza. Unfortunately, we were told that we must first go by ship to Palma de Mallorca and then catch a ferry to the smaller island. That didn't jive with what we were told back in Barcelona, so we decided to stay overnight in town hoping to find a more direct route in the morning. After eating around twilight we made our way over to the water to catch the sunset. No sooner did we settle in for nature's show than we were startled by hostile Spanish expletives coming from a wacked-out constable wearing a clown-like square-backed hat and swinging a Billy club. He was not clowning around. As he charged, we blocked his onslaught as best we could and got the hell out of there. Despite being forewarned to avoid Madrid because Dictator Franco's police did not take kindly to hippies, we had no idea that we would run into such crap along the coast. It was only later that we learned how lucky we were to have escaped with only Billy getting his forearm clubbed. We joked later that the pig's club had Billy's name on it. Billy called us assholes.

Next day we were totally happy to take the first available ship to Mallorca and find our way from there. Mallorca had a bohemian reputation in travel brochures, but seemed very commercial to us so we didn't stay long. Unlike the ship, the boat ride to Ibiza was a bit rocky, but we managed to survive by staring at the horizon to keep from puking. Someone had told me that trick years ago and it actually worked, for me at least. As soon as we landed, the nausea was replaced by the enchanting scene of a beatific white stucco village full of artisans. My eyes immediately found a slender dark-eyed girl with pale complexion, delicate features and wild hair. She was wearing a soft flowing dress that clung to her graceful body as if caressing each contour. I believe she looked right back at me with a captivating child-like smile, but only for an instant and then she was gone. *Okay! Alright! This is the place.* I couldn't wait to get off the boat.

Almost instantly we ran into "California" Jim who had been on both Ibiza and its smaller neighboring island of Formentera for over a month. His sun-bleached hair flopped into natural dreadlocks over his inebriated eyes as he gave us the skinny on the island scene. Getting around Ibiza was a hell of a lot easier in our van than hitchhiking, so he enthusiastically agreed to give us the grand tour. By twilight we arrived at a small hacienda where we were pleasantly welcomed by several nicely tanned European ladies who graciously invited us to have dinner and stay the night. I had been thinking all day, *I love this place!* Unfortunately, there were several male freaks hanging out inside and busily preparing the ritual sundown chillum. Unlike their friendly female counterparts the men were a bit standoffish at first, but they became more sociable as the pipe was passed around.

After a few hits, a French dude with eye shadow and liner began playing guitar and humming. Before long he was joined by some bongos and a cat on harmonica; although not particularly melodic, the "music" wasn't bad because the hashish was so good. Things went on this way for hours until, one by one, we each crashed where we lay.

Come morning Jim signaled that we had outstayed our welcome and suggested that we check out the mind-blowing beach scene on the island of Formentera. Cool. We figured we were in good hands so we let him direct us back to Eivissa (our original port of landing) so we could catch a ferry to the port of la Savina.

***

The seas were calm and the trip to la Savina was quicker than I expected. As we drifted into port, the lack of action was immediately obvious, and with it Jim's short-lived reputation took a serious hit. Doubting that we would stay on such a desolate island for long we, nevertheless, followed Jim's cues to the small village of San Fernando (which, along with its sister village of San Francisco made up the two most populated towns on the island). Pepe's, the only restaurant/bar in town was the main hang-out. It was there that I once again caught a glimpse of the captivating beauty I saw on the landing dock when we arrived in Ibiza the day before. She appeared somewhat anxious as she followed a huge, bald-headed black guy out the back of Pepe's. Pointing her out to Jim, I asked if he knew who she was. He had little info to offer other than that he thought she was French "which explains why she acts so weird," he said matter-of-factly. Somehow I was deeply attracted to "weird" and immediately made up my mind to stay on Formentera.

There were rooms for rent at Pepe's and over in San Francisco, but we followed Jim's lead out to the beach on the south side of the island. Although the whole island was only nineteen kilometers long, the shore seemed to stretch forever since there were no buildings or structures to obscure one's vision along the lone paved road. Jim ordered us to park by the hut advertising *agua*, Coca-Cola, and *huevos* sandwiches. As we made our way down to the rich blue water we instantly understood Jim's enthusiasm for Formentera. Heading straight for us (or actually the beverage hut behind us) was a tanned audacious babe wearing only a loin cloth. "Bonjour, mes amis," she sang in passing. We, of course, were speechless while Jim sported this big old "I-told-you-so" grin across his face.

After days of beach living, chillum parties, and sleeping under the stars, we were each stamped with Formentera tans (Elliott was pitch black) and decked out in the traditional uniforms of scarves made into loin cloths (tan lines and bathing suits were the stigmata of rookies). Of course, the lack of world news was inconsequential, but we were startled one day in mid July, after drifting into town, to hear of "The Eagle" landing on the lunar surface! Sure enough, on July 20th Apollo 11 carrying Neil Armstrong, Buzz Aldrin, and Michael Collins had landed on the moon. The local newspaper carried Armstrong's words in Spanish across the headline, "That's one small step for man, one giant step for mankind." Pepe himself translated the news for us. He was so excited; you'd think he was *Americano*. Unfortunately, mention of the youngest, and sole surviving, Kennedy brother (Edward M.) being drunk and driving his car off a bridge on Chappaquiddick Island, Massachusetts two days after the Apollo launch and two days before the moon landing tempered the locals' enthusiasm for American ingenuity with fodder for disdain. The sentiment was shared by everyone when we learned that Mary Jo Kopechne (a young former campaign aid to Bobby Kennedy) died in the accident under suspicious circumstances.

Later that night, as we toasted sundown to the west and the rising moon to the east, I recalled my many intimate encounters with the moon at Hamilton College and realized that they would never seem the same to me again now that I knew a guy had walked up there.

Speaking of being moonstruck, I finally found out the name of that sultry French chick that haunted my thoughts: Virginie. The guy she seemed to follow was called "Black George" (to distinguish him from "Blind George" who was white and legally blind because of retinal macular degeneration). Black George dealt heroin and, unfortunately, Virginie had a habit. *So much for hooking up with her*, I thought sensibly, until she approached me one day at a small villa rented by mutual friends of ours. She spoke only a few words of English and apparently found my broken French terribly entertaining. Before I knew it, I was swept away by her exotic charm. After making it clear that I did not do heroin or hard drugs she seemed surprisingly attracted to me.

As slow as beach life can seem on the surface, relationships moved very fast. Free love and the kindred hippy spirit of the '60s were powerful aphrodisiacs. To the best of my knowledge, Virginie remained clean (from heroin) for days as we enjoyed Formentera together. Then Julia popped up. This stunning blond teenager from Germany had a smile that weakened my knees—this was obvious to Virginie immediately. But the big surprise turned out to be that Julia felt the same way about Virginie, not me. Julia hung out with us because of her attraction to Virginie; I figured all this out during my first ménage a trois. Though incredibly frustrating at the time (certainly for me anyway), we laughed about it for weeks afterwards. Somehow this exciting intrigue created a deeper bond between Virginie and me; partly because I had no shot at Julia. So we were both particularly sad when the boys and I departed Spain to explore Morocco without her. The fact was, I asked her to come along, but she felt that she could not (perhaps because she feared being too far away from Black George and the comfort he supplied?).

As our ship pulled away from the Eivissa dock my eyes were locked with Virginie's and I promised myself that the next time I left she would be at my side. Like a Hollywood movie our gaze remained transfixed for what seemed like hours until the Island of Ibiza was but a stone in the vast Mediterranean Sea.

Our trusty guide "California" Jim, of course, jumped at the chance to come down to Morocco with us. We headed for Alicante and then drove down the Costa del Sol to Malaga. There we would catch another ship to Melilla, Morocco, in order to avoid landing in Tangier where "everyone gets ripped off." The trip down the coast was breath-taking, as expected, but I could not wait to get out of Spain hoping to escape the thought of leaving Virginie behind.

Melilla was an absolute culture shock for all of us. Our first experience in a Muslim town, devoid of all modern conveniences (unlike one might find in metropolitan cities like Tangier, Rabat, or Casablanca) was like setting foot on another planet or stepping back in time to the Middle Ages. But adventure was what we were looking for—the quest to experience the world and far-out places. Jim was wearing his I-told-you-so grin as we headed down the narrow mountain roads to Fez, then Meknes, and on to Marrakech! We were on the bus (a broken down VW, but a bus nevertheless) the whole way, playing Crosby, Stills and Nash.

In Fez we picked up a couple of sets of Moroccan bongos, some traditional shirts and vests (which I mailed back home to Marta for sale in Boston), and got turned onto to green tea and the local weed (called kif) smoked in a long pencil-thin pipe with a small clay bowl at the end. More *Marrakech Express* (this time with bongo accompaniment), kif, and an Italian hitch-hiker named Antonio. Meknes was fun and riding on the mountain roads past stretches of kif fields was positively outrageous, but arriving in Marrakech spelled CARNIVAL. Jugglers, snake charmers, hash cookies—the works! We were in freak heaven.

A shower at the hotel was bliss and cost three dirham (about 25 cents). We slept in the van with our ever-updated rock sounds and soon had curious hippy company including Christie, a chick I remember having seen hanging out with Blind George back on Formentera. She was no Virginie, but good enough and actually cute in her own way. The good times were rolling, no doubt, until one evening when the notion struck me: *At summer's end I will be returning to the States to start Cornell Medical School.* I quickly pushed the thought out of my mind as best I could and forced myself to live in the now.

Tony (Antonio) voiced (in his heavy Italian accent) his desire to go south to Mauritania in the Sahara, but we were willing to go only as far as Goulimim (the "doorway to the Sahara Desert" famous for its multicolored beads and enchanting Guedra dance of love) and no further. It took some doing (because of the language barrier) but we also convinced Tony to come back with us to Formentera once we left Africa. Elliott, on the other hand, had already decided to head back to the States via London. Perhaps a little sick of life on the road and desirous of American comforts (including soft toilet paper), he would leaves us in Ceuta, Spain.

I was ambivalent about leaving exotic Morocco, but was excited to reunite with Virginie. Unfortunately, upon my return she was nowhere to be found. The beach scene was much like we had left it with many of the same players (*sans* Virginie). The big talk amongst the Americans in early August was about crazy Charles Manson and his so-called "family" cult that went on a killing spree murdering among others, actress Sharon Tate who was eight months pregnant. We also heard reports that President Nixon was working on "Vietnamization" of the war and pulling out American troops. But news from overseas seemed so foreign in our supreme state of self-absorbed isolation.

Marc and his wife Julia,who was pregnant with their first child, were Brits who made the pilgrimage to Formentera every summer. He was well prepared with his fully loaded Land Rover, buckets of suntan lotion to protect their fair skin, and gray crystal acid he claimed was made by "Sir" Owsley himself. For days he prepared us for the August full moon party on the beach which he claimed would take us to another dimension, or at least knock our socks off. Word of the event spread across the island like wild fire and even attracted dozens of freaks from neighboring Ibiza.

At twilight, on the first day of the full moon, brown scantily covered bodies began pouring onto the white beach in anticipatory rapture. Some built bonfires; others sat in circles preparing chillums. Marc and his designated team (Billy, Tony, and I) were given folded pieces of newspaper each containing gray crystal powder about the size of a silver dollar.

"Blokes, this stuff is powerful, so meter it out carefully," Marc counseled.

I watched Billy show those gathering around him just how to take the stuff. He wet his index finger in his mouth, then touched the powder and delivered it to his tongue. *Easy enough.* As we continued the demonstrations, it occurred to me that the exact dosage of a single trip was unclear. *Maybe we should stop.* I handed what was left in my packet to someone else and sat down next to Julia near the bonfire. She handed me a plastic thermos cup of red wine and told me to take only a sip because it was spiked with gray crystal acid. I did so and passed the cup to Billy sitting next to me. Much to my surprise he drained it and handed it back. "What are you doing?" I asked in disbelief.

The next thing I knew I was flat on my back staring up at the full moon and thinking that I could simply will myself to float up to its surface and play Neil Armstrong. How it got so dark and the moon ascend so fast I had no idea. Then it occurred to me. I had taken so much LSD that maybe I overdosed. *Can you O.D. on LSD? What happens if you do? Maybe my parents were right; drugs are dangerous!*

Hours passed before I had the ability to sit up and right myself. To my astonishment most of the other revelers were sitting side-by-side in circles with their arms wrapped around each other, swaying back and forth, chanting, "We can make it. We can make it." Their bodies were outlined in day-glow colors as were others who were doing cartwheels and rolling around on the beach. Some were making love with desperate fury. Clearly, we all had taken too many hits of gray crystal, but miraculously survived.

The psychedelic scene went on this way for two full nights without any need (or desire) for more drugs. By the second morning the beach was strewn with fatigued freaks lying wasted in the sand and shallow tide.

Full physiologic recovery took me at least a week, but the experience was permanent. "Exciting" and "freaky" were balanced with "frightening" and "grateful" (grateful for having survived the mind twisting experience). The talk on the beach over the next several days was all about the August Full Moon Party, but mention was made about Bob Dylan's concert on the Isle of Wight, and something about a huge multi-band concert on a farm up in Woodstock, NY that got rained out.

My head was just about centered when we made the trip back up the Costa Brava, through the south of France and into Switzerland on our way up to Holland to meet my girlfriend Marta in Amsterdam. There was only one hitch: as we crossed from Basel, Switzerland into Lorrach, Germany we were asked to get out of our vehicle for a search by the border guards. Not surprisingly, they found a couple of pipes and some hashish. What was surprising was that they confiscated my van and threw us all in jail!

How I, a white upper middle class young American student on his way to matriculation at Cornell Medical School, could get busted and thrown in the slammer in Germany made no sense. Sure, I was scared (mainly that my parents would find out), but outrage and being pissed at my stupidity superseded my emotions. Dealing with the hegemonic border police was a game I was ready to play because I had been forewarned that they were in it for the pay-off. Recognizing that I was on to their money scheme, they let me out of the clinker next day—with the assignment of collecting five grand for the release of my comrades and the van.

My discussion with Billy's parents (both medical doctors) was anything but pleasant. I had to be careful because, although they did not know my parents personally, they certainly were capable of contacting them. Explaining that their son had been ripped off and needed about $1,000 wired to Germany in order to complete his trip and buy a new ticket home was easy. Why he had not made the call himself, I figured he could explain to them himself when he was no longer imprisoned. Evoud's dad in Holland sounded like he had bailed his son out before, so my honesty was appreciated. Jim's girlfriend in SoCal said to "tell the bastard that this was the last time," but agreed to sell his stereo and wire the money.

When the "Gestapo" readily agreed to accept $3,500 instead of $5,000 to resolve the problem, I realized that I could easily have kept the $500 (which I had received from Marta for the Moroccan goods) I threw in to sweeten the pot. *Idiot!* Not so smart, after all. Nevertheless, freedom and being back on the road was sweet. Really sweet.

Arriving in Amsterdam was a triumph. My two Hollander friends were incredibly grateful and helped me find Marta at the American Express center. They then took us directly to the famous Paradiso (the quintessential psychedelic discothèque) where hashish was legal and the international freak show was free.

Marta was wide-eyed and all ears as I, the world traveler, told her about Marrakesh and my imprisonment in Germany. Before long we were on a houseboat-like barge in one of the canals, where Marta witnessed people shooting up for the first time. Although I had already been exposed to this sordid behavior, it was no less repugnant to me so we worked our way out of there fast. The rest of the week was just heaven—my girl and me, and fantastic stories about Morocco, Formentera, and the full moon party.

Suddenly it was the end of August! The end of summer; one filled with the most amazing adventures, across two continents, in which I met the most spaced-out people ever. I lived nearly naked on a beach, had a romance with an exotic French junky, was on the African continent, and survived a night in jail. Now the prospect of starting my first year of medical school among the most conventional people in the world was a bit of a let down and, quite frankly, a mega-bummer!

***

BUMMER! BUMMER! BUMMER!

I can't believe they threw me in here! I'm educated! I'm supposed to go to medical school! I come from a civilized country! We have the rule of law! I'm an American! You can't do this to me! I'm innocent!

My cellmates don't give a shit about the injustice…*do you! Wake up! Don't you find me interesting anymore? I'm your entertainment, remember? Achhh! I can't stand it!*

This is the last of it. My refuge from Hell is just about gone. And who knows if I will ever see J.G. again; if I will ever see another American again…

Hmmf… hmmf…There we go… It's all good…and I can dream one last time.

***

Marta and I really enjoyed Al and Tipper's celebrity wedding in May at Washington's National Cathedral in D.C. J.G. was Al's best man and it was shocking to see the groom's mom come at Jimmy with scissors demanding that he cut his long hair to a "respectable length." J.G. was not about to surrender, but he did compromise by wearing his hair tucked up under a top hat. Few, if any, pictures of Al in his military dress uniform included the best man or any of us hippy friends wearing less than formal attire.

Aside from the lovely choice of *All You Need is Love* played by the organist, most of us were of the mind that the event was a warped springboard for Al's future political career. But hey, to each his own; the guy wanted to be President and outdo his old man who only made it to the Senate. I wasn't much different, come to think of it. I figured that becoming a cardiothoracic surgeon would put me one up on my father and make him especially proud of me. But now I was heading in an entirely different direction once the medical school year came to an end.

***

The day my parents took me to Newark Airport was anything but pleasant. Sure, the sun was shining, but not on us. Mom broke down and admitted that they had considered taking my passport to prevent me from leaving the country, for my own good. The words "for my own good" set me off. I told them how stupid and ineffective such a tactic would have been. That they just didn't understand; I must see what's out there. In a simplistic way Dad asked, "Son, why do you have to think so much?"

"You want me not to think; not to question? You think

you need to take my passport to save me from myself?" *Enough!* I was furious with them.

When asked how much money I had, I answered that it was not important. They begged me to take the money Dad put in my hand, but I refused—leaving with a hundred dollars in my pocket and a plane ticket to Paris. Virginie awaited my arrival (we had kept in touch via mail all winter) and I was excited to begin my new life's journey. My departure was blurred by tears and borderline hysteria.

***

Paris was very different; kind of like the flamboyant freaks that met me at the airport in a psychedelic van. But it was Virginie's familiar beauty that made me feel at home. The flat we stayed in was crowded with her friends. The food was expensive. Knowing that my hundred bucks wouldn't get me very far (not to mention that I had no wheels) I headed up to Koln, Germany with a cat named Petre to work in his friend's factory. After being joined by J.G., who flew out from the States to meet me as planned, we both got busy rolling up posters and stuffing them into cardboard cylinders. After several weeks we had amassed about a thousand dollars, which was plenty to live on for awhile, considering our vagabond, hippy lifestyle. Four hundred went to the purchase of a used blue VW van, which we drove south through Germany, France, and Spain to Barcelona. J.G. couldn't wait to see the spaced-out scene I had told him about in Ibiza and Formentera. I couldn't wait to see Virginie who had left for our rendezvous spot in the Balearic Islands shortly after I left Paris to make some money in Germany.

It took J.G. all of about twenty minutes to fall in love

with and become a beloved player in the bohemian lifestyle of the islands. It took me about the same amount of time to learn that Virginie was on Formentera. Though anxious to make the voyage, I acquiesced to J.G.'s desire to check out Ibiza first. After meeting up with who else but "California" Jim, we headed out to a villa in a secluded cove to spend the night. Jim was again wearing one of his patented "check-this-out" smiles. It was not long before we were sitting in a chillum circle and being fed as the pipe was passed around.

As a grateful gesture I offered to go out to the van to get our stereo tape player so we could enjoy some music. Above the giggles, I was told not to bother. Apparently, they had something better. His name was Henry, but they all called him Taj. Having gotten a glimpse of him earlier, I was struck by the black man's countenance and obvious respect he commanded from the others. As soon as he picked up his guitar and began to sing I fully understood "California" Jim's smile. This was Taj Mahal; *the* Taj Mahal! And all night long he played stuff from *Nach'l Blues* and *Giant Step*, as well as some new stuff, accompanied by amateurs on bongos and mouth harps. Too cool!

Nevertheless, come morning I was ready to get to Formentera and Virginie. So we finished the tour of Ibiza for J.G. and headed to the Eivissa dock in time to catch the last ferry. The seas were rough and while the others were focused on the horizon to settle their stomachs, my thoughts were focused on Virginie.

Upon arriving, however, it took me several trying days to track her down. *Was she back with Black George; feeding her smack habit?* I heard rumors that she had left the islands altogether with a Frenchman named Pierre; a pot-bellied, older, but very wealthy restaurateur. One of her French girlfriends said that Virginie had a baby over the winter and that Pierre had promised to provide for the child even though it wasn't his. J.G. tried earnestly to comfort me. I could not wait to introduce him to my exotic beauty and just like that I found I was but one of a string of men in her young life with whom she had toyed. Why should I be surprised? After all, she was a junky; a road person with no ties or sense of responsibility: not to her baby, not to me; not even to herself. *Forget her, you fool. The world lies ahead, ripe for exploration. It is the real reason why you are here.*

Fantasies are hard to get past, but I managed. There were plenty of other chicks and it was fun to watch J.G.'s child-like joy when we hit the beach scene on Formentera. I felt like "California" Jim's all-knowing smile was painted across my face. Running into many of my old acquaintances from a year ago (some of whom were players in the August '69 full moon party) was special; almost like I hadn't missed a beat. *Did I really spend a year in medical school?*

Feeling my independence was so intoxicating that I succumbed to the urge to get my ear pierced. There was some discussion about which ear I should have stuck. A certain side supposedly indicated that you were gay, so I had better choose the opposite side. Since most people I talked with believed that the right was the gay side, I opted for the left ear. The chick with the sewing needle told me that the ice would help numb the pain and proceeded to sterilize her surgical instrument with a match. After pushing the needle through my earlobe she left a loop of thread there (since no one had an earring I could borrow) in order to keep the new hole from closing over. Several days later, and with only a mild infection, I inserted my first gold stud. I was now officially a hippy!

CHAPTER 3

Peaceful Easy Feeling

It wasn't long before J.G. started asking about Morocco. I had talked it up so much he was itching to check it out. I stalled for a while, partly because I was having a blast right where I was and partly because I still thought I might run into Virginie. But after a couple of weeks we headed back to Ibiza to catch a ship to the Spanish coast. As we pulled into Eivissa I was slammed hard with déjà vu; on the dock stood Virginie in all the splendor of my first vision of her a year ago. She was with Pierre and they were arguing. When finally our eyes met her angry demeanor magically melted leaving that captivating child-like smile for which I longed. As I stood up above her on the ship, like a knight on his stallion, she seemed to instantly forget Pierre. J.G. later told me that all at once he knew that this girl was the fabled Virginie.

The very next day we stood on the deck of a ship to the Spanish mainland, Virginie by my side. It took her no longer to make the decision to come along with me as it did for me to tell her I was leaving for Morocco the next day. She managed a slight wave to Pierre as our ship pulled away. Not knowing the man, it seemed awkward that I felt a kind of kinship with him from knowing that we were both in love with Virginie and that neither of us could truly have her for long. But this was my time and I planned to make the most of it.

The ride down the Costa Brava was more beautiful than the first because I had Virginie with me—the ship ride to Africa like a dream. The whole Moroccan thing had familiarity, but with a new exuberance that was beyond words. Not only did we visit the coastal town of Essaouira (known for its black magic and whirling dervishes), but we traveled far south, well below Agadir and Tiznit, to the Oued Draa River just above Western Sahara. Virginie revealed to me that she had been to Moroc' (as she called it) before. The reason we stopped in Essaouira was so she could ask a Sufi if her travel with the American (me) would be fruitful. Apparently, she got an affirmative answer and so she became excited to get me to the desert. There we slept out in the open "with a million stars all around" (making the Eagles' *Peaceful Easy Feeling* a song that would always remain deeply special to me).

The days were unduly hot, but without the tortuous humidity that would have made it unbearable. Washing in streams required soaping up one body part at a time and then quickly rinsing off so that the intensely dry heat didn't have time to turn the coating of soap into a firm crust,nearly impossible to wash off.

The peacefulness of the desert was intoxicating, but J.G. eventually became hungry for some action, so we headed back up to the circus that is Marrakech. There he juggled with the jugglers, romped with the acrobats, and got his fill of carnival and hash cookies while Virginie and I watched (almost like doting parents). On our way back north, we passed through Fez to pick up shirts, vests, and Moroccan tapestries that we would mail to Marta so she could sell the goods to her college friends in Boston. She sent me the profits (and, to my surprise, took no commission). Sounded like a great gig to me, so I thought that I would keep the business going once I got to India. On the road there was no shame.

The shop owner from whom we bought the dry goods was so grateful for our business that he invited us to dine with him and his family. Hungry for food and the bourgeois experience, we gladly accepted. Leaving our shoes at the door we entered his humble abode as his curious children gathered around us. We were motioned to sit on a colorful Moroccan rug around the central, communal pot of couscous. Straw plates were handed out by a young girl; green tea was poured and the feast began. But then an obviously happy family, abounding with joy to share their food with guests, suddenly turned sullen and quiet. The abrupt change in mood caught us off guard. The shopkeeper motioned for us to get up and leave, which we did with some hesitation.

Once we were well down the street, Virginie, who understood some of the family chatter that was partly in a French dialect, explained that our hosts were deeply insulted when J.G. (who was a lefty) contaminated the communal couscous pot by reaching in with his left hand—the one used to clean one's ass! Ah, yes, a stupid, crass, Ugly

American *faux pas*. But what else can one expect from us culturally barren hippies? J.G. wanted desperately to go back and apologize, but Virginie insisted it would do no good and only make matters worse.

It was not long before Virginie was anxious to return to Ibiza. I couldn't help but think that she had the urge to nurse her smack habit, which she had so valiantly tamed for several weeks during our travels. My attempts to talk about her addiction came up short, as so many of our meaningful conversations had. After all, our inability to fully express our thoughts to one another in a common tongue had avoided conflict and probably prolonged our relationship. More than once she expressed the feeling that I was too good for her and that she would only bring me down. I, naively, felt that I was just what she needed to win the battle and triumph over her demons. "Tu fou," she would cry. "You are mad!" But the tears in her eyes made it sound to me like a desperate cry for help.

Back on Formentera the days were long and lazy. Reading Hesse, Gurdjief, Ospensky, and the *I Ch'ing* provided basic fodder for pursuit of the occult. Stories about gurus Meher Baba (who recently passed over) and Bagawan Sri Rashneesh who resided in Bombay were told by those who had journeyed east. Intermingled with the hippy beach scene of drugs and free-love, the fine line between the pursuit of Nirvana and hedonism was comfortably blurred beyond recognition. Summer passed gently in this way until the cool fall winds signaled that it was time to move on. Following the sun from the Balearic Islands in August to the warmth of Goa on the west coast of India in winter was what many referred to as the "hippy trail." It sounded awfully good to me; after all, India was my primary destination.

There was just one problem: Virginie was lonely for (or feeling guilty about) *L'enfant* (her baby whom she never named). The child was apparently living with her *grandmere* in Paris. For more than a month I tolerated living in a villa on Ibiza with about a dozen very spaced-out French freaks that did nothing but smoke and play musical instruments (badly) while Virginie decided whether to come along with me and J.G. to India or head up north to Paris. When she chose the latter, I robotically elected to drive her to France in hopes that she would change her mind and journey with us to *L'Orient*. J.G., despite thinking that I was nuts, graciously conceded. His free and easy manner was music to my ears (and dysfunctional mental state).

Paris turned out not to be the "City of Love" that I remembered. Instead I was damned to tolerate more bizarre goings-on, more freaky friends of Virginie who smoked all day and played bad music, a cute little blonde toddler (called Gwendol by his *grandmere*) that Virginie seemed not to want to coddle or even hold, and a grandmother who fought constantly with her granddaughter (thank God I couldn't understand a word of it). It was too expensive to enjoy the city, so J.G. and I primarily hung out in the flat. After weeks of this nonsense and the closing in of cold weather, I finally came to the realization (with the help of my side-kick) that I had to extricate myself from the dumpster. With or without Virginie we were heading east in the morning!

CHAPTER 4

The Razor's Edge

The road out of Paris was empty for me without Virginie. J.G. joked about "whispering French nothings in my ear," and asked me, "What, am I just chopped liver?" in an effort to snap me out of my depression. He was truly valiant in the face of my morose obstinacy. Surprisingly, however, we ran into Hannuke and Evoud in Switzerland. This time they had a VW van of their own, red to go with our blue one. They too were headed east so we started a small caravan. Initially, the addition of two more very warm traveling companions was uplifting, but soon, seeing the two of them act so lovingly together caused me to fall back into reverie over my loss of Virginie.

It was our unfortunate mistake to pass through Austria on our way to Yugoslavia. By this time we clearly bore the full stigmata of the hippy culture. (Months earlier I had even given up wearing underwear because it was just more stuff to wash and take care of.) The bohemian/gypsy look, no doubt, was a magnet for disdain.

While buried deep within our sleeping bags (or under blankets) to avoid being bitten by mosquitoes one night, we were brutally awakened by stiff boots in the ribs and back. While these Gestapo-like thugs worked us over, my mind raced back to Mr. Crouter (my high school world history teacher) who called Hitler "a carpetbagger, with paint chips under his nails, from Austria." With some effort we scrambled out of there fast, and I swore I would never even go near a Viennese dessert table ever again.

The coast of Yugoslavia was salve for our wounds; a seaside of extraordinary majesty. It was there in Dubrovnik that we hooked up with another VW van (this one green) full of Europeans also heading east. As our caravan grew and we meandered along the inlets and waterways of this enchanting country, I could feel my fixation on Virginie wane (with the help of Olivia, a British chick in the green van). Though not as captivating as my *femme-fatale* she made life and love open up again for me.

By the end of the year we were lucky to arrive in Greece; just in time to be spared the bitter cold of winter. It was there that we learned the inconceivable—the Beatles were breaking up! We spoke more about that tragedy (and the deaths of Jimi Hendrix and Janis Joplin) than the Kent State shootings.

I and my cronies celebrated the New Year (1971) by selling our blood in Thessaloniki for well needed cash (and free orange juice). While some wanted to head south to spend the rest of winter in the Greek islands, the mystical allure of India won out. By this time we were sharing books like *Autobiography of a Yogi* by Paramhansa Yogananda, *The Complete Works of Swami Vivekananda*, and the new *Be*

Here Now by Baba Ram Das (formerly known as Dr. Richard Alpert). Nothing would deter our rush to enlightenment.

The route we drew up was direct: Istanbul across northern Turkey (avoiding hang-ups in Ankara) and on to Iran. We were especially warned not to travel with those having passports with visas stamped in Israel for fear of rejection by Arab countries. While Istanbul (with its Blue Mosque and other fascinations from the Ottoman Empire) was tempting, we passed through rather quickly and headed for the lonely stretch of road just south of the Black Sea.

Travel along the two lane "highway" was desolate and boring; that is until we came upon an accident that clearly had happened just minutes before. A white, late model Mercedes with European plates lay flipped over on its roof, somehow run off the road, with its two passengers writhing in pain outside the vehicle. One had an obvious broken femur and the other abdominal injuries. Though sickened to my stomach I, nevertheless, summoned my experience from one year in medical school to help me make the diagnoses and act like I knew what I was doing. After carefully moving them into our vans, one managed to communicate to us in German/English that there was a hospital in Sivas some two hundred kilometers southwest. Without hesitation we changed course, anxiously hoping to get there in time. The thought of being in their predicament (in central Turkey with life-threatening injuries) put me on edge and filled us all with unspeakable doubts about the journey ahead.

We had the guy with belly pain in our van; moaning and begging for water. The cat with the broken leg was yelling so loudly from the green van, as it tossed over uneven roads, that we had to roll up our windows and speed ahead to mute his agonizing shrill. Three hours later we entered Sivas, a town without paved roads that somehow harbored a hospital. Finding the emergency entrance was easy enough, but explaining that we had a medical emergency and finding help was something far more daunting. It was left to us to carry the injured in and lay them down on stretchers. My companions filed out while J.G. and I looked for some reassurance that a doctor was being sought for care.

Before we ever saw anyone looking like a physician, several men in disheveled military apparel gruffly escorted us to a facility nearby. We were being thrown in jail!

Being locked up for no reason was insulting enough, but being thrown in prison in Turkey?! This seemed like the kiss of death after all we had heard about Westerners disappearing in Turkish jails for drugs; but for saving lives?! No way. This just could not be happening!

Unlike the cell in Germany, this place was a rat hole that smelled of piss. Meaningful communication with our captors was impossible. Even laidback J.G. was clearly shitting bricks. We had no idea where the others were and as we spent the night in that sewer we feared it might be the first of many more to come.

Miraculously in the morning, just like that, we were released and told to go, get out of town. To my exasperation, J.G. was looking for an apology as I quickly yanked him out of there. We found the others outside. They had not been locked up at all and managed to convince the police that we were not involved in the accident, but instead acted as an ambulance (drawing a Red Cross on a piece of paper that fortunately got the point across). For the second time in my life the appreciation of freedom from prison overwhelmed me.

As I was filling up the van with gas at a one pump station, my exhilarated feeling was suddenly eradicated by the eerie sensation of cold steel on the back of my neck. As I slowly turned around I was face to face with my leather skinned intimidator smiling through a mouth full of gold teeth and wielding a two foot-long machete. His wide-open smile emitted a rancorous odor that made me recoil, hitting the back of my head hard on the van. He and his Turkish audience found this very amusing as he played with the beads around my neck; moving them slowly one by one counterclockwise with his sharp sword. At that moment I feared that I might die for the second time in my life (the LSD overdose at the 1969 full moon party on Formentera was the first).

After a boisterous laugh, at my expense, my tormentor abruptly motioned with his weapon for me to move on. *Sucker, you are only being toyed with. Take your beads and Western hippy ways with you out of our proud land. You are an infidel, not worthy of our assiduity.*

Not being wanted was absolutely fine with me; and his encouragement to hightail it out of there was even better. Without looking back, our entourage wasted no time putting the lovely town of Sivas at a distance.

In our haste to abandon Turkey we drove nonstop through the night at nearly our top speed of seventy-five kilometers per hour. The only saving grace of our maddening run to freedom was the spectacular transformation of absolute night into the liberation of dawn.

Some five hundred kilometers from Sivas we reached the northeastern border of Iran near the town of Khvoy. There our Dutch friends found no trouble getting their passports stamped. In fact, they were welcomed and given open-ended visas, permitting them to stay as long as they liked. Apparently, the Shah of Iran got his beloved tulips from Holland, which translated into cart blanches for Dutchmen entering his country. We miserable non-tulip producers, on the other hand, were reluctantly given one-week passes through Persia (which I believe was granted only because our Dutch brother and sister were with us).

Our hasty one-week journey through northern Iran left us little time in Teheran and no time to explore the coast along the Caspian Sea. People were friendly and many whom we met made a point to emphasize their Persian heritage rather than be confused with Arabs. There was a definite western feel to this country both in dress, manner, and their acceptance of us. The warm sense of safety was a stark contrast to my experience in Turkey.

After leaving Taybad, the last Persian town en route to Afghanistan, the ambiance of the countryside seemed to change and take on a more Moroccan feel. At the border I sensed that we were once again being treated as nuisance hippies. The guards, who looked no more presentable than we road-dusted travelers, eyed us with obvious disdain, but waved us through nevertheless. A couple of hours later we reached Herat (a major city in this archaic land) and found that we were among our own tribe. The western freaks we encountered had passed this way before and explained our options en route to India.

The northern "Silk Roads" to China would take us up to Masar-e Sarif near the Russian border. The pressed pollen (a precursor to hashish) from that region was world renowned, but the unsavory mountain roads would make the journey rough. The flat "Spice Roads" to the south would bring us through Kandahar, but that meant missing Kabul and the enchanting little village in the hills of Pagman just above the capitol.

So we decided to take the central route, passing fabled tented Kuchis (meaning "nomads" in the Pashtu language) all along the way. The hot, dusty roads lent little to our heightened anticipation of things to come as we entered Asia with its archaic ambiance. It was not until we left the province of Ghor and entered Bamyan that signs of twentieth century technology (such as electrical wiring and gasoline stations) once again appeared.

Days later, when we reached Kabul my hunger for a shower was overwhelming. Throughout the journey I had kept up with my workout routine (daily runs, pushups and sit-ups) so that I, more than the others, stunk to high hell. I forked over five Afghanis (about 10 cents) at the first hotel I saw and sprinted to their shower. The soothing tepid water running over my body was revitalizing and somehow led me to chuckle over the time Marta had accidentally pushed me out of the shower on Billy's island. Later, a real sit down meal at the hotel for twenty Afghanis seemed terribly civilized (though the ingredients were suspect).

Refreshed and ready for more exploration we learned of Siggy's, a hippy restaurant hangout owned by a bloke from Liverpool. The enclave was isolated within an ancient ivy-covered stone wall that protected the goings-on inside from the very contrary monastic Muslim life outside. As Cat Stevens' *Tea for the Tillerman* album played loudly in the open courtyard we were greeted enthusiastically by members of our own tribe. Some looked healthier than others, with several so emaciated that the word "junky" immediately came to mind. Apparently living as an addict in the Orient was easy: the pharmacies actually sold cocaine and heroin OTC with minimal discretion and without breaking anyone's piggy bank.

Hanging out at Siggy's was entertaining and fun, in small increments. But the real find was Pagman in the hills above Kabul. This isolated, temperate community filled with shade trees (many bearing walnuts) revealed its secrets to us after just a few days camping on its outskirts. Raymond and Marie took a liking to J.G. and me. The handsome, articulate British couple had rented a white stucco villa which they had meticulously transformed into a palace filled with Oriental eloquence. The tapestries and nick-knacks of collector's quality seemed bizarrely out of place in this rather rustic land. But it was not long before J.G. and I discovered the truth: Raymond was a smuggler. Indeed, Pagman was a smuggler's community.

Most of the riches that were on display at Raymond and Marie's were acquired through illicit drug runs. While others in Pagman traded in anything that brought in a buck (including opium) Raymond was a purist; he only dealt with hashish. Though honorable, staying away from the hard stuff, he also knew it was a whole lot safer. Not only were the penalties for trafficking in narcotics stiffer, the suppliers of poppy products were ruthless. Instead, he bought bags of pollen (the precursor of hashish) from Masar-e Sharif, compressed and flattened it out in air-tight sealed plastic bags and hid the stuff in false paneled suitcases. "Runners" were hired to take the suitcases west where they were met, after clearing customs, by dealers in Europe and occasionally the United States. There the pressed pollen was mixed with water and turned into hashish. The water added volume and weight, which translated into more dollars for the final product. The runners were often young innocent looking kids who were returning to their western homes, often on student visas, after short sabbaticals in the East. They were paid handsomely (sometimes thousands) for taking the bulk of the risk.

J.G. and I watched the scene unfold like a suspense movie or international best selling thriller. The back room was filled with jumbo sized plastic garbage bags of loose cannabis pollen; the air so pungent with the mellifluous smell that just standing there induced an spontaneous high. Were Raymond and Marie not so very pleasant and down to earth we may easily have been scared off by their risky, treacherous business, but instead we enjoyed their hospitality.

Late one evening, as we lounged upon Tibetan sofas and Persian carpets listening to Crosby, Stills and Nash and Led Zeppelin, the couple introduced us to a white powder that J.G. and I had always looked upon with an odd combination of disdain and fascination. Raymond was very proud of his stash which was heroin actually refined in Marseille, France; not the Asian variety which was brown (as in *Brown Sugar* by the Rolling Stones). It was glassy-eyed Marie who offered us a snort, and wouldn't you know, my Harvard educated partner never hesitated. With a wink he cleared the line. Minutes later he had this look on his face that said, "You gotta' try this, bro."

Somewhere in the middle of *Stairway to Heaven* our

eyes connected and J.G. and I both agreed that the reason heroin was called *dope* (and all other drugs including pot should not be) was because it made everything seem so perfect; you could feel like you were sitting on a throne even if you were sitting on a pile of your own excrement. In other words, it turns you (the user) into a dope. The profundity was realizing that we were experiencing the ultimate mind altering drug, so powerful that the tranquil, secure feeling it produces belies its very own treachery. Somehow, even in the midst of its caress, we were both scared shitless of its power. I thought of Virginie and better understood the magnitude of her addiction. J.G. looked perplexed by my tears.

CHAPTER 5

The Incident

We stayed most of the time in a cement stucco house with eight or nine other freaks (the number varied on any given day) and, without assignment, we each assumed chores for the good of the group. I somehow enjoyed doing the dishes and general clean-up. No doubt Mom would have been mystified. J.G. was fascinated by cooking and really got into meal preparations (though shopping for ingredients, not so much). Others went into town to do the shopping. It was interesting how everyone seemed to gravitate to what they felt was needed for the communal good. Harmony reigned except for the hepatitis that was going around. Several jaundiced, lethargic house dwellers were diagnosed by a doctor in Kabul and placed on high dose vitamin C and herbal remedies. Incredulously, J.G. and I were not visibly stricken.

One bright sunny day we hopped in the van to check for mail at the American Express Office in Kabul. This weekly ritual did not always turn up word from loved ones back in the States, but the drive was always filled with anticipation and hope. Even world explorers get lonely and long for news from home.

The drive was bumpy and, as usual, I maneuvered the VW through a sea of bicycle riding Afghans. The sudden thud on the far right side of the van was accompanied by a sickening jolt that made my heart race as my right foot slammed hard on the brake. There is a travelers' aphorism, "If you hit something with your car in the East, don't stop. Keep on going." Harsh, words, but certainly profound as I should have realized from my experience in Turkey. Explanations about roadside accidents, especially from hippies, were seldom accepted. Nevertheless, always looking to rack up good karma, I picked up the kid (who actually ran right into the side of my van while horsing around with friends) as well as a nearby cop who told me that the kid was not looking where he was going; and we headed right to the hospital where (you guessed it) I was thrown into jail. *Come on! Where's the good karma? Where's God?!*

* * *

Forsaken! Abandoned in the worst damn place on earth! It was two days before J.G. managed to find out my location and got permission to come see me. He explained that the boy I hit ("That punk ran into me!" I yelled through the catcher's mask) happened to be the little brother of the Commandant. His leg was broken and I was to remain in jail until it healed.

"Are you shitting me? Get me out of here!" I ranted. "Where the hell is the U.S. Ambassador or Consulate? I'm a United States citizen!" J.G. calmly tried to explain that he

found me through the U.S. Consulate and they were working on getting me freed. He looked around and then passed me a folded piece of paper through the catcher's mask. "I'll be back tomorrow and every day you're in here until this thing is over. Don't worry I'm working on it." It was a sad moment when the guard pulled him away and all I saw was the back of J.G.'s long curly hair.

Stupefied, I suddenly remembered the folded paper J.G. managed to slip me when the guard wasn't looking. An escape plan? No; not a note at all. Instead, I found that it contained a gram of Raymond's white powder.

The putrid stench and bedeviled eyes of the rats I'm imprisoned with make this worse than a nightmare…I'm not waking up from this one. It's fucking real! And I have no more of Raymond's dope to get me through another day! How did I let this happen, after a life of such promise? My stupidity is overwhelming. My shame is immense.

What if J.G. can't get me out? What if I never see him again and I just rot here like these two hopeless souls…?

It's a miracle! J.G.! Jimmy! Get me out of here!

"Relax, bro," he says without having the slightest idea of what it's like to be in here.

"You try it for a day! You couldn't last one God damn day in this dungeon, son-of-a-bitch." His eyes transmit his pity and concern for me, and all at once my remorse for the outburst leads us both to tears.

"I'm trying. Believe me," he whispers earnestly. "Twice a day I go to the consulate. They know all about you, but the process is slow; very slow. Injustice is not a big concern to the Afghan authorities. But I will get you out somehow," he says reaching for my hand with another packet from

Raymond. I heroically reject his offer.

"If you are going to get me out I don't want to wind up a prisoner to that stuff." Filled with ambivalence, I make the stand based on anticipation of actually being released from the slammer sometime soon. Realizing that I will have to carry on in this hell drug-free weakens my knees, but I have no opportunity to renege as the guard abruptly pulls J.G. from the door ending his brief visit. "Come back tomorrow, Jimmy. Please," I shout after him. He raises his hand and nods reassurance over his shoulder while being gruffly led away.

After eight more days of excruciating mental anguish, sans pharmaceuticals, I am summarily extricated from the rat hole (twelve days in all); leaving behind the overwhelming stench of stale piss and my two cell mates, never once having had any meaningful communication with either one of them. I somehow managed to cope, despite the cramps, nausea, and shakes (early signs of heroin withdrawal), via shear faith that I would survive the humiliating injustice and be stronger for it. The theme of "ascendance through suffering" that permeated many of the occult books I had read gave me a target on which to focus...*a higher state of mind...the Holy Grail...the purpose of my journey.*

CHAPTER 6

Freedom Like No Other

Freedom this time takes on a whole new ecstasy. Germany and Turkey were overnight internments relatively free from the stench of human waste (though the latter was frightening because it was Turkey), but this imprisonment seemed to go on forever. Each day of bondage sapped me of my vigor, confidence, and faith; the very things that drove me east and inspired me to explore the world. My initial impulse was to get the hell out of this morbid country and even abandon my insane journey all together, but the spiritual call of India is overpowering.

J.G., on the other hand, does not want to leave because, aside from trying to correct my misfortune, he is having a gas. "Listen, man," I reasoned "these guys are nuts. They play by their own rules. We have got to get back to civilization." One small problem: the Kabul crazies took my passport on the day of my internment and won't give it back. I am still a prisoner in Afghanistan!

The daily waiting in government offices attempting

to retrieve my papers simply wears me out and gets me nowhere. Two months later, J.G. and I are fixtures in the Pagman/Kabul scene. Our caravan has long since dispersed, with Evoud and Hanneke moving eastward shortly after my incarceration. Before long my disdain for the Afghan way of life gets to me; especially after taking in a Buzkashi tournament (a form of polo played with a dead goat). As has been correctly said, this is a society that is an unpredictable composite of etiquette, honor, and extreme brutality.

As our money dwindles and my frustration about still being a prisoner in Afghanistan mounts, I begin listening to Raymond's plan to send a teenage Polynesian girl named Lei, traveling on a student's visa, back to her home in Hawaii with a sitar case concealing enough pressed pollen to split $40,000 three or four ways. He will finance the entire project, including plane fare for the runner and her hook-up, as well as arrange for the contact in Hawaii to complete the deal. Believing he can trust me to complete the transaction and send him his share of the take, he asks if I would consider being the hook-up. Still not having my passport, I simply laugh the whole thing off.

Miraculously, a few weeks later my passport appears on the desk of one of the government clerks, and without much ado he hands it to me. Just like that, I am free to leave the country after nearly four months in limbo. Meanwhile, J.G. has been in touch with "California" Jim who is now back home in Laguna Beach. He mentions the possible run to Hawaii and asks if Jim knows anyone reliable there who could complete the deal. The answer is unequivocally yes. Suffice it to say that our little trip to India is temporarily postponed while I take time out to see Hawaii and make some much-needed money.

As unpredictable as such drama can be, the caper comes off without a hitch. Lei is totally cool as she picks up the large yellow crate containing a sitar, clears customs, and is brought home by her parents. The next day Jim's man in Honolulu is given the crate in exchange for money. I give Lei her cut ($10,000) and wire the same amount to Raymond. After enjoying a few days on Kauai and eating potato chips on Maui, I take a plane ride to Laguna Beach to hang with Jim for a few days and give him his share of the booty. Can you dig it?

While in Southern California, I pick up *The Mucus Free Diet* written by Arnold Ehrets (some "professor" who cured his end-stage kidney disease by eating only fruits and vegetables) and decide to become a vegetarian. I exchange the rest of the money for American Express Travelers Checks and fly into Singapore on my way back to Kabul. My plan is to use the excess cash to buy a custom Mercedes van (knowing that the old VW bus is on its last legs) and a Nikon camera to help document my exploration of India.

Having already been warned that Singapore authorities frown upon long hair (apparently, even Robert Kennedy was given a hard time entering the Republic back in the '60s because his hair was not two finger breaths above his shirt collar) I purchase a short-haired wig in California and cram my shoulder length hair under it. Luckily there is no ban on beards so in no time I am strolling down Orchard Road, Singapore's main drag, absolutely amazed to be immersed in world of high-tech shopping centers contrasted with a myriad of archaic pushcarts and vendors selling food of every description.

In addition to making my purchases, I manage to run into other freaks (who, believe it or not, have also done the wig thing) and get invited to the Ming Court Hotel to watch their band play. Inside, the ballroom is opulent. As I watch the sailors dance with hot young Asian hookers, I am told a secret that these service men will learn much later in the evening: the hot chicks are all transvestites! Those big muscular navy cats gesticulating with other men are suddenly transformed into buffoons before my eyes. The scene is absolutely hysterical.

Singapore is unquestionably the cleanest city I have ever seen and the wide variety of international foods is beyond belief (especially when all the street carts from around the city gather in the Orchard for the evening feast). But once my shopping is done and the novelty of the Ming Court Hotel wears off, I am anxious to get back to J.G. and resume our overland journey to India. After arrangements are made for the custom Mercedes van to be delivered to the Port of Bombay for my pick-up two months hence, I orchestrate my trip back to Pagman. The simplest route at the time is through Hong Kong and then a direct flight to Pakistan followed by a bus ride through the Khyber Pass to Kabul.

Hong Kong is a more bustling, dirty Singapore, especially the Kowloon side where shopping reigns supreme. I have a couple of days to kill before my flight to Pakistan, so I decide to check out the city and get a tattoo.

I remember admonitions in the Jewish faith about having a tattoo. I vaguely recall it having something to do with the numbers branded on the holocaust victims by the Nazis. In any case, I choose a small, half dollar size, Sanskrit om (representing the "sound of the universe") to be placed on my right groin (just above the scar from my hernia repair when I was three years old). The tattoo parlor seems clean enough, and the proprietor promises that red ink inside the blue outline will not fade. (Just like Visine, six months later, there is not a trace of red left.) Now that I have an earring **and** a tattoo I am even more solidly a hippy than ever before. The commitment is irrevocable.

My arrival back in Pagman is celebrated for our successful run. My good work is met with offers from Raymond to continue the business with runs to Europe and Australia. J.G. surprises me by showing interest in the plan, but a slap upside his head gets us back on the road heading through the Khyber Pass to Pakistan.

The pass is about thirty miles long and cuts through the Safed Koh mountain range. At points it narrows down to just fifteen feet wide and is walled by cliffs one thousand feet high. "Khyber" is a Hebrew word meaning fort. The likes of Alexander the Great, Genghis Khan, Mahmud of Ghazni, and Zahiruddin Babar have all passed this way with mighty armies on quests to conquer the world. We are warned to stay on the narrow paved road which is under the jurisdiction of Pakistan. Wander off it and you are fair game for robbers and thieves. The village of Landi Kotal, within eye-shot of the road, is famous for its ambushing of unsuspecting travelers who drift just feet off the beaten path.

We emerge from this awe-inspiring piece of nature at Jamrud Fort on the Pakistani border, then drive on to Peshawar. It is already late fall and the idea is to cut through Pakistan into India, pick-up the new van in Bombay and then head south to Goa for the winter. Peshawar is rich with history, being the first real city one comes to after leaving the Khyber Pass. It is the cultural capital of the Pashtun people who, at the time we arrive, are buzzing with news of the impending war with India over independence for Bangladesh (previously, East Pakistan). We are advised to go east through Rawalpindi then stay just south of Islamabad (the Capital), and, at all cost, avoid Lahore where most of the Pakistani troops are mobilizing.

As we drive east and approach Rawalpindi, military troops become evident for the first time. At first they are not terribly distinguishable from ordinary civilians except for their firearms. In Rawalpindi, however, some semblance of military uniformity and decorum can be recognized. Having heard about the beauty of Kashmir and the serenity found by those living in house boats on its lakes and rivers, we are tempted to take the northern route into India. But concern about possible fighting in this long disputed territory (between not only, Pakistan and India, but China as well) makes us cross the Indo-Pakistani border just south of Jammu.

I commemorate my passage into India by sitting on the earth and watching the very same moon rise that I warmly embraced at Hamilton College and thought I could reach, if I so desired, while tripped out of my mind on Formentera. Now, more than five months after my twelve-day imprisonment in an Afghan jail, I appreciate the magic of the mind that lets me forget much of the abuse and allows me to feel, once again, the inner power to explore. Perhaps there is a bit of Neil Armstrong in all of us.

Moving down through Punjab, well west of New Delhi, it is days before we reach Bombay. Already I sense a spiritual uplifting as the Hindu images of God I have read so much about seem to appear on every billboard and way station we pass. The women in saris with the "third eye" dot displayed boldly on their foreheads are a stark contrast from hidden faces under burqas I witnessed for so many months in Muslim countries. At last we arrive in Bombay, the city of mystery that I have so very much identified with my quest to reach Nirvana. Unfortunately, that very night, instead of enlightenment from above, I experience my first real air raid complete with sirens and artillery blasts. It is the first week in December, 1971. The Indo-Pakistani war has broken out. Take cover!

***

The war officially lasts just under two weeks, but the dust doesn't settle until after the New Year. Bombay is the most laid back big city I have ever experienced. Despite the war, unpretentious life goes on. Huge cows roam everywhere while cops drink chai tea and smoking beedes (sometimes charas, aka. hashish) while hanging out on street corners. A naked man covered in grease wobbles down the middle of the main drag and, just as amazingly, only J.G. and I turn around to stare. The rest of the crowd, including Johnny (our newly found resident friend), takes no apparent notice.

Johnny is a British citizen who has lived in Bombay for so long he speaks with a Hindi cadence. He lives with Vani, his longtime Punjabi girlfriend who takes good care of him. Johnny has an opium habit and visits the dens at least twice a day. J.G. and I check it out, but the smell is so overpoweringly noxious that I have to hang by the open door. My adventuresome sidekick partakes and pays the price with twenty-four hours of nausea. He tries to overcome the sickness by drinking some orange juice from a street-side vender, but throws up after downing half a glass. The OJ, heavily laced with pepper as is the custom, further shocked J.G.'s system. The vendor tries to apologize to sahib, but J.G. is too consumed with his retching to care. Two lessons well learned. The East has its way of teaching.

The plan is to head south to Goa and enjoy the rest of the winter in a beach scene not unlike that on Formentera. But before leaving Bombay we cannot resist the urge to see a real live guru. Vani prays several times a day before her shrine of Shirdi Sai Baba. She claims that, as a devotee, more than once she has been blessed with *vibhuti*, a holy gray ash that appears from his picture. Unfortunately, Sai Baba is no longer bound to his earthly body (giving it up in 1918) so we have to find someone else.

The buzz around town is that Bhagawan Sri Rashneesh is headquartered in Bombay and open for business. This guy has been making international news with publicity ranging from him being a reincarnate eastern mentor for Hollywood stars to a licentious con man that uses Bhakti yoga to seduce young ladies from the West. Having seen several of his Western disciples on the street wearing his regalia (swami orange Samana robes with Bhagawan's smiling picture dangling from rose bead necklaces), we set out to find "the man."

In no less than half an hour we are being led into an air-conditioned, second floor room in a rather modern building overlooking Shivaji Park. Sitting on mats, surrounding a throne, are rows of peasants like us awaiting the Bhagawan. Pamphlets describing "his holiness" are passed out. The God of Night (translation for Bhagawan Sri Rashneesh) has returned to his homeland, after extensive travel throughout America, in order to reacquaint himself with the ascetic life. It turns out that the guy owns numerous Rolls Royce limos, Rolexes, and Sony TVs, among other Western frivolities.

Before long, in he strides. The height of an average Indian, bald on top with graying long hair that flows into his even longer salt and pepper beard, he wears flowing white robes and a similar rosary around his neck (resplendent with his own likeness at the bottom) as worn by his followers.

Instantly the room goes silent though there is a frenetic buzz that seems to heighten as he majestically takes his throne. Like two little kids at the opera, J.G. and I struggle hard not to burst out laughing. Luckily, the theater is short. The Bhagawan says a few silly words in a high-pitched Hindi rhythm and then rises to bless us all. As he makes his way to each of the mat sitters, he is followed by a Samana robed disciple carrying a plastic bag filled with rosary necklaces. Welcome into the fold is consummated with a peck on the top of the head by the Bhagawan's own lips after he puts a necklace with his picture around your neck. I am struck by the gaga-eyed freaks sitting all around me (especially the chicks) who seem entranced by the moment.

Suddenly he is standing right over me. Sensing an impending curse, I irreverently throw up my hands to fend off the Bhagawan's offering; and just as quickly both J.G. and I are firmly ushered out of the air-conditioned suite to find ourselves sucking up the heat of Mahableshwar out on the street. It was not a good first guru experience. Maybe we just didn't take the moment seriously enough? Or maybe the Bhagawan's act was just second rate? We certainly wanted to believe, but come on; this was right out of *Rowan and Martin's Laugh-In.*

Next day at the port I sign the import papers accepting Blue Ganesha (our name for my custom Mercedes from Singapore) and pay the tariff fee. Excited to see how she performs on the road down to Goa I am struck by J.G.'s silence. Something is up. As I work through the instruction booklet and figure out how to manage the choke on the diesel engine, J.G. confesses that he has decided to head back to Afghanistan. Only the tears in his eyes make me take him seriously.

CHAPTER 7

Alone At Last

On the road you learn that each person is a world unto himself; that attachment carries weakness and is the harbor for disappointment. Loneliness is an illusion that impedes one's personal evolution. J.G. and I will see each other again when the time is right. Letting go is supreme. So off I go south, alone on the road to Pune.

There are bicycles everywhere. Pune (pronounced *Poona*) derives its name from the Sanskrit Punya Nagari meaning "City of Virtue." Pune lies about one hundred-sixty kilometers south of Bombay, and as soon as I reach its outskirts the bicycles appear—not just a few, hordes of them; like being on the Long Island Expressway, but with everyone on bicycles instead of in cars. The other striking idiosyncrasy is that everyone is wearing white clothing (which no doubt reflects the suns strong rays and protects from the heat). The beauty of white robed people riding bicycles around perfectly clean streets makes the "City of Virtue" absolutely enchanting. It is here that I run into (or am found by) "Blind" George and his girlfriend Lydia. This is the same Blind George whom I met briefly about a year ago on Formentera. They, too, are on the road to Goa. There is plenty of room in Blue Ganesha, so off we go together.

The company feels good and takes my mind off of missing J.G. and, yes, Virginie. George, who is at least double my age, suffers from macular degeneration, an inheritable disease of the retina that he shares in common with his younger brother who is back in the States. The difference is that his brother has peripheral degeneration so that he can see only objects that are directly in front of him; George's degeneration is central and so he needs to look at things with his peripheral vision. He is able to read by holding the page off to one side. He tells me he is lucky because, unlike his brother, he can see the ground down by his feet when he walks and therefore does not need to use a cane, yet.

George is thin (as are most of the roadies) with doll-like features despite his age, striking (though malfunctioning) blue eyes, and curly blond hair that just meets his shoulders. He is lovingly tended to by charming Lydia whom I am sure is younger than my twenty-four years. There is something attractive about George that makes those around him care. I see this with those who know him well, those who meet him as strangers, and I recognize this in me as well. George has been to Goa every winter for years. He is bringing Lydia there for the first time. As I am soon to learn, Blind George brings a new young babe to Goa every winter. His charm never lets him down.

From the time that Vasco da Gama landed in 1498 until India reclaimed it in 1961, Goa was under Portuguese rule. The European influence (in language, food, and architecture) is strikingly evident. But out on Anjuna and Baga beaches, where we naturally migrate, the flavor of India predominates. The dark skin Goan natives make ready their dug-out canoes and fishnets as we freaks sit on the shore, sharing chillums, playing music, and watching the magnificent sunset on the Arabian Sea. The brave fishermen push off at dark each night, staying out at sea until the next afternoon when they arrive back on shore with catch that make fish stories credible. They freely share fresh shark and barramundi steaks, the likes of which unquestionably put Western sushi bars to shame. The days are warm, but not unbearably so. The nights are tranquil with a tender tropical breeze that is hard to forget. The papaya and mango are sweet beyond imagination and are everywhere for the taking. Never in my life have I experienced a portion of this earth that more deserves to be called paradise.

The winter passes quickly in paradise, especially with characters around like "Chicago" Jack, his woman Katherine, and Neal "Chicky" Phillips whose passion for the sweet candy called "chicks" (similar to balled up Cracker Jacks) branded his nickname. Jack is a muscular, dark haired, tough looking cat; so proud of his guns that he never wears shirts that covers them up. He does push-ups on the beach while beguiling Katherine looks on in a state of rapture. She is stunning despite her long prematurely gray hair. Like most of the chicks on the beach she is scantily clad in thin linen cloth that serves to barely cover various body parts depending on her mood and circumstance. She speaks very little, with Jack providing most of the phonics. I need not be warned of her seductive ways, nor the stories of her delight when C.J. pummels those foolish enough to succumb to them.

Laughter is sacred and plentiful. "Chicky" is particularly upbeat and joyous, understandably so when you know his story. Having once worked as a beat writer for the *Village Voice*, his "job" took him to Turkey and two years in jail for attempting to smuggle hashish out of the country. The actual details of his bust and incarceration are as protean as the number of times the tail is told. (Years later, the word on the street is that the book *Midnight Express*, and subsequent movie of the same name, is based on the experiences of both Billy Hayes and Neal "Chicky" Phillips.) "Chicky's" mantra, "Freedom is never ending" is absolutely contagious and brings back my own memories of prison life in Germany, Turkey, and horrific Afghanistan. I swear to myself that I will never forget to appreciate my freedom.

Paradoxically, I begin to find that living on the beautiful Goan beaches in an age of free-love and narcissistic excess is a disquieting freedom. My quest to find Nirvana has somehow stalled. Having a driving, type A personality I revive my guru hunt by asking around for sages. It is not long before the idea of checking out the faith healers in the Philippine Islands becomes a fascination I cannot resist. After all, at one time I wanted to become a doctor, so learning from a wise man with powers to heal would be even better than just finding some ordinary guru who sits around all day giggling under a banyan tree while being served by disciples. I even go to the library in Panaji to read about the many devotees of spiritualism and the abundance of psychic surgeons and faith healers found in the Philippines.

Months pass by, eating papaya (India is the best place in the world to be a vegetarian), writing letters to Marta (explaining my state of consciousness) and enjoying the fascinating "road people" as I ponder my next move.

It is my loneliness and stagnation that finally motivates me to take action in March, as my twenty-fifth birthday approaches. I entrust Blue Ganesha to Johnny and Vani (I figure Johnny is staying right there in Bombay near his opium dens and Vani, whom I have come to call Mataji, meaning "mother" in Hindi, has no other needs but to take care of Johnny) when I leave from the Bombay airport on my trip to Manila.

CHAPTER 8

The Land of the Little People

From the moment I exit the baggage claim in the Philippine capitol I am barraged by jeepney drivers vying for my business. Jeepneys are colorful, customized open-air cabs that compete with the gaudy Afghan trucks and overdone Harley road bikes for transport vehicles' ultimate circus award. The carnival atmosphere, however, is tempered by the pervasive carrying of firearms. The gunslingers are everywhere reminding me of the western movies on which I grew up. The difference is that I am no longer safe at home in my den watching Roy Rogers or Gene Autry on TV. The visible machine guns probably do not outnumber the concealed hand guns and the thought begins to freak me out. Then, suddenly, right there at the airport I run into Kerry (we literally collide as we both scramble to avoid the crowds and gunmen), a very tall lanky cat in suit jacket and tie with a close-cropped beard and disheveled black hair. The rather hysterical collision and obvious fact that we are both Americans makes for a bonding moment. We share a jeepney ride to his hotel in Makati (Manila's ultra rich high-end district).

It turns out that Kerry is a B movie director working for New World Pictures in L.A.; shooting an action film on Luzon (the Philippines' most populated island) because labor here is cheap. Getting past his Hollywood "dear" and "dude" chatter is easy because I am grateful for American company. Before long he starts introducing me around. His assistant and stand-in actress is a petite blond with a conspicuous belly ring that she proudly displays above her very low cut hip hugger shorts. Her name is Joy Bang. Kerry tells me that he rescued her from the porno industry back in L.A. and she has been his loyal side-kick ever since (a fascinating story I will no doubt relate to my grandchildren some day).

I meet Norma Japitana, a fashionable Americanized Pilipina (colloquially *Pinay*) who is an up and coming celebrity newspaper journalist. She also happens to be the sweetheart and fiancée of Domingo ("Sunday," Americanized to "Sandy") Lopez, the nephew of the Vice President of the Philippines. Sandy is a lawyer who hardly works because he doesn't have to. He and Norma throw lavish parties and are excited to include me on the guest list. I somehow become their resident American hippy; and the connections just keep on flowing thereafter.

My appearance at this time is much like the images of Jesus Christ seen throughout this spiritual Christian country. My tall, thin frame (my body weight has dropped to under 160 lbs., no doubt due to my daily three mile runs and vegetarianism), long hair and beard cause many Filipinos to call me Jesus. I get used to children following me on the street and to unsuspecting women clutching their bosoms and crying out, "Dios!" when I suddenly come into view. In effect, I become sort of a celebrity in the Islands and, therefore, am in demand for parties, celebrations, and—on occasion—as a conspicuous house guest. I am even introduced to Nora Aunore, the biggest recording and movie star the Philippines had ever produced. My mind set, at the time, however, is not to get caught up in material things because (from all the occult I have read) that would be the kiss of death to achieving my ultimate goal of attaining enlightenment.

I am invited to Bacolod on the island of Negros to stay with Sandy's parents and to Iloilo on Panay to stay with the Figueroas, both of whom are medical doctors educated in the States. I also head to Cebu to partake of the largest and sweetest *lanzones* (a remarkable tropical fruit that defies description) in all of Southeast Asia. Everywhere in the Visayas (a southern Philippine island chain) I am catered to and treated like a long-lost son. The venerable treatment is definitely something I could get used to, but I fight the impulse all the way. I remind myself that I am here for a purpose: to explore Filipino spiritualism with a particular eye on their form of alternative medicine—faith healing. So I start asking the question, "Where are the psychic surgeons and the faith healers?"

Before long I am up to my ears in tales of fairies and spirits and magical events that only true believers get to see and experience firsthand. I am taken to a house, which I'm told has been blessed. Smack in the middle of the living room is a good size boulder—home of fairy spirits. It erupted there one day years ago when the father of the household was just a boy. The rock is treated with solemn respect, and over the years, each member of the family has seen fairies emerge from it, especially in times of personal need. I want so very much to believe in another dimension and a higher order of things, *but fairies?!*

One day, Sandy (who always seemed to be quite cynical of the whole "spiritual world thing"), tells me that he has arranged a meeting for me with Bobby de Leon, a bona fide and very powerful faith healer. When I chide Sandy about playing along with the medicine man stories and setting me up with a charlatan to keep up the hype, he suddenly gets serious. The sweat on his brow and above his lip tells me that he is not joking. Apparently, sometime ago he was unfaithful to Norma who consulted Bobby to remedy the situation. Before long, Sandy was suffering from intractable migraine headaches, which only remitted when he stopped his womanizing. Regardless of the veracity of the tale, I cannot pass up the opportunity—after all, the tales of faith healers was the impetus for my journey to the Philippines.

Sandy, who comes from wealth, drives me into a squatter's area on the outskirts of Queson City (near Manila) in his stylish late model Jaguar. The "village" is located next to a huge garbage dump many stories high; apparently, most of the Philippines' urban impoverished set up makeshift houses out of cardboard, wood, and metal debris that they find by rummaging through such dumps. The garbage also serves as their main source of food and clothing. It is absolutely shocking and very sad. Sandy is obviously uncomfortable there and does not stay long after introducing me to the village shaman.

Bobby is an unassuming, rotund man in his mid-thirties. He speaks little English and is not very talkative. Though not discourteous, he motions me into his house (which is far superior to the others I see) and shows me where it is I am to sleep. The thought of spending the night on a dirt floor is not exactly foreign to me, but the reality of actually living in such poverty is disturbing. Before I can set down my knapsack, in comes the community, curious to see the white American who looks like Jesus Christ. The children lay on the dirt floor transfixed as if watching television for the very first time. At first, Bobby seems to wallow in the notoriety that he, the celebrity sorcerer, has attracted from across the seas: a foreigner who wishes to be his disciple. I am absolutely pissed off at Sandy for dumping me like a piece of garbage in a sewer to be made a trophy and sideshow for this most unlikely sage. But Bobby senses my consternation and shoos the onlookers away. It is late in the day, and having no way to reach Sandy, I decide to accept supper and stay the night.

That evening, I see a constant flow of helpless souls come to Bobby for resolution of their maladies. Some are ill and some just in despair. He treats them all with a gentle but firm hand. Many are women who complain that their men are unfaithful. Each gets a small vial of mixed oil and herbs with instructions to read prayers from the Bible and place a drop of potion on the forehead of her lover during sleep. *Interesting.* So I decide that night to stay for a while to see what happens to his "patients."

The longer I stay, the more intriguing the man becomes. His remedies seem to work for both the physical and emotional complaints of his people. He is able to recognize injuries that require hospitalization, and does not hesitate to take those so stricken to the hospital Emergency Room himself. They also come to him with disputes and grievances. He is both doctor and judge, a savior and a devil (to those who are guilty of sin). The respect and fear he commands is attractive to me, so I allow myself to believe that he has something to teach me. And so my internship begins.

CHAPTER 9

Test of Faith

I am given prayers out of the Bible to memorize. "They bring power to those who know how to use them," he says in broken English, repeatedly. I even go to Catholic Church with him two times per week. And although we never stay long, it is there that he says he gets recharged. For the spirit to remain strong within him he clings to celibacy. The results of his mastery over those who see Bobby de Leon as their link to the divine are spectacular. The ill recover, the unfaithful change their ways, and disagreements are settled quickly and without malice.

Bobby is powerful and makes me a believer over the months that I stay by his side, until the evening that we go out with his amigos to celebrate his thirty-fifth birthday. It starts out innocently enough, with music, dancing, and beer at a barroom in Manila. I am a bit surprised to watch this man of God down each beer that is handed to him, and suspect that he has the ability to minimize the alcohol's effect. Though courteous to all, Bobby gets near no women, who themselves appear smitten though in awe of his persona.

Late in the evening we pile into Bobby's open-air jeep, and although his eyes are glassy, I have faith in this man and his judgment. No sooner does he hit the gas with a heavy foot than I realize that I am as much a fool as the others who are sitting beside me. As we fly down the winding street, each holding on for dear life, I beg Bobby to stop and let us out. His laughter and insensitivity to my profound fear all at once make me think that this is the end. *I am going to die right here in the Philippines at the hands of a drunken spiritulista who is no closer to God than any other DUI felon.*

Somehow we make it to a red light and Bobby actually stops. Two of us jump out. The other two idiots stay with their hero as he speeds off just as the light turns green.

The last time I see Bobby de Leon is several days later when Sandy (who is deeply disturbed by my recount of the incident) brings me back to the squatters' area to retrieve my belongings. Though he is still without apology, there is some remorse in Bobby's eyes. I almost think that he was testing me on that night, wondering if my faith in him was strong enough to look death in the face. My conclusion: Bobby de Leon may possess unique powers, but the asshole risked my life and I am a dolt for getting suckered in.

Both Sandy and Norma obviously feel responsible for my harrowing experience and try to set things right by catering to me as much as I am willing to permit. The parties in Makati and introductions to members of Philippine society resume in earnest. Though the parties are fun, I am still disappointed, having not found that mystical connection for which I came to the Islands. Under duress, Sandy decides to take me to see Impagwa, the renowned psychic surgeon.

We drive miles up to Baguio, through magnificently terraced rice fields, until we reach the quaint village. It is anything but a squatters' area and is overrun by well-dressed foreigners also attracted by tales of supernatural powers that permit the practice of psychic surgery. One gentleman from Canada tells me that he saw Impagwa on the *Joe Pine Show* and has come to have his tumor removed.

Near a tent, chairs are set up for the audience, many with cameras and home video equipment. A line has formed for those who seek removal of their unwanted growths. One by one, they file up to the thin little man speaking Tagalog and waving his arms like a Las Vegas showman. Some lie flat on their backs while he digs his bare hands into their bellies. Blood spurts from between his fingers while the audience gasps. Into pans he throws the disemboweled body parts. They clang as they hit the metal bottom. More gasps.

It occurs to me that I have a chic pea size fibroma just under the skin of my right upper arm where Dr. Wiener used to give me my allergy shots when I was a kid. *Let's see if this guy can remove that thing without an incision.* I get in line.

The show is pretty good. And then it is my turn. He has me sit on the table facing the audience and then wastes no time going right at my lump. He presses so firmly that I nearly fall off the table. Blood shoots down my arm, but I feel no pain. And then comes the clank in the bottom of the metal basin. Next. I am flipped a wet paper towel by his assistant and asked to rejoin the audience. Sandy's mouth is hanging open as he asks me how I feel. "Fine," I tell him, and then reach for my fibroma. There it is, right where Dr.

Weiner used to stick me. "Let's get out of here." For me the magic show is over.

***

By September I am Philippined-out, especially after being thrown in jail (for the fourth time to date) when I was picked up by a police patrol for ignoring curfew. Apparently, President Ferdinand Marcos (whose supporters compare him to John F. Kennedy because, as a young man in World War II, he fought valiantly against the Japanese occupation) had declared martial law and ordered that no one be on the streets past 10:00 PM. His aim is to usurp complete control over the press and all private armies that might jeopardize his power. Fortunately for me I was released in the morning and told that I was detained for my own protection. An old hand at imprisonment, I was actually pleasantly surprised by their efforts of atonement.

Sandy and Norma are, of course, all apologies, but I tell them that I have business to take care of back in India. I must go.

In a matter of days I am passing through Bangkok on my way back to Bombay. It is a surprise to find myself in a modern metropolitan city with a mix of Asian, European, and Western flair. Still, ancient elements are evident as both the rickshaw carriers and bald monks are plentiful in the streets. It is here amidst the large crowds that my Nikon camera and invaluable film (documenting my travels) are ripped off. I feel sickened and sad all the way to Bombay.

Upon arrival I am struck by the long-lasting jubilation of India's victory over Pakistan and learn that Bangladesh has secured its independence. Even Johnny, who lived through

India's struggle for independence from Great Britain, but always claimed disinterest in international politics, seems deeply moved by the outcome. "How is it this third world country can win a war in a couple of weeks when your almighty America does not know if it is coming or going for years in Vietnam?" he jousts rhetorically. Though my proximity to Southeast Asia is greater these past couple of years than it had been during my college days, the Vietnam War seems more distant to me than ever. Somehow I feel momentarily embarrassed by my shameful self-absorption, but am not particularly disturbed at hearing that Richard Nixon has been re-elected. After all, he is working hard to end the war.

Johnny and Vani look well. Above all, they have taken excellent care of Blue Ganesha for me. I pay them handsomely (an amount worth at least a year of visits to Johnny's favorite opium den) and then ship the thing back to the States. For one thing: I am not in need of Ganesha because my travels are no longer confined to the road; and secondly, it is an opportunity for me to show my parents that I have achieved some element of financial success. After all, a customized Mercedes Benz camper is quite the trophy. (Little do I know that "Big Blue" will cause my dad a world of further grief.)

Hanging with Johnny and Vani gets old fast. After some three years on the road, with the last half-year devoid of my anchor, J.G., I begin to admit to a sense of loneliness and void of purpose. *Can I really find the Holy Grail here in India? Come on, now. Don't let doubt set in—it's the kiss of death!*

Before long it is back to the Philippines through

Singapore, one of my favorite cities on earth (now painted with monumental sized portraits of Mohammad Ali, the world's most famous man) and, of course, filled with amenities that remind me of home, like soft toilet paper and ubiquitous air conditioning. But my visa grants me only two weeks. Having overcome my disappointment with Philippine spiritualism, I am excited to explore the monetary opportunities that Sandy's affluent family in Bacolod has offered me. Being wined and dined, after sleeping in a VW van, a squatter's area next to a garbage dump, and a jail cell in four different countries, is quite the turn on.

I am picked up at the airport by the Lopez contingent. No Jeepney drivers are allowed to rush me. After getting cleaned up at the Hilton in Makati, I am escorted to the clubs and given the full rock star treatment. It is absolutely groovy. The next day we travel by boat down to the island of Negros in the Visayas. This trip is even better than the first. In Bacolod I am given custom hand-tailored clothes and a culinary spread so magnificent that I have no trouble deserting my vegetarian ways (even trying *Lechon*, roasted pork).

After days of play, including riding horses along the countryside and beach, I am introduced to some of the family enterprises. Sugar cane and rice farming occupy thousands of acres of land and employs hundreds of workers. But it is the fishing business of which they are most proud. While both fish and rice are the food staples of Southeast Asia, it is the fishing industry that can bring the Lopez family an international market, they explain. Unfortunately, a recent hurricane scuttled their fishing fleet and it will take American dollars to help restore it. Sandy points to two very large shrimp boats that lie just off shore. The *Lolita*, named after Sandy's mother, is the bigger of the two. It lists to one side because of damage to her hull. It will take $10,000 to make her seaworthy again, but once she is back in action her profits will easily pay for repair of her sister ship. Once that is accomplished it is just a matter of time before the Lopez fleet is back to international trade. New hurricane precautions have already been instituted around the Visayas to prevent future catastrophic damage to its fishing industry.

Excited to have a tangible mission, I pass the news of this opportunity on to my parents. Surprisingly, the response is favorable. In fact, they are anxious to take a trip out to the Philippines to see me and check out the scene. Dynamite! I couldn't be more excited at the prospect of showing them that there is more to my life than becoming a doctor stuck in an office all day long.

CHAPTER 10

No Deeper Love

The day of their arrival is special. I, the world traveler, will reveal to my parents things they have never seen, or even dreamt of, before. With Sandy and Norma at my side I watch from afar as they clear customs. It has been three years since I last saw them—hard to believe. They look older to me now and certainly not as spry. Once they see me, Dad comes rushing over with tears in his eyes. We embrace. He is not nearly as tall as I remember him to be. Mom seems stuck, not sure what to do, almost as if she does not recognize me. As I speak the word "Mom" and hug her, she feels heavy in my arms, almost unable to stand on her own. "Bobby, you're so thin," are her first words. I had planned a raucous jeepney ride to the hotel, but clearly that amusement will have to wait. Instead, a comfortable ride in the Jag with me pointing out the sights (while Mom and Dad sit speechless) brings us to the Makati Hilton. Dad is impressed that I have taken care of the bill (with Sandy's help).

The next day, after touring Manila and pointing out the diverse sectors like the strip of nightclubs in Queson City, the tough urban section of Tondo, and of course, the many squatters' areas juxtaposed to affluent gated communities like Makati, we take a short jeepney ride. Although Mom is put off by the noise and fumes from the traffic, I am confident that she will love the peace and fresh air down in the Visayan Islands. It is important to me that my folks see that I have not been idle. I have made friendships in a land of opportunity.

My parents fill me in on world events from the American point of view. My New York Yankees have not been playing like the team I was used to as a kid. So when they tell me that CBS sold the team for about $10 million to a consortium headed by a guy named George Steinbrenner I'm thinking *that's a lot of money, but hey, it didn't come out of my pocket; and this guy has to be better than a media network that never gave a damn about baseball or us Yankee fans anyway.* They are excited about the end of the Vietnam "conflict" and that our troops are coming home. Amid the nation's joy over the end of this infamous war (and the credit taken for it by Nixon) there looms the humiliation of the Watergate scandal. In a letter to Judge John Sirica, Watergate burglar James W. McCord admitted that he and the other defendants had been pressured to remain silent by Attorney General John Mitchell. A month later top White House aids H.R. Halderman and John Ehrlichman resigned. Shortly thereafter the U.S. Senate began televising hearings on the matter. The entire country, my parents say, is locked in on the drama as if at a three-ring circus. By fall, Spiro T. Agnew resigned as Vice President, and pled no contest to charges of income tax evasion while governor of Maryland in 1967. Congress confirmed Gerald Ford as the new Vice President and Nixon ordered Attorney General Elliott Richardson (whom he had replace Mitchell) to dismiss Watergate Special Prosecutor Archibald Cox. Richardson refused and then resigned himself. The Nixon administration was unraveling.

Dad goes on to tell me of a surprise he got not long ago that knocked his socks off (and gave him agita). Informed of a shipment that arrived for him from India, he cancelled office hours and headed down to the docks in Manhattan. Knowing that I had proudly sent over a Mercedes van, he decided to bring Hal, a neighbor and golf buddy, to share his good fortune. They immediately saw Blue Ganesha. It is impossible to miss because of its size, two tone blue color, and distinct customized body. They did not, however, think that it was the vehicle I had sent because they were expecting a van and this was a truck! When the customs officer brought them over to Big Blue, Hal had all he could do to get my father to sign the acceptance papers and pay the stiff tariff charges.

Then came the task of starting her up, not to mention working the clutch and maneuvering the monster through heavily trafficked Manhattan streets. Not having used a choke or clutch since the '30s both Dad and Hal were at the mercy of karma while New York (and later Jersey) profanities were slung at them from all sides.

After a long day, Ganesha finally sat obtrusively in the driveway at Berdan Avenue in Fair Lawn. After several days of pondering, Dad enlisted the help of another of his golf buddies, Malcolm Konner, who owned a large Chevrolet automobile dealership on Route 17 in Paramus.

He graciously took Ganesha off Dad's hands to sell from his lot on consignment. (Years later, after no takers ever materialized, Big Blue was donated to charity with the meager write-off justly going to the Konner's car dealership.)

The news of Dad's tribulation with my prized Big Blue is brutally disturbing and demoralizing. I catch Mom's cynical eye as I struggle to handle my latest screw up. Just then, my folks and I are greeted in royal fashion at the docks in Negros. I am relieved to have the pressure temporarily off me. Not only are the accommodations at the Lopez compound luxurious, my parents are provided with round the clock attendants to serve their every desire. The local touring, entertainment, and feasting are tastefully mixed with opportunities for privacy. Somewhere in there (just man to man, without Mom's presence) I offer Dad my humble apology for his hassle with Big Blue. He graciously accepts, in his usual loving manner, and I am miraculously absolved of my profound guilt. *Dad is quite the dad.*

We travel around the Visayan Islands visiting sugar cane fields, rice patties, and exotic fruit orchards. A special trip is made to Cebu where relatives of a Filipino physician colleague of my Dad's back in the States live. We are treated regally.

The people here love Americans and our culture. After all, it was our armed forces that liberated them from four years of hell under Japanese occupation during World War II. Even Tagalog or Filipino (the official language of the Philippines) is a mix of Spanish (Spain ruled the islands since the 16th century) and Americanized English. American movies are revered and our Hollywood stars worshipped. It is common practice to spend a whole day jumping from one theater to another, seeing movie after movie. The nature of the people out in the provinces is so warm and hospitable that I can see my folks are really enjoying themselves.

CHAPTER 11

The Deal

Dad had taken a full two weeks off from his medical practice, something I believe he has never done before. The bonding experience flies by. Two days prior to my parents' departure we are brought out to see the disabled ships, the *Lolita* and her companion. I can see the uneasiness in my father's face. He already knows the deal: I want him to invest in the Lopez fishing business. He is about to get hit up for ten G's. Deep down inside I know why they are coughing up the bread for me: to salvage their son from the grips of an enticing, but selfish world. But I honestly believe that the venture is sound because we are investing with "family" who care about us and whom we can trust. We will all become rich together!

Good-byes at the airport are tough. Mom tries one more time to get me to say that there is still a chance that I will return to medical school. Dad promises to have his lawyer review the Lopez contract proposal for making the Schultz family partners in their fishing enterprise. After their plane takes off, I head back to Negros to be with my Filipino family.

A few weeks later all the papers are signed, the money changes hands, and the deal is done. The Schultz family is a 50% owner of the *Lolita* and her sister ship. Once the salvage of the damaged vessels is completed the fishing operation will get underway and we will be in business. I am very excited. Not only did I have a wonderful two weeks with my parents, I have given them a taste of the orient and gotten them involved in my world. The sky is the limit for us now!

For the next few months I am treated like a rock star and communications with my folks are pleasant and upbeat. By the end of the year, however, the fishing boats still lie stranded on the reef. Despite my obvious concern, the questions I ask about the progress of the ship restoration project go essentially unanswered. Excuses for the delay become ever more overt and difficult for me to accept. My relationship with Sandy and his family becomes strained. Even Norma has angry words with Sandy on my behalf, resulting in her return to Manila and breaking off their engagement.

The New Year is celebrated in the Philippines just like we do in the States. After the parties come the resolutions. For me number one is to return to Manila to discuss with our designated family lawyer the options for recovery of our investment. The Lopez's continue to assure me that, although things move slowly in the provinces, our restoration project is underway. Towing the boats to the shipyard requires permits as well as the availability of expert repairmen experienced in damage of this magnitude; neither comes easy. I want more than anything to believe them, but I am already feeling uneasy that I have gotten my parents into a bum deal and am loath to admit it.

My time in Manila is spent trying to get the local lawyer to communicate with our family lawyer back in New Jersey. The phone calls and wires are tedious and not very productive. Weeks seem to pass by between communications. While my guilt mounts, I receive a letter from Mom that ends abruptly with the words, "Nana passed away last night, thanks for not being here."

In four years of traveling I have experienced my share of loneliness and doubt, but nothing as profound as this. Never wanting a safety net, I always fancied myself the independent road warrior who someday would find the Holy Grail. Now I find myself questioning everything and feeling ashamed of my actions for the first time in years.

Booking my ticket to New York is the easy part; making up a good excuse for bailing on my dream is quite another thing. Instead, I buy two plane tickets: one back to the States and the other a ticket from New York to Bombay. I will make amends with my folks and Marta (whom I still call "My Sweetheart" in all our correspondence), visit with friends, and get recharged. Then it is back to the Orient and the road to enlightenment.

The transcontinental flight on Pan Am is via the polar route with only one stopover (in Tokyo) to change planes. The journey is normally about eighteen hours, but a few hours in the air out of Tokyo a near inaudible announcement from the pilot says we may have to make an emergency stop somewhere over Canada due to technical trouble. The jumbo jet is losing power in one of its engines, but our flight crew seems well in control. *No big deal* I figure, since we still have three more turbines working just fine. It is not until I hear the stewardess stammer and the other passengers mumble something about the number four engine (next to the faulty number three) also failing that I wonder if I will ever see New Jersey again.

Our speed noticeably slows and it seems that the aircraft is laboring. The silence in the plane is thick and tenacious, almost as if all breathing has ceased. When the woman just in front of me begins to cry, the flood gates open and there is sobbing everywhere. The passengers are officially in panic mode with the young stewardesses also collapsing under the pressure. After at least ten minutes of immersion in this hysterical milieu my mind suddenly becomes quiet as I reflect on all the sports I've played, my years of schooling and college, the places I've traveled, and the far-out people I have met. I have done more than most in my short life and am grateful for that. The sadness I feel for my parents, sister and Marta who love me, is relieved only when we actually touch down in an emergency landing somewhere north of Minnesota. The eighteen-hour trip becomes a twenty-four hour one, but not one of my fellow passengers complains.

For me the experience of landing safely on the ground is akin to getting out of jail; the same instant ecstasy and gratitude that only "new" life brings. I promise to never forget what almost happened and how every day from here on in is gravy. I'm playing with house money, so let's get it on!

Mark and Julia Halliday during full moon party, 1969, Island of Formentera, Spain

Bob shaving; living on the beach, 1969, Island of Formentera, Spain

Bob (standing), Julia (standing), "California" Jim (sitting in middle), among others in villa, 1969, Island of Formentera, Spain

Elliott, 1969, Island of Formentera, Spain

Billy, "California" Jim, two hitchhikers, Antonio, Elliott, 1969, Atlas Mountains, Morocco

Bob, 1969, Marrakesh, Morocco

"California" Jim, getting out of prison, 1969, Lorrach, Germany

View from Johnny and Vani's window, 1971, Bombay, India

Vani (right) and friend, 1971, Bombay, India

"Bombay" Johnny, 1971, Bombay, India

Bob and Blue Ganesha, 1972, Goa India

"Freaks" gathering for sunset ritual, 1972, Goa, India

Bob, 1972, Goa, India

Bob with Domingo "Sandy" Lopez, 1973, Island of Negros, Philippine Islands

Edna and Irving Schultz (Mom and Dad), 1996, Boca Raton, Fl

Carl, Elliot, Bob, reunion at MacDougal St., 2004, Greenwich Village, NY

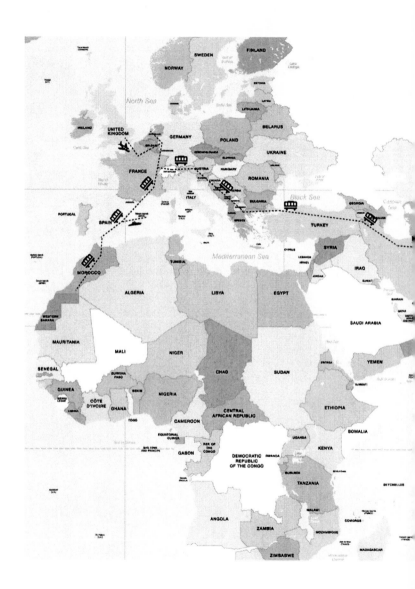

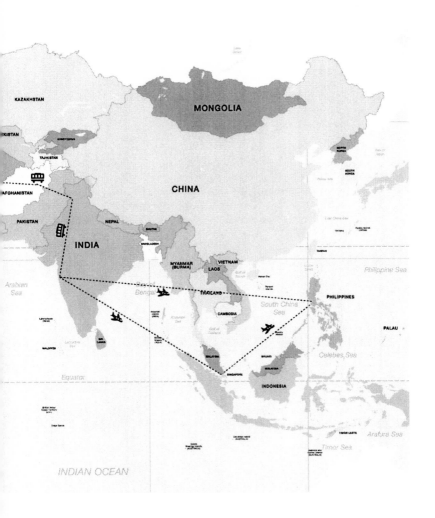

Part Two

CHAPTER 12
The Day From Hell

I know that things beyond my control will go wrong today, but I will weather the storm and act like a man instead of an asshole. Mantra said (with eyes closed, mind you): I enter the O.R. and greet the staff and anesthesiologist. As the patient is wheeled in, she is comforted by the nurse circulator and then positioned strategically next to the operating table for transfer off the stretcher. While Dr. Blady checks the IV access and further prepares his subject, I carefully check the instruments and verify that the holmium-yag laser is in proper working order.

I have come to do all my knee arthroscopies under local anesthesia so that the patient not only benefits from the procedure, but gets a real-time education about her condition. Preparation begins weeks before in the office when I explain the advantages to watching one's operation, while in progress, on the T.V. monitor. Having undergone the experience as a patient myself, four times (both knees and both shoulders), I can empathetically describe the initial trepidation; the pressure one feels as the instruments are inserted into the joint; the wonderment of seeing the inside of your very own knee (or shoulder). Above all, by seeing the pathology (disease/damage) first hand you gain invaluable understanding of it (well beyond words) that obliterates the fear of the unknown and lets you deal with the issue rationally. Invariably, my patients come away with the exhilarating feeling (akin to conquering a marathon, or as one patient told me, skydiving) of triumph, in addition to the gift of personal knowledge.

After sterilely injecting the knee joint and portals (entry sites for instruments) with anesthetic, I leave the O.R. for the customary three-minute scrub. It is 7:45 in the morning and standing alone at the scrub sink (since I don't need an assistant for this case, or the two that follow) is boring...

It wasn't always like this... Back in the day I was in a new country nearly every month. No routine. No three-minute scrubs. Four years, four continents; forlorn at times—yes, but the freedom from responsibility was entirely awesome. As a citizen of the world I thought at times that I might never return.

CHAPTER 13

New York, New York

Having been away from my roots for so many years never seemed like much to me until I smelled mainland America. Seeing all the big American-sized cars on the road and hearing brash New York accents from people dressed to the nines, all at once made me realize that the "common place" has everything to do with one's perspective. Mine had been drastically altered. I had become used to less creature comforts and extravagance. Even the royal treatment in the provinces of the Philippines paled with respect to the opulence we Americans take for granted daily in the United States. From the monumental size of our buildings and shopping centers to the uncanny softness of our toilet paper and astonishing lack of flies in public areas, I find myself marveling at what I left behind.

Nevertheless, I need to validate my journey through the third world by rejecting the prosperity around me. My mother is particularly troubled by finding that I prefer to sleep on the floor instead of in bed. Although I am no longer a vegetarian, my eating habits (mostly fruits and vegetables with absolutely no red meat or sweets) drive her crazy because I am, in her eyes, too thin. Dad encourages me to cut my hair and beard, but is simply so happy to have me back home that he wisely does not press the issue. I do not have the heart to tell him or Mom that I will be returning to India in a few short weeks.

Marta, whom I can't wait to see (and apologize to for running off for so long), has a big surprise for me. His name is Michael. He is a graduate student in biology at Harvard and a "Dead Head" (Grateful Dead fan). This smack to my ego lets me know, in no uncertain terms, that my spiritual evolution is pitiful at best. I am actually upset that this hot young babe did not wait for me ad infinitum (while I was globetrotting and taking full advantage of the free-love ethos). Michael, on the other hand, turns out to be a very cool cat; a soul-mate that someone as sweet as Marta truly deserves. So I respectfully withdraw to a corner and brood.

And then along comes Peter. The very same Peter Peuler with whom I went to Hamilton College and who led our yoga exercises years ago at Billy Hardy's Island in Upper Saranac Lake. It is really good to see him. Turns out that he has been on a similar journey to mine, with his path taking him to the island of Eleuthera in the Bahamas where he spent a year exploring the metaphysical. Upon returning to the States he decided to study chiropractic and enrolled in a school in New York City. There he met several classmates who were studying spiritualism with a psychic medium across the Hudson in Paterson, New Jersey. He joined them one evening and has been a dedicated follower of Bill Daut's ever since.

Would I too like to meet this man? Without hesitation I say, "Let's go." *Imagine if I traveled all the way around the world in search of a spiritual mentor, a guru, and all the while he was right here in Paterson, the city in which I was born? Too far out!* I am excited.

The day I enter the small split-level house on Hazel Street, not more than twenty minutes from my home in Fair Lawn, I am filled with euphoric anticipation. The old man is sitting upstairs in his kitchen wearing shorts and an undershirt. His cane is positioned awkwardly between his legs. A good amount of the vanilla yogurt he is eating rests in his bushy gray beard as he reaches a hand out to greet me.

"Welcome Doctor," he belches with the warmest smile a stranger has ever given me.

"I am not a doctor. My name is Bob," I respond shaking his sticky hand (more yogurt, no doubt). "As you wish, Bob," he giggles.

Hanging out with Bill is absolutely ordinary and yet extraordinary. There is a single black and white TV in the small bedroom next to the equally small kitchen. The living room has about a dozen folding chairs on a less than clean rug that are used by the students during teaching sessions and séances. The first floor is more of an entrance than living quarters, and the stairs are fitted with an electric seat that helps Bill negotiate his way to and from the second floor living area. It is obvious that he does not go out much.

His students (many of whom are chiropractors from "New York Chiropractic," where Peter studies) are absolutely in love with Bill. They kiss him smack on the lips (regardless of gender) during greetings and give him an equally loving kiss (along with saying "much love") when leaving. I detect no pretence or rigidness here, in stark contrast to my experience back in Bombay with Bagawan Sri Rashneesh. From that very first day in Bill Daut's house it occurs to me that maybe I should delay my return to India so I can check out this curious scene further. It will also help me delay confronting my folks with the news that I am off again.

But if I am going to stay here longer, I will need money. So I begin making trips down to the gigantic flee market in Englishtown, NJ in hopes of selling old stuff I find around the house. I go through the storage room in our basement asking Mom if there are things she doesn't need anymore. Among the old clothes and toys are my collections of marbles, rare rocks, sea shells, stamps, and even cleaned wishbones. But most valuable of all are my baseball cards dating back to the '40s! Shoe boxes full of them. I even find the 1952 baseball signed by the entire Yankees team. Unfortunately, having played with it as a kid, the names are barely legible; and I curse my youth for such stupidity. The cards actually bring me several hundred dollars, a pretty good take, but it's not going to keep me out of having to get a job.

My brother-in-law, Cliff, has a sister who used to be a high fashion model in New York and has some connections. Modeling sounds easy and lucrative so, with Diane's guidance, I put together a picture portfolio, which means I have to fully shave and cut my hair at least to shoulder length. Traumatic, but I need the money. Meanwhile, Dad is doing his best to find me employment. He even contemplates buying into a fast-food Chinese joint on Route 17 so I might get the opportunity to learn how to manage a business. In the meantime, Vince, a friend of his at Apple Ridge Country

Club, owns an advertising agency in Mahwah and agrees to let me start working in his copy department for minimum wage. Having always fancied myself a writer, I am willing to try it out. Of course, this necessitates a new wardrobe and further clean-up of my appearance.

Over at Bill's (where I can dress any way that I choose) things are moving along rapidly. I visit every day; sometimes only for an hour or so. I learn that Bill is a sensitive or psychic through whom the spirit world is channeled. His main spirit guide is Dr. James who passed-over around the turn of the century. Bill works as a "trumpet medium;" meaning that he uses a trumpet (actually a long slender metal cone) as the instrument through which spirit voices, other than that of Dr. James, emanate. The trumpet stands peacefully over in the corner of his living room and really looks like nothing special. I do, on occasion lift it up, handle it, and look for electronics or attached wires. No one, including Bill, ever seems to mind.

Finally, after nearly two months of hanging out at Bill's, I am invited to join in on a séance. Having dealt with faith healers, gurus, and fairies, I prepare myself with a healthy amount of skepticism. The folding chairs are set up in a circle taking up most of the perimeter of the living room. There are about ten of us including Bill. We sit close enough to one another that, when asked, we can reach out and touch the hands of those on either side. The trumpet is placed on the floor (with its apex pointing straight up in the air) in the center of our circle. As my excitement mounts, I am dismayed to find that the blinds are drawn and the lights are fully extinguished before we get going, igniting my cynicism.

We are asked to hold hands. No references are made invoking Jesus Christ or any other religious icon. Bill simply sighs and takes audible deep breaths as he asks if Dr. James is willing to talk with our group. The transition from Bill's voice to that of the British spirit is gradual and uncanny. I am introduced as a new member and greeted by Dr. James with a high-spirited, "Oh, we have another doctor among us!" Similar to the greeting Bill gave me when we first met—I do not feel it appropriate to argue. As the séance proceeds, several of our members receive answers to questions they had asked at previous sessions and a few are told of well wishes from relatives "on the other side." After perhaps half an hour, the voice of Dr. James seems to weaken signaling that the end of the session is near. I am disappointed that, as far as I know, the trumpet has not moved and I have experienced nothing concrete to dispel my cynicism. It is precisely at that moment that Dr. James feebly says, "Dr. Bob, Grandpa Harry sends his love." Seconds later the lights go on. The trumpet is in exactly the same spot in the center of our circle as at the start. Bill looks sweaty and fatigued, while the others appear happy and refreshed.

Much later Peter asks me how I liked the séance. "Did I ever tell you that I had a grandfather named Harry? Be honest with me, Peter. We are fellow seekers. This is very important to me," I say looking deep into his eyes. "No never," Peter responds without hesitation. I am speechless. My recently deceased Nana (Mom's mother) was married to Harry who passed away from rheumatic heart disease long before my sister and I were born. We rarely spoke of him even during family gatherings. My shock is mixed with hope; that at long last I have a non-drug related experience that points to the existence of a metaphysical world. Peter has that "California Jim smile" on his face, like "see I told you… India's got nothing on us."

CHAPTER 14

Trumpet the Call

I learn that the trumpet does not always spring into action during a séance. In fact, each one is different and unpredictable. The most unforgettable moment for me comes during a rather long session in which one of our psychic science members is being counseled by a spirit through the trumpet. She is sitting right next to me and I can hear a voice sort of hovering around her head. The words are somewhat muted, but audible. I think to myself, *there must be someone standing next to her whispering in this pitch-black room.* Not an instant later, I feel the trumpet whip around pointing its opening, like a megaphone, right up to my ear. "This is Nana, Bobby. Mother did not mean to hurt you for not being around at my passing. She was just upset." Totally freaked out, I instinctively brush my right hand by my ear like swatting at a fly. My hand smacks into a firm, but movable object. Immediately, the lights go on and I am looking down at the trumpet at my feet. All the others, including Bill, are sitting right in their chairs. No one is standing.

The abrupt end to the sitting is entirely my fault, and the obvious stress it has placed on Bill disturbs me to no end. But it is worth the embarrassment because I have proven to myself that the trumpet really does levitate and communicate through metaphysical energy. It is time to cancel my plane ticket back to Bombay. I have found my wise man right around the corner in Paterson, New Jersey!

While séances with Bill are most exciting, aura-reading sessions are also pretty darn spacey. It is Bill's belief that all of us have potential to see auras, but we must open ourselves up to it through practice. Visualizing the energy field around a person is best learned by using one's peripheral vision, especially when there is a solid dark background (like the deep green surface of a pool table) behind the subject. Once auras are consistently seen, the interpretation of the colors becomes the focus of study. Sensitivity training is the key to opening oneself up to the spirit world and other dimensions around us.

Knowing that my mother is an artist, believes in ESP (often joking that her name Edna Phyllis Schultz bears the same initials), and enjoys being hypnotized I decide to tell her all about Bill Daut and even bring her to meet him. She is absolutely delighted with my story and is quick to suggest that I continue keeping this a secret from Dad. "He has this science background, you know, and doesn't believe in such things. We'll let him in on it in due time," she giggles.

Wasting no time, she insists on going over as soon as possible. Having already gotten the okay from Bill to bring Mom over "anytime," we head for Paterson. As we enter the Hazel Street house she appears a bit uncomfortable, but greets Bill like a member of the family. Before he can get a word in edgewise, she tells him that whatever he is doing to keep her Bobby here "where he belongs" is fine by her. They hit it off splendidly.

Before long, she actually visits with Bill on her own several times, always reinforcing the need for him to keep me from running off. He tells her not to worry; that, in fact, I will be staying for the foreseeable future and will be returning to medical school. He warns her not to discuss his prediction with me until after it comes to fruition. Needless to say, she, too, loves Bill Daut.

***

For me money is still an issue. I am twenty-seven years old and feel odd living off of my parents. The modeling attempts are falling short; there is nothing left in the storage room to sell; the copy writing gig is boring as hell. So I decide to write a book on Filipino faith healers since their psychic surgeon counterparts have been getting a great deal of press world wide. Having firsthand knowledge makes me, more or less, an expert on the popular subject. During my research of the published literature, I come across a book that describes the author's personal experience with psychic surgery while in the Philippines. From the start I see his lack of depth and understanding of the island culture and its spiritual fascination. I am convinced that the writer simply took a one week "psychic surgeon tour" of the Philippines and got his book published because he had M.D. after his name. And so the seed is planted: I will get myself an M.D. degree so that I too can have instant credibility and get my books published. *Brilliant!*

While my parents are vacationing in Portugal with

friends I get up the nerve to call Dr. Buchannan, my old dean at Cornell University Medical College, to ask if there is any chance of my resuming my medical education. While he remembers me with fondness, he tells me that were I to be taken back into the program I would be the first student to be readmitted after being away for more than two years. After all, I have been gone for over four years and Dr. Ribble, who is now Dean of Admissions (and was my original Admissions Committee advisor), will not likely look upon me with favor since I proved him wrong once, already. Nevertheless, Dean Buchannan promises to check into things and call me back.

A man of his word, Dr. Buchannan calls me the very next day—the prognosis is not good. Although Dr. Ribble is willing to meet with me, he believes there are several committee members who just do not want to consider my request even though I completed the first year satisfactorily and was granted a leave of absence at that time. My plea is that they give me the chance to personally speak with each of the naysayers so that I may convince them that I am not only worthy of a second chance, but that I have gained worldly experience, which will benefit my fellow classmates.

Remarkably, interviews with the six Admissions Committee members who are the most negative about my case are scheduled: three per day for two days. Both overjoyed and nervous I drag out my modeling suit, get a shorter haircut and shave off my sideburns, goatee, and mustache. After rehearsing my entreaty in front of the mirror for hours, I drive into the City with sweaty palms and a pounding heart.

As it turns out, the first day of interrogatories are all with professors who had taught me in the past. They primarily want to know that I am healthy, not hooked on drugs, and serious about wanting to complete my medical education. Two seem extremely interested in my travels.

The second day is a different story. My self-confidence is shattered when a woman cardiologist points out that it costs a million dollars to educate and train each medical student to become a worthy doctor. I have essentially pissed away a fortune for the university and contemptuously given up an opportunity that a myriad of other bright young people could only dream of. "And your parents, young man—have you stopped to think what your running away did to them? And I see that your father is a doctor," she sneers. "What is it you expect us to believe this time?" As unexpectedly as her sharp words assault my very soul, the tears spill out over my cheeks in a deluge. Through my congestion I manage to say, "I will become a doctor even if I have to return to the Philippines to study. And I will make whatever institution that gives me the chance, proud that it recognized my passion and renewed commitment." Leaving her office for the final interview seems empty and pointless.

The next few days are filled with shattered self-esteem and anger. When Dr. Ribble calls to tell me that I will be accepted back into the program as long as I am drug tested, deemed healthy, and serve at least one year as a student member of the Admissions Committee, I am speechless. He seems to know how overwhelmed I am and simply suggests that I think about whether I want to resume my studies with the class of '78 that is already in the middle of its first year (which I completed successfully back in 1970) or wait to matriculate with it in July when it begins its second year.

Without hesitation I ask to start immediately (feeling that repeating some of the first year courses will get me back in the groove of being a medical student). I am overwhelmed by my good fortune.

CHAPTER 15

Back in the Game

So I am back in medical school: originally in the class of '73, now in the class of '78. When my parents return from Portugal (one of their scarce vacations outside the country) I greet them at the door with my new CUMC picture ID in hand. Mom looks at it, fills up with tears, raises her eyes to heaven and says, "Thank you God. I will keep my promise and never smoke another cigarette again." Dad, who now holds my ID like he is cradling a newborn baby, perseverates, "What's this? What's this? What's this?" over and over again.

Somehow the scene reminds me of a poignant joke: The priest is asked, "When does life begin?" He responds, "Life begins when the egg is fertilized by the sperm." The minister is asked, "When does life begin?" He thinks a bit, and then answers, "When the fertilized egg embeds in the uterus." Finally, the Rabbi is asked, "When does life begin?" Without hesitation he replies, "When you get into medical school!"

Beyond the joy I have given to my parents, I am fortunate

to find out (after numerous tests, including a painful bone marrow biopsy) that the amoebiasis (systemic infestation by amoeba protozoans) I picked up in my travels is to be treated by Dr. Kean, Cornell's world renowned parasitologist. My yellow skin color turns out to be carotenemia (deposition of carotene from excessive ingestion of carrots and other vegetables), and not jaundice from liver disease. Best of all, I no longer have to philosophize when asked, "What do you do?" I can now simply answer that I go to medical school. The response is always extremely positive. Oh yes, and then there is the fact that I am actually going to be a doctor.

I am back in mainstream society where events like Watergate, Nixon's resignation, the Patty Hearst kidnapping, and Hank Aaron's assault on Babe Ruth's thirty-nine year old homerun record matter.

Initially, medical school is only a means for me to get M.D. after my name so I have credibility with publishers and can get paid for writing books. But the fact is I like the favorable response I get from people when they hear that I am a medical student. I no longer have to give a long philosophical explanation of how I see life and why it is I am not on any conventional path. My parents are pleased as they can be, and Dad is not at all upset that when I started back in '69 my medical school tuition was $800 and is now up to $2,000 per year. The biggest surprise, however, is that I actually enjoy going to class and learning about the human body and what makes us tick. Studying and simply passing tests is a whole lot easier than coping with the world and dodging trouble.

I am several years older than most of my classmates and carry the aura of an experienced world traveler. So the laugh is on me when I accept Dr. George's invitation to attend a party at his Central Park West apartment. He is, after all, my pathology professor and world-renowned in his field. When I arrive at his door I am greeted warmly and hand him the customary bottle of wine as I enter his abode. *Where are the other guests? I must be early.*

With classical music playing softly in the background he motions me over to the sofa and offers me a cocktail. Before sitting down I ask if I have come too early and when the others are expected to arrive. "This is our night," he whispers. *Uh Oh!* This is not good at all. "Ugh...I don't go that way, Sir," I say in a panic and bolt through the door. "Keep the wine!"

Next day in class it seems that everyone knows that I, "Worldly Bob," fell for the old come-on by "Georgie." It is really tough to take, but not nearly as embarrassing as going to pathology lab; despite my professor acting as if sexual rejection is an ordinary part of his week. Surprisingly, I feel more accepted by my classmates after this humiliating incident than before it; as if I have gone through hazing or a right of passage to emerge as one of the gang.

Earlier in the year, after playing basketball in Olin Hall, I notice that my left knee feels tight and swollen. Subsequently, every time I pivot or cut on a basketball or tennis court I get a twinge of pain on the inner side of it. Back in Jersey my dad arranges for me to have an arthrogram (pre MRI days) in which dye is injected into the joint and x-rays are taken looking for a torn cartilage. The test is brutal, but worst of all it is turns out positive and I am told that I need surgery. My knee is to be cut open so the torn meniscus can be entirely removed. After consulting with Dr. John Marshall, the head of the Sports Medicine Service (and The New York Football Giants' orthopaedic surgeon) at Hospital for Special Surgery, I agree to a surgical date.

Two weeks later, in a pro-section (special anatomy) class, taught by Dr. Marshall with the help of some of his residents and fellows, I meekly approach my professor and explain that I read that removing the entire meniscus may have long term ill affects on my knee. Dr. Wantanabe in Japan has developed the arthroscope for removal of only the damaged piece of cartilage, which spares the rest of the shock absorber. I want to wait for that technique to come to the United States. "You're not as dumb as you look, Schultzy," Dr. Marshall responds with an arm around my shoulder. "We'll have that surgical technique down in another year or two." *Phew…a temporary reprieve.*

The basic science years (the first two of medical school) are interesting, but really get exciting towards the end when we begin training in Physical Diagnosis. Under the tutelage of Drs. Barondess and Gardy, we are taught how to take a history and perform a physical exam on patients in preparation for our upcoming clinical years. It is at this point that I begin tasting what it might be like to be a real medical doctor. My thoughts of being a writer (or a model, or a faith healer, or one of the enlightened here on earth) readily evaporate.

Because of my busy medical school schedule I only get to hang out at Bill's on weekends. Even Maddie, one of my cousins whom I turned on to Bill, has been going to see him on a more frequent basis than I. Although I miss the connection with the metaphysical that the psychic spirit sessions provide, Bill reassures me that I am doing exactly what I am meant to do and that my seeming diminished contact with him and the group matters little towards my spiritual growth. "You will be a wonderful doctor and bring comfort and healing to your patients. Dr. James and I, and everyone here are very proud of you," he reminds me often. But I do notice that my focus of exploration is changing from the existential to the concrete world of medicine. After all, it is necessary to learn a whole new language in order to grasp and communicate the concepts of medical knowledge. I can see that this is a full time task that leaves little room for diversion.

As I blend more into the mainstream, my parents ask if I would speak with the Landaus, their longtime friends (Dr. Landau is a colleague of Dad's), about one of their three sons. It seems that Jonathan also ran off to explore the world some years ago, but is now in Tibet with the Dali Lama. Since I am living proof that a wayward son can come back to traditional reality, perhaps I could be the bearer of hope for Johnny's distraught parents. I reluctantly consent, although I know full well that Johnny will do whatever the Dali Lama wishes him to do until disillusionment takes over. After listening to their tale of woe, I simply tell his folks to have faith in their son and to be patient with his process of discovery. Many of us who turn to Eastern philosophy for answers to our existential questions eventually learn that we are, indeed, Westerners after all and that there is no place like America. Johnny will eventually return. When asked if I thought drugs are the cause for his fall from grace, I explain that while I believe psychedelics may have initiated Johnny's search, it is my understanding that drugs are not part of Buddhism. I am warmly hugged by both parents and, to say the least, admired and praised by my folks.

Dad encourages me to become a surgeon of some sort because I will make a good living and, as he puts it, "There is nothing liking being in the operating room." To reinforce his point he gets me a summer job as a scrub tech at the Barnert Hospital in Paterson. Initially, I am a bit put off by his guidance (*Why so pushy? I'm already back in the fold for God's sake!*), but once I see the goings-on in the operating room I am completely mesmerized. After being trained in proper sterile surgical technique, I am introduced to the instruments, their complex names, and how to hold and pass them. Before long I am scrubbing in on biopsies, hernia repairs, and eventually big stuff like bowel resections and hip replacements.

The O.R. drama and excitement is a rush, but there is more: Suzanne! She is a circulator and scrub nurse, not just a tech like me. Above all, Suzie is hot and very sensual. Before long she is gowning me in the most provocative way and, on one occasion when a case is cancelled, encourages me to get to third base with her in the autoclave room. By the end of the summer I am making regular trysts to her apartment for outrageous fun. Unfortunately, as with most summer romances, fall intercedes and I must leave to begin my third year of medical school. Besides, sweet Suzie is moving out of state with her fiancé. *Here's wishing all the best to the lovely couple.*

It is 1975 and the "Thrilla in Manila" between Mohammad Ali and Smokin' Joe Frazier has special meaning for me. The pre-fight coverage, with footage of jeepneys in downtown Quezon City and exposés on Imelda and Ferdinand Marcos stirs up memories of a not-too distant-past, though it somehow seems to border on the surreal. Mom and Dad don't watch.

CHAPTER 16

Ben Casey's Got Nothing On Me

My clinical years involve rotations through various medical services with an emphasis on internal medicine (the foundation of the art of medicine). Rotations are generally three months long with time on subspecialty units, such as rheumatology or ophthalmology, cut to six weeks or less. As a medical student on the team I am low man on the totem pole and used for "scut" work such as finding medical records or lab reports. In return I am taught how to write orders, draw blood, work-up patients for admission to the hospital, and be respectful of the Art and my superiors. Despite being just a "go-for," I do get to wear a white coat and carry a stethoscope. The coat, however, is short (like a suit jacket) and quite distinguishable from the long lab coats worn by the real doctors.

In preparation for actually drawing blood from patients we medical students practice on each other. Because I have prominent veins in my forearms (no doubt from working out) I become the class guinea pig. The problem is that big veins do not necessarily stay in place when a needle approaches; they tend to roll away unless anchored down by the venapuncturist. Unfortunately, this "advanced" technique takes time to learn so I am left to constantly explain the etiology of my colorful, bruised arms.

Each of us is given an elective month in which we can choose four weeks on a specialty service or split the month into two-week rotations. Since I am convinced that I want to be a cardiothoracic surgeon (because it sounds cool) I select two weeks on the thoracic unit. And because I am into athletics I ask for two weeks with Dr. Marshall on the Sports Medicine Service.

Heart surgery carries with it a mystique and prestige unlike any other service in the hospital. The residency training is several years longer than for general surgery and New York Hospital has an entire high tech wing dedicated to the specialty. So it is even more remarkable that on the last day of my cardiothoracic rotation I find myself sitting alone with the chief of the department who is in tears after losing a patient on the operating table just minutes before.

The asymptomatic fifty-year-old airline pilot was scheduled for coronary artery bypass surgery because he was found to have a blockage (on the arteriogram) after his routine stress test was positive. While the actual surgery went well, tragically they could not get him off the bypass pump at the end of the case. They tried for hours, but his heart would not beat on it's own.

Now, as a lowly third year medical student I am at a loss for words of consolation for my mentor. All I know is that cardiac surgery can be very unpleasant and has certainly lost its luster as far as I am concerned.

The very next day I begin my stint on the Sports Medicine Service at the Hospital for Special Surgery. New York Giants' fullback Larry Csonka has torn his anterior cruciate ligament and is being admitted to the hospital for surgical intervention by Dr. Marshall. The reporters are everywhere, the excitement is awesome, and I am the medical student assigned to the case. Most importantly, there is no life and death element to the admission. Too groovy!

Not only do I get to watch the All-Pro athlete's knee surgery and round on him with the team, I am mistakenly asked by a young reporter to comment on his prognosis. It is at that very moment that the notion of switching from cardiothoracic surgery to orthopaedics solidifies in my brain. I mean, who needs the life/death drama, anyway? Sports medicine is dynamite; and nobody dies from an ankle sprain.

Now that I have made my mind up to pursue an orthopaedic residency, I need to get honors in my studies so that I can get accepted into this very popular field. Working in a research lab is also helpful on my resume, so I ask Dr. Becker (a very cool cat) if I can work with him. He is studying Berger's disease (*thromboangitis obliterans*). This bizarre ailment is a vascular allergy to tobacco glycoprotein, a caustic substance in cigarette smoke that closes off small arteries in the body of certain vulnerable smokers. These patients come into the hospital for amputations of fingers and toes and sometimes arms and legs.

The amazing thing is that Berger's disease, unlike

atherosclerosis (also often a product of cigarette smoking and high cholesterol), is fully reversible if the person simply stops smoking. As I interview patient after patient lying in their hospital beds awaiting amputation, the absurdity of their "logic" given between drags on cigarettes (which each so gravely covets) is absolutely mind boggling. The only thing more frightening is watching a patient with laryngeal carcinoma (voice box cancer) smoking through his tracheotomy (breathing hole cut in the throat). The similarity to the pathetic junkies I saw on the road is striking and briefly sends me into a reverie about Virginie.

There is more research in store for me out in Colorado during the summer. Fortunately, it is strictly lab work (studying the in vitro effect of calcium blockers on smooth muscle) with no patient contact. My sister has invited me out to Denver where her husband Clifford is head of a pulmonary lab; studying the likes of the great marathoner Frank Shorter and his family members who have blunted hypoxic responses (they tend not to get short of breath during exercise). He arranges for one of his associates to take me on as an assistant for a couple of months.

Helaine and Cliff's two kids, Julie and Todd, are all about swimming, hiking, and bicycling just like their parents. The outdoors and mountain landscape is a huge relief from the overbearing urban life in Manhattan. Being out there for the nation's bicentennial celebration of our independence is particularly far-out. We also spend two weeks in July sucking up every televised event of the Summer Olympics in Montreal, Canada. Nadia Comaneci's seven perfect scores of ten in gymnastics could not be more awe-inspiring (unless she represented the United States). The Winter

Games were held in Innsbruck, Austria despite the fact that they were originally awarded to Denver, Colorado. It seems that the expense of putting on the Games and residual fear of violence held over from the 1972 Summer Olympics in Munich caused the Colorado voters to reject the event.

As always seems to be the case, the summer passes quickly. My final year in medical school makes me feel almost like a doctor. Psychiatry and Ob-gyn rotations are exciting because of the one-on-one patient contact granted to us medical students. At the Payne Whitney Hospital I am assigned two patients. The teenage chronic drug abuser admitted for "dry out" and counseling makes me appreciate how lucky I am that my years of substance experimentation never put me in his pitiful state. My other assignment is to an attractive woman in her mid thirties with the diagnosis of "borderline personality disorder." To say that she is manipulative is to suggest that the "Son of Sam" is rude to ladies. Her disorder is not classified as one of the two psychoses (schizophrenia or manic depression), but something well beyond a neurosis. Between her attempts to convince me that she is saner than Dr. Michaels (head of the institute) and her outrageous "come-ons" to me (and the other male practitioners) I realize that psychiatry is not my calling.

On obstetrics, at Lying-in Hospital, I actually get the chance to deliver babies (from uncomplicated "multips" who have little difficulty bearing children). Despite playing little more than catcher, the thrill is just as Dad always describes it, "A miracle!" Although he has delivered some two thousand babies, he remains in awe of nativity.

Staging the uterus' preparation for delivery is done

by pelvic exam. Naturally, we are closely monitored by the obstetricians or nurse midwives. Trying to act as a seasoned professional. I enter the birthing area to check on a patient already up in stirrups. As I lift the sheet I am conscious of the nurse sensing my hesitation. Suddenly we are both speechless. It is the young mother-to-be who finally breaks the silence. "My Yosemite Sam always steals the show," she says proudly. The tattoo of cartoon character Yosemite Sam chasing Bug's Bunny into her A-hole is unforgettable.

Not everything during the year is quite so memorable. In fact, the daily routine starts to intrude on my free spirit. Winning a $1,000 scholarship and a three-month externship at The Royal Hospital in Edinburgh, Scotland, is an honor, but more importantly it gives me a chance to escape the noise and griminess of New York City. Living right next to the hospital with its ambulance sirens and relentless hum of activity is, at times, beyond annoying. The thought of getting back on the road again and visiting another country rekindles my sense of adventure.

With the get-away bug up my ass, and the trip not until September, I head off to Miami Beach where Gayle, a cousin of mine, and her husband, Eric own a hotel. Nothing fancy, mind you (catering to the elderly), but on the ocean, nevertheless. The scene is subdued and very hot (temperature-wise). So it is surprising to learn that on January 19th Miami, Florida had its first (and only) snowfall. As I lay out by the pool in mid-August cooking like a burger on a grill, envisioning myself basking on the beach in Goa, I hear the loud sobs of several women, "No, not the King!" "He can't be dead." Indeed, Elvis Aaron Presley is dead at the age of forty-two; found on the floor at Graceland by his fiancée Ginger Alden (he and Priscilla separated back in '72). Not surprisingly, the autopsy report indicates that he died of "combined drug intoxication." Another great one self-destructs with the help of drugs—one more reason to appreciate my good fortune.

CHAPTER 17

On the Road Again

Come September, I find myself back on the road: this time in Edinburgh, Scotland where I discover that the city is pronounced "Edinboro" (not "Edinberg") and that a surgeon is called "Mister" (with "Doctor" reserved for the non-surgeon physician). Among the many culture shocks is finding that the nurses in the Royal Hospital always immediately stand and give up their seats when a male physician enters the charting area to write orders. But there is more: while taking a history from a woman (to whom I am assigned for hospital admission) I ask the routine question, "Have you ever had surgery before?" She says, "Yes, indeed. I had my uterus removed." When I ask if there were any complications ,she mentions that she had to spend three weeks longer in the hospital than expected. It seems that during the hysterectomy, both her ureters (tubes connecting the kidneys to the bladder) were cut. Shocked at hearing that **both** ureters were mistakenly transected during surgery, I ask her what she did about it (anticipating hearing of a hefty law suit). She responds calmly, "I did whatever the doctors asked me to do," with the look of what-else-would-you-expect-me-to-do on her face. *And I thought the people in Goa were laid back!*

Actually, being laid back is an understatement. During a *duodenojejunostomy* (small bowel rerouting) procedure, I am the only person in the operating room laughing when Mr. Johnson, the primary surgeon, suggests that we break for tea and biscuits about ninety minutes into the case. Believing that it is a joke, I awkwardly stand there as everyone breaks scrub and exits the theatre, leaving me and the nurse anesthetist to tend to the patient. "Go," she says shooing me away, "get refreshed, young sir."

I find the crew sitting in an antechamber taking tea and discussing football (soccer). All are relaxed and in no apparent rush. Some fifteen minutes later Mr. Johnson slowly rises and says softly, "Shall we have at it?" The leisurely return to the operating theatre sees everyone in good spirits and ready to perform the anastomosis (sewing the bowel together), the most critical part of the procedure (requiring a water tight closure to prevent catastrophic leakage). All in all, the entire operation takes no more than two and a half hours, skin to skin (about the same time it would take back in the States without the outlandish tea and biscuits break). Of course, the patient goes on to do beautifully.

I learn a lot about Scottish temperament and their perspective on things. But it irks me to no end when, on October 18th (after catching the game on Armed Forces Radio) I ecstatically run out of my apartment into the streets and find no one with whom to celebrate the New York Yankees' World Series win (the first since 1962) over our rival Los Angeles Dodgers. No use bragging about Reggie Jackson's or Ron Guidry's heroics. In fact, one guy on the street has the audacity to say, "You Americans have your nerve calling that tournament the 'World Series.' After all, it is just your country's players participating." A bit deflated, I go have a celebratory beer by myself and ponder the painful veracity of the cat's remarks.

The British Isles have a celebration of their own: 1977 is the Silver Jubilee of the reign of Queen Elizabeth II. The twenty-fifth anniversary is marked by pictures of Her Majesty surrounded by red, white, and blue ribbons in store windows, on street posts, on buses, and on bumper stickers. Her likeness is ubiquitous and her subjects just can't get enough of her. For me the upbeat atmosphere has a good vibe, but after a while I start seeing that face beneath the tiara in my dreams. Before long, however, I am back in the States and Elizabeth's face is replaced by John's; John Travolta, that is. *Saturday Night Fever* has come out and the disco craze is taking over.

***

My last year of medical school is all about securing a spot in a good orthopaedic surgical residency program. Yep: five more years of specialty training after I graduate from medical school (most of it learning how to operate). Knowing that I want to spend as much of that time as possible learning orthopaedics, I look primarily at "one-four" programs; meaning one year of general surgery (mandatory for learning basic surgical techniques) and four years of orthopaedic surgery. I apply to three residency programs: Hospital for Special Surgery (HSS), New York University

(NYU), and Harvard. The last one is a "two-three" system (two years of general surgery and three of orthopaedics); not exactly what I prefer, but I apply there mainly to appease my brother-in-law who did one year of training at Mass General Hospital and thought it was "the end all" in medicine.

I have good credentials, coming out of Cornell and having been elected to AOA (the national medical school honorary society, similar to Phi Beta Kappa in college), so I figure my chance of getting into the "one-four" program at HSS (my first choice) is good. But it is not meant to be. Instead, I am only offered a position in their "two-three" program. With a bruised ego, I consider taking the NYU "one-four" spot granted me. And then I get a call from Harvard to come up for an interview. Still pissed off about the HSS snub, and kind of fed up with New York City anyway, I make the trip to Boston.

There I find myself competing with numerous other candidates, all AOA from outstanding medical schools. After a series of interviews (in a group, one-on-one, and one-on-three) I am certain that it was a wasted trip. I stand no chance, particularly because the interviewer with the mustache and long hair (no doubt the psychiatrist everyone says is thrown in there to evaluate each candidate's squash) kept asking me about my fascination with India and why I bummed around the world for so long.

Once back in New York, I am about to take the NYU position because of the "one-four" opportunity and the desire for a change of scenery—HSS is part of the Cornell medical complex where I have already spent nearly five years. The only bummer is that I will have to live five more years in Manhattan. But then the letter of acceptance to the Harvard Combined Orthopaedic Residency Program arrives. *Are you kidding me?* I actually call the residency office to make sure there is no mistake. While I'd rather spend only one year doing general surgery instead of two, don't know a soul up in Boston, and hate the Red Sox and Boston Celtics, my parents and brother-in-law all tell me that this is the opportunity of a lifetime. They say that my fear of being intellectually blown away up there is a bunch of insecure nonsense.

Okay, then. Having made the decision to head to New England in 1980 (after two years of general surgical residency at, you guessed it, The New York Hospital), I can finish out the rest of my final medical school year knowing that my future is secure. I am even getting off to the fact that my acceptance to Harvard is already paying dividends from my parents and every soul they tell. Even my fellow classmates seem impressed. My impulse is to resist the primal baseness of it all, but the high is just too cool so I indulge myself. HARVARD... HARVARD... HARVARD!

CHAPTER 18

The Graduate

I am happy with my new digs on 72nd Street and York Avenue. It is a walk-up apartment that provides me with a respite from the maddening pace of the nearby dorms and hospital employee housing. It is there, late one evening, that I hear a rhythmic tap on my front door. There is something familiar about it, as I extricate myself from my medical books and open the door. *No way!* Standing there, looking like Grizzly Adams, wearing a blanket like a poncho and a big shit-assed grin on his face is J.G.! The hug is immense; the buzz spectacular.

After telling me that he tracked me down through my parents in Jersey (whom he swore to secrecy) he proceeds to fill me in on the last five years. After leaving me in Bombay he made his way back through Pakistan and the Khyber Pass to Pagman, Afghanistan. Teaming back up with Raymond, he did a few "runs" and made some mad money. The whole thing ended abruptly for him when he found himself on the wrong side of a gun and promised himself that if he survived he would get out of the business for good.

It was then back to Europe where he got "on the bus" (the European version of Ken Kesey and the Merry Pranksters' bus) in southern France. He says that was such a heavy drug scene that he was sure he was going to lose himself, but he stayed as long as he could because of this outrageous chick. At some point, he too found himself in need of reparations with his father (J.G.'s mother had passed away long ago) and brother so he made his way back to the States and his home in Cedarhurst, Long Island.

"So you're going to be a doctor after all!" J.G. says like a proud brother. "Far freaking out!"

I tell him about Goa, Singapore, the Philippines, and Peter introducing me to Bill Daut. He can't wait to meet the man whose power kept me in the States. I feel a twinge of guilt for having lost touch with Bill and the whole psychic scene for a while.

We talk about Raymond and Marie, "Blind" George, "Chicky" Phillips, Virginie, Marta, Elliott, Billy, Carl, "California" Jim, and Johnny and Vani. I am transported back to the magical road where anything can happen and freedom races just ahead of loneliness. We laugh about how I was blown off by Lenny Berman, an old childhood friend of mine from Camp Indian Trails, whom I contacted after seeing him anchor sports on the NBC evening news here in New York. J.G. says he hasn't tried to contact his old college roommate Al yet, but supposes that the young Congressman might pull a "Lenny" on him as well; adding, "Especially with the way I look right now. Remember how his mom attacked me at the wedding because of my long hair?" We go on into the night laughing and reminiscing until I realize that I have class early in the morning.

When I finally get J.G. over to Bill's in Paterson it is just as I expect. The two of them wear the same "knowing" smile and, for a moment, I think that they have met before. Bill sees a wonderful family, with adorable kids, in J.G.'s future. J.G. seems quite agreeable to that notion. (It will be years before J.G. and I hook up again; both with our own families.)

Graduation from medical school is far different than from college, especially for my parents. My goatee is gone (though I still have a mustache and longish hair) and my crimson robes are neatly closed over a clean white shirt and tie. Most of all, I appreciate how much this day means to them. Dad whispers that the shrimp boats and blue monster Mercedes van were all worth it just to get to this day.

In July of 1978, after getting my medical degree in May, I begin my internship like so many other new doctors. Though still in training each of us has earned the right to be called doctor even though we are greenhorns at best. That is why it is not very smart to be admitted as a patient to a teaching hospital in July, unless you are at death's door. The competency level of the new "house staff" (as we are called) rises logarithmically over the next several months. Initially, we rookies are seldom asked to do much more than draw blood and start an IV.

I am on the Yellow Surgical Service and awfully excited about entering the operating room for the first time as a doctor. But first I have the responsibility of drawing the morning bloods. Knowing that I am damn good at venapuncture I make my way from room to room without a hitch, depositing the properly labeled vials of blood with the clerk at the nurses' station. Looking at the clock I realize that

I have only a few minutes to make it to the O.R. in time for the first case.

As I hustle to the elevator I hear the clerk call me back. "You have missed Mr. Clots, Dr. Schultz."

Damn! He's all the way down the hall; half a block from his room and hooked up to an IV pole. With no time to usher him back to his bed, I decide to draw his blood where he stands; just one tube for a CBC; no big deal. "Good morning, Sir. This will only take a second," I say with a hurried smile. Knowing that I have to take the sample from the arm without the IV, I strap on the rubber tourniquet, ask him to open and close his fist several times to pump up his veins, and swab his antecubital fossa (area in front of the elbow) with an alcohol sponge. *Nice looking vein; piece of cake.* Next thing I know Mr. Clots is lying at my feet having had a vaso-vagal attack (sudden drop in heart rate) from the noxious needle stick. Fortunately, he did not break a hip or suffer a concussion. Needless to say, I am late for the O.R. and have some real explaining to do regarding the infamous "Clots episode."

But little can compare with my first stint on the Burn Unit. The New York Hospital had recently opened its state-of-the-art burn treatment center under the guidance of the trauma physicians originally from Parkland Hospital in Dallas (the very same individuals to whom JFK was brought on November 22, 1963). Each of the general surgical residents rotates through The Unit for three months each year. If you survive, you get a tee-shirt that says "I Survived The New York Hospital Burn Unit."

It is in The Unit that I learn to do escharotomies (where a large "H" is made with a scalpel through the leather-like scar tissue on the chest of a badly burned victim to allow the chest to expand and the patient to breathe), tracheotomies, intubations, and insert A-lines (arterial lines to measure blood oxygen). The patients are so very sick and the place so hectic that even interns are often enlisted to do procedures on an emergency basis. New burn victims bring with them the smell of burned flesh and anguish beyond words. Even with the preoccupation of having to quickly gain access to their veins and airways, and balance their fluids and electrolytes, the tragedy of what we witness is staggering and, at times, horrific.

***

By the time 1979 rolls in I am half-way through my rookie year and infinitely more competent than I was six months prior. After rotating through the Yellow and Blue surgical services (not to mention the Burn Unit) I am now stuck on medicine (a non-surgical rotation) where all we do all day long is round on patients and write notes in their charts. Without the excitement of surgery to break up the day I find myself withering into a nerd.

Every chance I get I throw on my sneakers and run along the FDR Drive (wondering if the exhaust fumes are negating the benefit of the exercise) or skip rope. Playing basketball or tennis still hurts my left knee and at some point I will have to get it arthroscoped.

After a late lunch break, during which I spend essentially the whole hour skipping rope on the pavement outside the cafeteria, I notice that my right foot is swollen and once I take my sneaker off I can't get my dress shoe back on it. Fifteen minutes later I can barely walk. At the clinic an x-ray shows a stress fracture of the third metatarsal bone.

As I sit on the stretcher getting casted (with a new product made of fiberglass instead of Plaster of Paris), the other two medical interns are signing-out to me. "All my patients are fine. You should have no problems," Ruth says. The other simply hands me his list. Neither makes so much as a gratuitous offer to switch call with me despite my obvious lower extremity trauma. After all, it is Friday night! @#!

Considering the fact that our patients span three floors of the hospital (and I routinely take the stairs) I realize that I am in for one hell of a night. Even healthy hospitalized patients need PM bloods drawn (for potassium, glucose, and hematocrit levels), and IVs commonly need to be restarted. There is no way I am ever going to be able to keep my newly casted foot elevated for the first twenty-four hours as instructed. All I can do is drag my progressively swollen foot up and down the damn stairwell (cursing out my "brethren" associates) knowing that one of the two elevators is out of commission for servicing (and the other is slower than hell).

As aggravating and dispiriting as the lack of compassion from my fellow interns is, I am absolutely demoralized by the treatment Peter, a PGY-2 (second year resident), dumps on me several weeks later. Being one year behind him in training, I have known Peter for years in medical school and throughout his internship. We played basketball together and hung out with the same crowd. It was he who helped convince me to take my general surgical residency at The New York Hospital. "You know the whole scene here and we'll have a blast," he said to me more than once. Well, there must be something evil that warps a resident's brain into sadistic cravings once he moves up the ladder and has an intern below him.

It is after 6:00 PM; surgery is done for the day, and there are hospital admissions to be done (for tomorrow's surgical schedule) before we can go home. I have a list of six patients that need H&P's (history and physicals) and their pre-op bloods drawn. At my novice stage, each will take me at least one hour to do. "Hey Pete, help me out here buddy. Do a couple of these admissions. Take the two women in for breast biopsies. Enjoy yourself. You can knock them out in no time," I suggest. Ever so slowly Peter peers out from under the sports section of the newspaper and says, "You've got to be kidding me. It is my job to see that you get every bit of training available to you," he says with a malicious grin on his ugly puss. I am sure he is kidding until four hours later, as I am just getting to the fifth admission; there is no sign of Peter. Okay. I get it. It's a dog eat dog world out here in these hallowed halls.

Even the honchos in the Department of Surgery seem to get off beating up the house staff. I distinctly remember Dr. Shire (department chairman) telling us prospective candidates for his residency program that being on-call occurs every third night. Keep in mind that, when one is on-call, it is not unusual to be kept up all night tending to IVs, emergency admissions, and anything else the nursing staff may need you to do. So when the truth comes out, that the on-call schedule is every other night, instead of every third, it hits me and every other sucker hard. How many times do I get back to my apartment well after midnight, so tired that I can't decide whether to eat, take a shower, or just go to sleep? Waking up in the morning with shredded wheat and half dried milk all over me and the bed becomes routine.

The only benefit of being overworked is that it teaches me the uncanny ability to grab a catnap at any time, anywhere, and when I am awakened from a sound sleep I can respond alertly just as if I had never dosed off. On the other hand, sound decision-making when unduly fatigued certainly comes into question, but it is not macho to complain. Under the circumstances I often wonder why there are not more serious iatrogenic (doctor caused) errors made in teaching hospitals.

The lack of sleep puts us all on edge and I am sure it played a roll in my near physical encounter with Dr. Brown, my chief resident. But the real genesis of our argument is two fold: firstly, I am considered an outsider, as is any intern or resident going into a specialty other than general surgery. It's as if I am only hitching a ride for two years and not committed for the duration. Secondly, Brown is a bully and constantly on the look out for someone to push around. (Probably a member of the same lame gang as my sixth grade nemesis Ralph.)

As it happens, I am on Emergency Room rotation (which I like because I get to see orthopaedic stuff like broken hips and multiple trauma). I diagnose an acute appendicitis, so I call my chief who sees the patient and books him for emergency surgery. While this is going on, a car accident victim comes in with several musculoskeletal injuries. The orthopaedic residents are all over this one and, of course, I find it fascinating. Despite having plenty of help for the appendectomy, Brown orders me to leave the E.R. and accompany the hot appendix to the O.R. I can see his fiendish grin as he bellows the order.

"You can't be serious!" I retort, doing my best John McEnroe.

Sensing insubordination Brown gets right in my face. "I have never been more serious in my life, Doctor!" he blasts.

Instinctively, I reach up and fortunately a couple of the other residents step between us. Brown looks pleased that he got me to "lose it" and knows that it won't end here.

The appendectomy is unexciting (I actually do not even get to scrub on the case since there are already two other assistants). My meeting with Dr. Shires, to whom I am reported for reprimand, does, however, get my attention. Apparently I have come within a hair's breadth of losing my residency. Just as in the military, there is a chain of command; break it and you are dead meat!

"Do you understand, Doctor?" "I do, Sir, but..." Dr. Shires interrupts with, "Had you hit your chief, you could have kissed your surgical career good-bye. There is nothing more to understand."

Doing my best to extricate myself from the general surgery milieu, I volunteer as often as allowed to take E.R. duty. In addition to the orthopaedics exposure there, I get to experience the craziness that can only be found in an emergency room. From having to dis-impact (digitally break-up fecal matter) Truman Capote after he had eaten unshelled sunflower seeds earlier one night at a Ranger game, to dealing with DB's ("dirt balls") who pathetically feign illness just to get drugs and a stretcher to sleep on, I find E.R. duty full of surprises and reminiscent of being "on the road."

Like the character that drifts in with abdominal pain at 3:00 in the morning... I am awoken from a sound sleep (we sleep in a small on-call quarters right there in the E.R.) to see this "sad sack" with belly complaints. As I examine his soft, benign abdomen I ask how long he has been hurting. "Oh, for years now," he says with a perfectly straight face. "For YEARS?!" I shout incredulously. "Then why do you come in now, at 3:00 in the morning?" Without hesitation he responds earnestly, "Because as I was lying in bed I got to thinking that if I've had this pain for so long, it must be serious!" Okay, it's funny now, but at 3:00 in the morning it was all I could do not to give him a real injury.

And then there is late October when the whole hospital is a buzz about Mohammad Reza Pahlavi, the Shah of Iran, who has come to The New York Hospital with non-Hodgkin's lymphoma to see the famous biliary surgeon Dr. Thorn Bjornson. On October 26th the E.R. is suddenly overrun with mountains of fresh floral arrangements sent in honor of the Shah's birthday. The flood of flowers not only impedes the flow of E.R. traffic, it causes a rash of allergic fits among patients and staff alike. The Shah occupies the entire 17th floor of the hospital, also known as the "Penthouse," replete with carpeted floors and mahogany doors. Even his greyhound dogs are allowed to stay up there with him. And instead of a lowly intern drawing his daily blood samples, the chief resident gets the assignment.

All of this is a bit opulent and pretentious, to say the least, but the consequences of President Carter's decision to allow the Shah to seek medical care here in the United States is far more grave. For on November 4th some three thousand Iranian radicals (mostly students) invade the U. S. Embassy in Tehran and take ninety hostages (fifty-one Americans), demanding that the former Shah be sent back to Iran to stand trial. The blindfolded hostages are seen, on every newscast, being paraded through the streets like criminals.

Eight days later Carter orders a halt on all oil imports from Iran and three day after that freezes all Iranian assets in the United States and U.S. banks. On November 21st the crisis escalates further when the Ayatollah Khomeini (who took over Iran when the Shah fled to Egypt ten months before) falsely reports to the Muslim world that Americans took over the Grand Mosque in Mecca (which, in fact, was taken over by armed Islamic fundamentalist dissidents). In response, the United States Embassy in Islamabad, Pakistan is attacked and set on fire.

The Shah remains at The New York Hospital (due to surgical complications) until December 15th, then heads down to Panama, eventually returning to Egypt in March, 1980 where he dies in July from his lymphoma.

***

Moving up the ladder to PGY-2 (postgraduate year two) gives *me* interns to step on, but (as tempting as it may be at times) I swear not to take advantage of them. My noxious experience with my supposed friend Peter (and some of the other sadistic members of the general surgery hierarchy) makes me loathe to pull rank on the poor bastards. I refuse to join the tight knit fraternity of abuse. Next July I will be gone from this New York inferno and begin to learn my real trade as an orthopaedic resident up in Bean Town.

But before springing the coop I have much to get through including another three months' service on the Burn Unit.

It starts off with a bang. I am assigned to pick up a transfer from the Shriners' Burn Hospital in Boston because the patient's family resides in New York. He has been temporarily stabilized and it is my job to be sure he remains that way on the helicopter ride back. That's right; I am making the trip by helicopter!

The ride up to New England is spectacular; the view awesome. But on the way back, the term "crispy critter" (irreverently used by the staff for comic relief) is never more pungent. The smell of decomposing flesh and unrecognizable human form only takes a back seat to my preoccupation of maintaining fluid resuscitation and a stable heart rate. The fact that I am even in a helicopter on the return trip barely enters my mind. Perhaps the saddest part of the whole experience is my knowing that this poor soul attempted self-immolation by putting his head in a gas oven and lighting it. Of course, we medical professionals will not let him succeed and will do everything in our power to keep him alive (with monstrous physical scars that are only matched by his emotional upheaval).

Unfortunately, this crispy critter story is unique only for the helicopter ride. Sylvia, another attempted suicide that we "saved," survived with self-inflicted burns over 80% of her body nearly two years ago. I met her on my first rotation through the Burn Unit and participated in many of her skin graft operations. I watched her progress from the critical care area, where strict sterility is maintained at all times, to the step down facility that is more like an intensive care unit. Now she has made it to the third stage, which resembles a regular hospital ward. Here she is preparing for life outside in the real world beyond the protective hospital walls.

Instructions on use of her custom elastic body garments to keep the cicatrix (scar) in check and daily exercises to maintain joint range of motion are blended with psychiatric care so she has some cognitive means of coping with life's vicissitudes.

Though Sylvia barely remembers me (as a minor player in her last two years of hell) I am astonished by her apparent calm and graciousness during morning rounds. These qualities are particularly striking on the day before her discharge. So it is absolutely eerie when, the next morning, we find her dead in bed with no apparent explanation other than she willed herself to die before having to face the ruthless world again. Somehow the unearthly experience makes me think of Bill and I regret having abandoned his teachings which may have given me answers to this uncanny mystery.

Being one rung up on the ladder of medical hierarchy does, however, have some advantages. I am no longer a simple "go-for," nor am I responsible for drawing the morning bloods (and, of course, I get to go on helicopter rides). I also get to rotate through the private services where some of the "big-cheese" attendings (medical staff physicians) house their "hot-shot," celebrity patients. That does not mean that as an intern I did not participate in the care of celebrities (e.g., Mr. Capote in the E.R.). While on-call for the medicine service, Isaac Stern came in one evening with chest pain after a violin concert. A preliminary check was made by the E.R. physician and then I was given the task of admitting Mr. Stern (taking a history and physical and getting blood work).

The next morning as I presented the case at chart

rounds, I gave the run down of systems on physical exam. I included that "the prostate felt benign and the stool was guaiac negative" (no blood). The chief resident (who just so happened to study the violin) flipped out.

"You did a rectal exam on him?!" she stood screaming over me.

"Of course," I said without hesitation. "On surgery we are taught that the only time you don't do a rectal exam is if you don't have a finger or the patient doesn't have an anus" (the actual quote is "asshole," but I thought it appropriate to clean things up in the presence of the opposite gender).

"Do you realize, Dr. Schultz," she blasted, "that performing a rectal on a rule-out MI (myocardial infarction, aka. heart attack) patient can precipitate further heart damage?"

And it didn't end there. She was on my case the rest of the day; so much so that Mr. Stern heard about it. Being good spirited, and learning that his cardiac enzymes were not elevated (he did not have an MI), he graciously invited me to his room that evening to listen to him and his daughter play their violins. As awesome as that was, it didn't compare with the satisfaction I got knowing that the chief resident heard of the personal concert Isaac Stern put on just for me. I told her she could ream me out any time she liked.

Of course, the star quality up on the private service is much more prevalent. Dr. George Wantz, the hernia surgeon of luminaries is quite the socialite himself. When the fashion designer Hubert de Givenchy underwent a herniorrhaphy by Dr. Wantz it was I who tended to him post-operatively. A pleasant man who seemed to act without pomposity, Mr. Givenchy startled me one day when he suggested that I come with him to Paris. The offer was made without pretence and right in front of his handsome young companion who had been at his bedside throughout the hospital stay. As I uncomfortably passed on his offer I left the room a bit disturbed (remembering my encounter with Dr. George, my pathology professor) and questioning my virility considering that this was another come-on from a gay dude.

And then there was the Mafioso who was so impressed with my attentive bedside manner that he asked for my business card. When I told him that I was still in training and had no card, he laughed and asked for a way to contact me in case of an emergency. My suggestion that he use the emergency room prompted him to speak bluntly, explaining that he wanted to avoid the wait and the publicity that came with going to the E.R. Besides, tending to him personally could be very lucrative for me, if I knew what he meant. Growing up in Jersey (and having read Mario Puzo), I sure did and I knew that getting on his payroll was like selling my soul to the devil. So I managed to worm my way off of the guy's treatment team, all the while praying that he did not take offense to my disappearance.

My rotation out at North Shore Hospital on Long Island (a Cornell affiliate) is most memorable for the night of February 22nd when I was tending to scut work and being furious that I could not find any more IV fluid to hang. Apparently a whole case of bottles busted because of carelessness (IV fluid in plastic bags was still years away from becoming routine). But suddenly a roar penetrated throughout the ward, "The Americans are winning! We are beating the Russians!" It is the "Miracle on Ice" and suddenly no one cares about IVs or broken bottles. Patients and caregivers alike huddled around TVs watching the amazing show in black and white, but as far as we are concerned it is all red, white, and blue! My joy shortly thereafter was unfortunately tempered by the devastating news that the man who got me interested in orthopaedic surgery, Dr. John L. Marshall, had just perished in a plane crash while flying up to Lake Placid, New York to help cover the XIII Winter Olympiad.

Come July, my two years of general surgical residency are at a glorious end. Not only do I get far away from the Mob guy, I leave The New York Hospital insiders for an orthopaedic brotherhood that will accept me with open arms. At first I am fearful that I'll be surrounded by Harvard eggheads and geeks who will blow me away intellectually (and rant and rave about their beloved Red Sox and Celtics). But the reality I find is one of scholarly pursuit devoid of arrogance. My conclusion: I left a community of "wannabes" and landed in a haven of those who have nothing left to prove. I would even encounter a few Yankees and Knicks fans among them.

CHAPTER 19

Bones and Joints

The orthopaedic residency hierarchy, unlike general surgery in New York, is all about teamwork and the learning experience. There is no dumping on the juniors; in fact, we generally get first dibs on doing most surgical cases, with the seniors (and attendings) acting as our mentors. At the Mortality and Morbidity Conference (quality assurance meetings) "bad outcome" cases are openly presented and discussed so that everyone can learn from them. There is no hint of cover-up or reluctance to disclose the facts. It is a breath of fresh air in a medical world of uncontrollable egos.

The history of Massachusetts General Hospital alone goes back to the mid 19th century when, in Mass General's Ether Dome, the first demonstration of anesthesia using ether was presented to the medical world. The term "anesthesia" was first coined for the insensible state by Oliver Wendell Holmes, then a professor of medicine at Harvard Medical School.

And then there is Brigham and Women's Hospital newly built from the merger of Peter Bent Brigham Hospital, Robert Breck Brigham Hospital, and Boston Hospital for Women. In its first few years of existence it becomes world renowned for its treatment of rheumatologic diseases. Although we residents also rotate through several other highly regarded institutions, MGH and BWH serve as the illustrious cornerstones of Harvard's medical educational system. Being part of it is awesome.

***

I am fortunate to get an apartment in Charles River Park, well within crawling distance of MGH. It is expensive, but definitely worth it. The traffic on Storrow Drive can put the L.I.E (Long Island Expressway) to shame (almost) and the aggressiveness of Boston drivers is matched only by the "gladiators" of Rome.

So it is, one evening when I am coming home from a date in my two-tone Toyota Supra, that I spot an opening in traffic. Without hesitation I fill the void and the next thing I know a motorcycle cop pulls me over to ticket me for not stopping long enough at a stop sign.

"Are you serious?" the McEnroe in me bursts out.

With a fiendish smile he simply says, "Indeed, Doctor," duly noting my MD plates.

Silently wishing him ill I have no idea that the very next day, while on call in the MGH E.R., I will find myself standing over the very same "pig," now helplessly lying on a stretcher with a tib-fib (lower leg) fracture. Of course, he recognizes me immediately and simply squeals, "Uh oh." With immense satisfaction I explain to him the extremely serious nature of his injury (despite the fact that the bones are well aligned and do not involve the knee or ankle joints) and top it off with the fact that despite his treatment of me last night, I am a professional and will not compromise his care. Vindictiveness can be sweet! Instant karma, even better!

E.R. call at The General can be exhausting and it can be heart breaking. Our team of ortho techs is absolutely amazing and, no doubt, many of them could be orthopaedists themselves. As I often take a cat-nap (well trained from my New York Hospital general surgery days), it is the tech that sends the patients for x-rays and then lines up the studies for my review after allowing me as much time for sleep as feasible.

So it is one night that I walk by the rows of view boxes (assessing each x-ray) and, disturbingly, come across a thoracic spine film showing marked displacement of the spinal column. This is not good. So I hurry to find a handsome young man with his lovely young wife and child next to his stretcher. He is already dosed with morphine and joking with his family. My exam shows spinal shock (from which some recovery of motor and sensory function might be expected), but the x-rays forebode a bleak prognosis. He is turned over to the spinal service, but I elect to follow him over the next week using his dislocated thumb (which I reduced) as an excuse for the visits. As the gravity of his paralysis sets in on the family, I find myself emotionally no longer able to drop by. What I see in my chosen profession can be heartbreaking. I remember the words: "There but for the grace of God go I."

Days later I learn of the murder of John Lennon. Perhaps

I am still deeply affected by the passing of Dr. Marshall and the recent tragedy of the handsome young family man, but I am distraught and feel that the joy of my youth has somehow been squeezed out of me.

***

At the start of 1981 I am still a greenhorn ortho resident and extremely grateful for meeting up with Jay who is doing a visiting pediatric rotation at Boston Children's Hospital. Jay is in his early thirties, but looks like a teenager. He is from Lincoln, Nebraska where his father is a well-established orthopaedic surgeon. Along with the knowledge his father has imparted, Jay already has two full years of orthopaedic training at Lenox Hill Hospital in New York under his belt. He has helped take care of the Jets football team and been to the NFL combine. He dreams of becoming team physician for the Kansas City Chiefs one day. After his six-month rotation in Boston he will return to his primary ortho program in New York City.

We become instant friends and he is kind enough to take me under his wing, easing some of my growing pains. It is out of shear gratitude and respect for him that I try my damndest not to laugh when I see him drinking a small, cold bottle of Magnesium Citrate (a strong laxative) late one night when we are both on call in the hospital. But as he describes how thirsty he has been all day and explains that he lucked out by finding a few of these lemon sodas in a refrigerator, I just can't hold back any longer.

"That's Mag Citrate, brother," I obnoxiously spit out as I crack-up right in his face.

"Awe shit! This is my third one!" he says expelling what's

left in his mouth with the most helpless look on his face. Needless to say, my pal Jay spends the rest of the night in the head paying penance for his cathartic mistake.

Jay is madly in love with his wife, Marilyn whom he says "keeps me out of trouble and heading in the right direction." They have two little kids whose pictures he cannot stop showing. Among the normal vices that are part of all men's DNA, Jay is a cigarette smoker despite having been a gymnast and swimmer back in Nebraska. My single status makes me a bit of a devil for Jay who certainly enjoys a beer and a smoke on the town. But somehow he always remembers his commitment to Marilyn when the action gets hot.

I, on the other hand, am a free spirit and absolutely delighted to find a connection with my old hippy days through Steve, an impresario from Worcester. The cat puts on outrageous rock n' roll concerts with the likes of Bonnie Raitt and Richie Havens, with whom he is personal friends. The scene is absolutely wild! Jay heads back to New York just in time.

Of course, I miss Jay, but keep in close touch with him. I tell him about the thrill of covering the Boston Marathon in April and that just before the start of the race (with an abundance of medical volunteers) some of us were given the opportunity to run in it. Never having run more than twelve miles at a clip before, but having done that distance often for years, I raised my hand actually expecting the offer to be a joke. Surprisingly I and two others were escorted into the crowd near the starting area and given numbers.

Figuring I would simply get my day's run in, drink a lot and just take it easy, I am amazed that at the twenty mile mark "it ain't so bad;" I'm in a rhythm and cruising. Then, suddenly, up comes Heartbreak Hill and the "doubts" creep in. No sooner do I conquer the Hill than I feel the burning pain in the front of my knees as I decelerate down the slope. At the end, I sneak in at just under four hours (certainly better than that cheat Rosie Ruiz last year). Unfortunately, it takes me a week to recover and another week before I have any inclination to resume my daily run.

After my pediatric rotation at Children's Hospital I am back at The General and find myself on the hand service when a devastating upper extremity injury comes in. The victim of a lawn mower accident has lost four digits on his dominant hand; along with a "spaghetti wrist" (laceration with exposed tendons). The amputated parts fortunately had been packed in ice at the scene and appear viable. The plan is re-implantation of the digits and repair of the wrist structures.

The restoration of the small vessels and nerves in the fingers (as well as the slightly larger structures of the wrist) requires magnification. The operative microscope has viewing portals for both the surgeon and assistant who sit opposite one another during the case. As the assistant I am asked to retract tissue, irrigate the wound, and clear blood from the viewing field with a small suction device. Every motion made looks gigantic through the scope, so it takes intense concentration to keep my hands from shaking.

Each digit takes several hours to reconnect. So in a case like this we have teams that work in six to eight hour shifts. After looking intently through the focused field of a high powered microscope for hours at a time my mind simply wants to shut down. So when the new team scrubs in to relieve us I am positively thrilled to relinquish my seat.

Having started the surgery at about 4:00 PM., it is just after 11:00 PM. when I reach my apartment door. I am dog-tired. The phone is ringing inside so I hustle to insert my key and manage to pick up the receiver before it stops. It is Dad on the other end and he sounds excited. "I have been trying to reach you all day," he says in an octave higher than his normally subdued voice. "Dr. Wilson has set up a laboratory at the Barnert Hospital here in Paterson, dedicated to developing microsurgical operating techniques. They practice on rats. He says microsurgery is the wave of the future. Have you ever thought about getting some experience in that field?" Dad is the sweetest man ever and in my heart I know he means well, but his timing could not be worse. "Microsurgery sucks, Dad! And I have to go back there in six hours. Tell Dr. Wilson he can take my place and work on a real live human being if he can get up here in time. I'll even pay for his plane ticket!"

Actually, at the beginning of the case, microsurgery seemed pretty cool, but now it sort of reminds me of the time I ate so much curried rice at a smorgasbord that, for years afterward, I couldn't stand even looking at rice.

Fortunately, my next rotation is sports medicine with the venerable Dr. Carter Roe who is an icon in the field. He has been the team physician for the Boston Bruins hockey team forever. Although I am not a fan of the sport, I am enamored with the dream that one day I will be the orthopaedist for a pro team. So I work my way into covering some of the games (usually attended by a junior attending or fellow). Between periods one night a player with a twisted ankle asks me for a shot so he can get back out on the ice. When I tell him that I don't think an injection is a good idea he calls over the trainer who tells me to shoot him up; this is the pros and it is done all the time. Not feeling comfortable numbing up the guy's ankle so he can possibly do more damage by continuing to play, I call the sports medicine fellow who impatiently tells me that these guys are not treated like normal patients. "So give him a squirt and don't worry about it." Like a punk I do just as I am told, but that very night I decide that treating professional athletes is not for me.

More disturbing is a study handed to me by one of my friends on the medical service. Back in June the CDC reported on five active homosexual males in Los Angeles that had a rare form of pneumonia (pneumocystis carinii) seen only in patients with severely compromised immune systems. Initially the term GRID (Gay-related Immune deficiency) was used to describe the new disease, but that has been changed to *acquired immunodeficiency syndrome* (AIDS) since it is not confined to the gay community. She advises that I pass the information on to my surgical buddies since the contagion may well be blood borne and perhaps we should take special precautions in the O.R.

CHAPTER 20

Holding Tight on the Rollercoaster

Halfway through my residency I learn that Mass General Hospital is getting a new general director. Initially, it is of little interest to me until the name J. Robert Buchanan, M.D. appears in the hospital bulletin and I hear it through the gossip stream. After leaving Cornell, my old Dean became director of the prestigious Michael Reese Hospital in Chicago and now, somehow, fate has brought him to the same Mecca of medicine to which I have also been blessed.

Daily, for weeks, I peek into the administrative office to ask if Dr. Buchanan has yet arrived; until one day, at the height of pedestrian traffic in the great hallway of The General, I see his towering figure (all six foot, six of him) above the crowd coming right at me. The slow motion scene from the movie *10*, when Dudley Moore and Bo Derek run toward each other on the beach, idiotically replays in my mind as I anxiously approach the new director and he surprisingly races towards me. Startled that he even recognizes me, his embrace and words are typical of the great man that he is. "Dr. Schultz, I always knew you would make it here. I am simply grateful that I too have arrived." His fervent faith in me is awe-inspiring and no one is more touched by this than my father who wells up with emotion when I tell him of the reunion.

Arthroscopy and NMR (Nuclear Magnetic Resonance; later to be called Magnetic Resonance Imaging or MRI in order to eliminate the fearful word "nuclear") are in their infancy. The latter is still in the experimental stages and not yet used commercially. But working on the knee joint through tiny incisions with the aid of the arthroscope (and specially designed instruments) is here and is a huge advancement. No longer do patients have to suffer the morbidity that comes with an "open" operation. So it is imperative that I learn the technique, no matter how steep the learning curve may be.

The camera (attached to the slender, pencil-like arthroscope that is inserted into the knee) is bulky, weighing about a pound and nearly ten inches in length. It has to be cradled on the forearm while the scope is held in the "prayer position" to keep it from falling on the floor. This is actually an advance from just a year earlier when the surgeon had to put his eye to the scope in order to see through it into the joint. Viewing on the TV monitor markedly increases the field of vision and allows the assistant (and OR personnel) to see inside as well. Along with this TV advance, of course, comes the added difficulty of looking up at the television monitor while working with your hands down at the operating table below.

Needless to say, the skill needed to become an expert arthroscopist takes time to develop. I try to tell myself this as I leave the hospital late one evening after struggling earlier in the day with a simple arthroscopic partial menisectomy (removal of torn cartilage). Being on the clinic service and not having an expert attending surgeon with me during the case, I simply could not get back in the corner of the knee adequately to remove all the torn cartilage. After logging in (participating in) nearly five hundred cases I am deeply distraught at my ineptitude. Wiping away the tears with the sleeve of my white coat, I question whether I will ever be able to master this "bread-and-butter" surgical procedure that is becoming routine for all orthopaedists. Unable to sleep, I punish myself thinking that I will have to find another way to make a living rather than hurt people with my lack of arthroscopic skill. Fortunately, this very same year, the advent of the tiny immersible camera that actually fits in the palm of one's hand makes arthroscopy much easier. With renewed effort, I begin to see the light at the end of the tunnel. *I can master this!*

But my training continues to be a rollercoaster ride. Just as I start to feel confident in my abilities it is time for me to rotate through Dr. Mankin's oncology service. Dr. Mankin is chief of orthopaedics at MGH and often flies around the country attending meetings and performing as a guest speaker. So it is that he is leaving for Chicago and has left his oncology fellow and me to do a simple AKA (above the knee amputation) on a lovely eighteen-year-old girl with a telangectatic osteosarcoma (cancer) in her femur just above the knee.

He leaves specific instructions that the amputation must be done at a high level in her thigh because of the aggressive nature of the bone cancer. Yes. Sir! But during the operation we elect to leave her with a few more inches of thigh so she can better be fitted with a prosthetic leg. After all, she is young, engaged to be married and the tumor is way down by her knee.

Upon his return, Dr. Mankin looks at the post-operative x-rays and immediately blows his top. "Idiots!" he shouts, showing us no mercy, "I tell you to give her a high AKA and you don't listen! Suzanne has a telangectatic osteosarcoma! That kind of tumor is notorious for skip lesions that can be remote from the main tumor at the knee. Pray that you two didn't kill her with your imbecilic decision to leave too much femur!" Mike and I are devastated (and do not truly exhale until her one-year follow-up scan shows no recurrence of the cancer. Miraculously, we are both graciously invited to her wedding in late 1983.)

Feeling inadequate and stupid is demoralizing at best, but there are times when the tables turn and the impeccable attending surgeons are trumped. It is such a day when Dr. Leffert, world renowned for his expertise in neuromotor function of the upper extremity (arm and hand), is doing a consultation for none other than Mr. Isaac Stern. It seems that the virtuoso violinist has pain and stiffness in his fingers that is interfering with his ability to play. While Dr. Leffert examines the maestro's arthritic digits I enter the office to give report, expecting to find my mentor alone.

"Dr. Schultz," Dr. Leffert bites, "I am extremely busy. Your report can wait."

As I attempt to slither out of the room Mr. Stern quickly

interrupts. "Dr. Schultz," he says enthusiastically as he rises to shake my hand and pat me on the shoulder. "How have you been, my friend?"

"Well, Sir," I respond, noticing the sudden depth of Dr. Leffert's jaw.

"I see you gentlemen know one another," Dr. Leffert manages to get out.

"Intimately," Mr. Stern quips, no doubt referring to the rectal exam I stupidly performed on him a couple of years earlier at The New York Hospital. Enjoying the private joke and fully pumped from my instant notoriety I float out of the office and back to my menial tasks.

***

Fully immersed in the daily grind of learning to master the demanding skills of orthopaedic surgery I am suddenly and profoundly shaken to hear that my spiritual mentor Bill Daut has passed over. It is August, 1982 and although I know that he was never in the best of health throughout the eight years that I knew him (in his earthly form) it seems to me that his death, at age sixty-five, is sadly premature. Perhaps because of the shocking news or some more ethereal reason, I dream that Bill is soothing me in his usual warm way by telling me that now I have another spirit friend on the other side. He comforts me by asking me to call whenever I think of him or am in need. It actually makes me feel guilty and self-absorbed knowing that I made very little effort to visit with him once I began my residency. He was always the one to make excuses for me, saying that I needed to focus all my attention on my studies so I would become a great doctor and minister properly to my patients.

Being up in Boston and getting notification of his passing several weeks late did little to soothe my conscience for not having attended his funeral. I simply lost touch with him, as well as with my spiritual quest.

***

The last six months of my residency come quicker than expected especially as senior thesis day rapidly approaches. Before graduating from the program each of us is responsible for presenting a thesis paper on an original research project. For two years I have been working on proving the existence of microscopically small mechanoreceptors in the human anterior cruciate ligament (ACL). Prior research has found that such structures exist in cats and other animals. If they are, indeed, present in ligaments (structures that hold joints together) then one might suppose that a sprain (disruption of a ligament) might not only cause pain and render the joint unstable, but also interfere with messages sent to the brain that help stabilize the joint through recruitment of nearby muscles (mechanisms called proprioception and stereognosis).

After harvesting numerous ACLs from knee replacement surgeries and postmortems I am able to prepare the specimens for microscopic study and painstakingly go through hundreds of slides looking for the tiny nerve endings. The reward is finding the type of receptors that are described in animals; having the morphologic potential to act as feedback messengers to the brain. It takes me more than six months before I finally hit pay dirt (and find a true Golgi body-like structure). The fact is that I was initially looking in the wrong places: aged knees that require joint replacement have so much degeneration that even the mechanoreceptors (in addition to healthy cartilage) wither and disappear. Once I realized this and began to harvest otherwise healthy tissue (ACLs) from young autopsy specimens, I began finding what I was looking for.

Taking the study one step further, I decide to act as my own guinea pig. Since my left knee still has a torn cartilage and I need to have it fixed anyway, I elect to have it done essentially without anesthesia (only the skin portals for the instrument insertion will be numbed with lidocaine). Once the meniscus tear is removed, the experiment will begin. An electric probe will be used to stimulate my ACL and I will then see if I perceive a change in position of my knee or if the muscles around my knee fire (proving the existence of a neural reflex arc). Anesthetic in the joint itself, of course, might interfere with such action so I must do without it.

The day of the surgery is exciting and nerve-racking (no pun intended). As I lay on the operating table getting prepped and draped I remind myself that I have traveled the world, been in jail several times, thought I was about to die more than once, and have always survived. *This too is just another experience*; something to weather and come out on the other end more tested and worldly. But Christ, I also have seen infections and irreparable joint damage! And God only knows what that damn electric probe will do to my knee and its cartilage surfaces! *Too late to punk out now.*

I bite down on a sponge (gauze pad) and feel the pressure as Dr. Zarins inserts the arthroscope and fills my knee with fluid. As I watch the TV monitor and the trimming of my meniscus I start to relax feeling very little discomfort and enjoying the show. Twenty minutes later it is time for the experiment. I see the electric probe making its way to my ACL and then rest on the lower most portion of it.

"Ready, Bob?" Dr. Z rhetorically announces. "Here we go," he says as he steps on the stimulator pedal.

The burning pain is immediate and immense as it tears through my knee! The electric charge, no doubt being enhanced by its transmission through the liquid medium, is no more shocking than the frickin' smiling onlookers calmly asking me what I am feeling. "STOP! For God's sake, STOP!"

Once the torture subsides and we discuss the situation, I "bravely" allow one more attempt at ACL stimulation, this time dry without any fluid in my knee. Although the pain is less severe, it is of sufficient magnitude for me to abort any further attempts. The experiment is over, leaving me to wait and see if I suffer any long-term ill affects of having my knee fried. A bit bummed and knowing that I will receive no extra credit for my bravery/stupidity I cling to the knowledge that I have racked up yet another far-out experience.

Thesis day is exciting and taxing, but all in all signals the end of a long research and clinical apprenticeship. The papers are of high quality and presented well. What else would one expect at such a prestigious institution? In the audience sit all the high ranking professors, honored guests, emeritus legends (including Dr. Otto Aufrank), and even the editors of the JBJS (*Journal of Bone and Joint Surgery*), orthopaedics' most prestigious publication. It is therefore incomprehensible to me that as we file out of the auditorium after the presentations, Dr. Curtiss (editor-in-chief of JBJS) grabs my arm and suggests that I submit my research thesis to him for consideration of publication in The Journal. Walking on air, I have no vision of the fact that I will need to work diligently for the next year, while in private practice, to tighten up the article so it is fit for publication.

***

The most important time of my last days in residency is dedicated to the pursuit of a job back in Jersey. Though offered an opportunity to stay at Harvard doing further research on mechanoreceptors in various other tissues of the musculoskeletal system, I opt to go out into the community to make a living rather than stair through a microscope in a laboratory.

The job interviews are varied and, for the most part pointless, since I have already made up my mind to join Paul (the debonair sixty year old orthopaedist who treated my Osgood-Schlatters knee condition when I was fourteen years old). He offers me $50,000 per year salary, exactly half of what the others put on the table for my services, and says we don't need a contract; among men a handshake will suffice. He promises that one day I will be driving a late model Cadillac just like him.

When I find out that he has contracted his practice to the point where he is operating only one or two days per week and closes the office by 5:00 on weekdays (and at 3:00 on Fridays) I negotiate a bonus based on productivity. He agrees to instruct the staff to stay open later if I can bring in more patients and I will be paid the income (after overhead is deducted) above and beyond his previous collections. Again, the deal is confirmed by a handshake.

Leaving Boston is professionally difficult because I know I will never again be surrounded by such a wealth of intellect and skill. Going out on my own is liberating (and what I always fancy myself to be about), but somehow leaving the Harvard nest is traumatic for me. I soon replace the MGH blanket with an air of arrogance that I struggle to contain when, rarely, I recognize it. This is not good. It can only make for bad relationships with my colleagues and patients and will, no doubt, eventually get me into trouble.

CHAPTER 21

Jersey Boy

Back in Jersey with my people. The "return of the prodigal son." I am ready to tear up the world. But first I am in need of living quarters. Mom had been gracious enough to hunt down an apartment for me in Ridgewood, but the tenant decides not to vacate at the last minute and I, a 36-year-old orthopaedic surgeon, am forced to spend the night in my parents' house.

Going to sleep in my boyhood bed, remembering sleeping on the floor next to it upon returning from India; seeing the college and Yankees pennants still on the walls where I carefully placed them decades ago; recalling how still I used to lay in bed during the dog days of August to keep from sweating before central air conditioning became commercially available (Mom was not in favor of fans because she believed they made you sick), and sweetly reliving the stories about the Prince on the White Horse that Mom used to softly whisper to help me get over those frightful night-terrors, makes me embrace the significance of one more night at home. But, of course, living with my folks at this stage is unacceptable.

The next day a realtor at Quail Heights apartments in Hackensack tells me how lucky I am to get the only one bedroom available in the whole blasted city. A girl just vacated the apartment so she could save money by sharing a two-bedroom unit upstairs with a girlfriend. Not spectacular, but I'll take it, especially since the building has a reputation for housing hot single girls. "And don't miss the July 4th party tonight out by the pool," she says with a wink. "I met my future husband down there a few years ago." Even though, in the last several months, I am starting to have thoughts about not being so young anymore and fearing that I could miss out on becoming a father, my main object is to get laid, not married.

Without question I decide to check out the "talent" at the poolside celebration. Within minutes a blond and brunette come over to me. Debbie, the brunette does most of the talking. She asks if I am the "hot guy" that she heard about who moved into her apartment today. *How the hell does she even know of the transaction that I completed just hours ago?* There is something about her voice and the entire freaky circumstance that makes me nervous. I can't put my finger on it, but since the girls are both cute I go with it. I have a really good time (despite only a goodnight kiss).

Quail Heights (commonly known as "Quaalude" Heights) is a bachelor's delight. But despite the talent and play, my relationship with the brunette gets serious. The evening I enter the apartment house elevator to find myself alone with Debbie and her dentist boyfriend Steve, is monumental. Despite his handsome 6'4" frame and relative youth, Debbie later tells me that it was that elevator ride that made her break off their relationship and focus her attention on me. Far be it for me to question the logic of a woman.

Despite the QH distractions I am working my ass off to build up Paul's practice so I can make some real money. I take Emergency Room call every chance I get because it is a major source of new patients. Those referred to the practice by other docs or patients see me by default only when Paul is too busy. Even those that I do see invariably ask for Paul to do their surgery (even if it involves a procedure in which I am the expert, like arthroscopy which is still relatively new). I am clearly second fiddle until three months into our partnership when, unexpectedly, Paul has to scrub out of a total hip replacement surgery because of difficulty breathing. After finishing the case alone I find him in the surgeon's lounge sweating and looking sallow. The subsequent shadow on his chest x-ray and the fact that he is a big time cigarette smoker leads to a thoracotomy. Instead of finding cancer they say it is a form of tuberculosis. In any event, Paul is out for the year and I am left solo to run the practice.

Despite the tragic opportunity I still have to find my patients in the E.R. Not knowing how long Paul will be incapacitated, the referring physicians advise their patients to wait until Paul returns before having elective surgery. So, in order to secure more surgical cases, I get on staff at two other hospitals and put my nose to the grindstone.

Paul, understandably, loses heart for participating in the goings-on of the practice. Even though elated that cancer is not his diagnosis, he does not take well to being an invalid. I visit him regularly at his home. We drink cocktails, watch Yankees games together, and I try to stimulate him by discussing cases and going over x-rays. I even tell him about the hot babe that sat naked on the exam table with the dressing gown down around her waist when I walked in. He admonishes me not to fall for that crap like he did years ago with a scrub nurse who got him divorced for dipping in. "If she's that spectacular," he laughs (for the first time in months) "end the doctor-patient relationship before partaking." It would be one full year before Paul returned to the practice.

***

1984 is here already! Eric Arthur Blair, using the pen name George Orwell, in 1949 predicted an all-knowing government (Oceania) who, through the Ministry of Truth and strong arm of the Thought Police would keep constant surveillance of the populace. We all read the novel and feared a totalitarian state in which "Big Brother" would watch our every move and rule our lives. But here it is 1984 and it just isn't that way in America (maybe in the Soviet Union, China, and Cuba, but not here in the United States). No way.

For me it is time to get my name out there and make some money. Paul is grateful that I have not only kept up the practice, but have actually increased its gross revenues in his absence. For this he offers me a $20,000 bonus to be paid at year's end. I remind him of our agreement; that I would receive the profits above and beyond his previous year's take since they would represent my personal hard work. "Of course," he says "let's see how that shakes out once I'm back in the swing of things."

Having no reason for distrust I step up a gear and actively

pursue as much emergency room call as my colleagues are willing to give up. Many of them are older and already established in the community. Taking E.R. call, to them, is a real pain in the ass; it is arduous and time consuming. Being on-call means that you must remain within twenty minutes of the hospital for the full twenty-four hour shift and respond promptly to a page for orthopaedic care. So once I put the word out that I am looking for more on-call, the others on staff come running. Taking as many as eleven or twelve days/nights per month from them becomes routine for me and I readily pick up patients through the E.R. who like my care and wish to continue seeing me in the future (as do many of their family members and friends). Aside from working-out, finalizing my research paper for publication, and seeing Debbie, I am all about orthopaedics.

The good news is that Debbie is also a gym rat, so I get to kill two birds with one stone (I figure I'm safe saying this because she is generally so busy with stuff that she will never actually get around to reading my book). Our crowd at the gym (Elmwood Park Athletic Center) is diverse: from Sonny and Michelle (the Italian stallion and his hot blond Jewish princess) to Mark and Pam (the Jewish karate instructor and his petite, stacked babe whom he never gets to see sans full makeup) to Dr. John (the outrageously muscled, suave chiropractor who never practiced his trade a day in his life).

EPAC is also a big source of patients for me. Injuries abound among the aging fanatic handball players and the "never-big-enough" body builders like Billy S. whose intense training protocol and juicing regimen eventually gets him all the way to winning the Mr. Universe title (amateur body building's ultimate championship) in '91.

The whole gym scene is all about hard bodies and looking good. The sexual ambiance is always strong and propels Debbie and me to reunite in a frenzy after one of our classic break-ups. Avoiding one another at the apartment house and not having spoken for two weeks, we make eye contact at the gym and immediately head for our cars; then drive like maniacs back to my apartment to reconcile our differences.

The rest of my time is consumed with what seems like the one-millionth draft of my research paper that never seems good enough for publication in the *Journal of Bone and Joint Surgery* (my profession's bible of research publications). But then on September 1, 1984 in the JBJS Vol. 66, Issue 7 there it is: *Mechanoreceptors in human cruciate ligaments. A histologic study.* By Robert A. Schultz, M.D. et al. A triumph and relief that, quite honestly, is only matched by the moment, six months later, when the braces I have had on my teeth (to correct the malocclusion that resulted from my automobile accident in '67) for a solid year are finally removed. Of course, getting out of prison was more liberating than either of these experiences, but who's counting?

By the end of the year I have acquired a good enough credit rating that I can purchase a condo in Washington Township. The end unit on Winchester Court in Washington Commons seems like a good investment and is certainly better than pissing away the monthly rent at Quail Heights. Debbie visits frequently and at times moves in, but we both agree that she should keep her apartment in QH.

Foots Walker, Michael O'Koren, and Harry Carson are just three of the professional athletes living in the Commons.

It is exciting to play pick-up basketball with these guys until I rupture an extensor tendon in my right index finger during a game. It is so embarrassing that I pretend it is just jammed and tough it out. But I subsequently have to splint the mallet finger for several months, making it really hard to do things, especially operate. After that I just keep making excuses about not having time to play, figuring the pros can just beat up on themselves since they are, no doubt, used to it.

Because of my friendship with Jay who trained at Lenox Hill Hospital in New York (the guy who drank the Mag Citrate laxative at Boston Children's Hospital four years earlier) I am referred football players by the NFL Players' Association for second opinions about their injuries. Not permitted to treat them, I am simply asked to give my opinion about their diagnosis and when they can safely return to play. Having no pressure on me to send them back on the field "as quickly as possible," I am conservative in my recommendations (as I would be with any patient). Of course, come Sunday I see just about every one of them right back in the game, rendering my consultations meaningless.

Sensing my frustration, Lenox Hill takes me off the NFLPA second opinion list, but continues to refer athletes to me who live out in New Jersey. Most memorable is Sparky Lyle who, although retired from Major League Baseball, is still a Yankee hero of mine. His supposed Achilles' tendon rupture (suffered on a racquet ball court in Closter) turns out to be a simple calf strain. While no further treatment from me is necessary, several of my male patients are extremely impressed to see Sparky in the waiting room. I momentarily revisit the thought of getting involved with pro sports.

***

Being on call for emergencies on Christmas day (common for me each year, being of the Jewish faith) is usually uneventful since most people are hunkered down at home with family. But early in the morning I get a call from the E.R. doc who tells me that he believes he can reduce the dislocated thumb of a young boy and is asking for my permission, as the orthopaedist on call, to proceed. He explains that he will apply longitudinal traction by pulling on the digit to "pop it back into joint" as he has done many times with others. The x-rays show no fracture. While enjoying the comfort of my living room I agree to let him give it a try while I hold on the phone.

Next thing I hear are the agonizing cries of the boy. "Stop! Stop!" I shout repeatedly. "I'm coming in! I'm coming in! Damn it!" Finally, he comes back on the line telling me that he can't seem to get it back in place. Disturbed by my decision to let the guy do my job I frantically jump in the car and race to the hospital.

It is Christmas morning, mind you, so there are no cars on the road except mine and the little old lady driving incredibly slowly in front of me. Wasting no time I pass her and immediately hear the siren of a cop car pulling me over. Here we go again: the John McEnroe rage is building. "You can't be serious! It's Christmas morning!"

"You just crossed a double yellow line, Doc," he says obviously noticing my M.D. plates.

"But I wasn't speeding and I am on my way to an emergency," I say incredulously. "Come with me, you'll see."

"That's okay, Doc. I won't detain you," he says matter-of-factly. "The ticket will be mailed to your home address. Just don't pass over the double yellow line again or *you* might be the next emergency."

Still upset when I enter the E.R., I am suddenly disarmed by a cute little black boy lying in the lap of his mother who sees me and starts praising Jesus for sending the thumb doctor to take care of her child. My first impression is that these are poor people and this will be a freebee (I am not getting paid). But it is Christmas and despite the damn traffic ticket I have a job to do.

After looking at the x-rays and anesthetizing the boy's thumb, I gently reduce the joint without further anguish for the child. As we wait for the post-reduction x-rays to be taken the mother says softly, "Yes, we are blessed. Jesus sent you to us today; and yesterday he blessed us with a winning lottery ticket. Praise the Lord." *Uh, say what?* She hands me the newspaper article showing her and her husband holding the poster sized check for $2 million. *Glory be!*

As I drive back home in my car, after splinting the boy's thumb, I can't help but think how incredible a Christmas story this has turned out to be; and I will actually get paid for my services. Unfortunately, the Christmas spirit is nowhere to be found when I go to court to dispute the traffic ticket. I am simply shown the New Jersey State ordinance (highlighted in yellow) clearly stating that a physician on the way to an emergency may not be detained, but is still responsible for obeying traffic laws. I must pay the fine in full, though the judge is gracious enough to give me only two points against my license instead of three for a moving violation. Even Christmas has its limits.

By this time, Paul is back to work having been out recuperating from his pulmonary disease for a full year. He looks good and seems ready to work hard and get in step with the pace I have set for the practice. Super!

It is just my second year in private practice and boom; I get indoctrinated into the malpractice arena first hand.

After admitting one of Paul's patients late one evening through the E.R. for septic arthritis (joint infection) of his knee, I proceed to wash it our arthroscopically in the operating room. I have to do this several times during the patient's hospital stay in order to be certain the infection is completely eradicated. Upon discharge the grateful patient has no further fever; his blood work has returned to normal and he feels well.

About two months later I receive an attorney letter stating that I am named, along with my associate, in a negligence case involving this patient. As it turns out, the guy claims that Paul had caused his knee infection and, despite my proper and vigorous resolution of the problem, I am also named in the suit because I am Paul's associate and have my name all over the hospital records.

According to the office notes Paul had drained the knee several days before the patient saw me in the E.R. complaining of pain and swelling. Paul had written that the fluid from the knee was cloudy (commonly an indication that infection may be present), but he elected to inject the joint with cortisone anyway. Since corticosteroids decrease inflammation by making the white blood cells (that fight infection) go away, administering cortisone in this setting is contraindicated (i.e., a big fat No-No).

But I am not Paul! And I did the right thing, so how can I be sued?! After months of ranting and raving about the injustice of it all, my name is finally dropped from the suit (which is eventually settled by Paul and the insurance carrier). An attorney friend of mine explains to me that every doctor even remotely involved with a malpractice case is named initially until discovery exonerates those who shall be dropped. This way the lawyers make sure that everyone is included so they can "recover" as much money as possible. "No hard feelings," he says. "It's all part of doing business." *You can't be serious!* Welcome, Doctor, to modern day medicine and its challenges.

CHAPTER 22

The Hotshot Newspaper Doc

As luck would have it one of my patients is an editor for The News (formerly The Paterson Evening News). The newspaper has a large circulation in North Jersey and he suggests I write an article about sprains and strains for the Sunday health section. Naturally, I jump at the chance to get my name out there. Fortunately, the response is favorable enough for him to offer me more press time. Eventually, I have a column called *The Doctor's Office* in which I answer questions sent in by readers regarding musculoskeletal diseases and injuries. My picture appears next to the byline. Before long the North Jersey News and the Bergen Record (now The Record) are including *The Doctor's Office* in many of their issues. Patients in the E.R. and locals on the street recognize me as "The Newspaper Doc." It is little wonder that this free publicity raises the ire of many of my colleagues.

As in past decades, advertising by physicians is frowned upon by our profession. *But my column is an "educational tool"* I tell myself. My dad doesn't seem to mind (in fact, he is proud of my notoriety) and he is from the old school.

Although Paul is somewhat concerned over my cutting edge endeavor, he is enjoying the flood of patients that the practice is experiencing and therefore keeps his mouth shut. As our revenue grows I naturally expect appropriate remuneration for my efforts, but again I am told to be patient; that in another year I will be an equal partner and my salary will reflect that. Perhaps as pacification, he and his second wife, Poo Poo, make an effort to set me up with young ladies, much to Debbie's indignation.

At this point I am starting to feel hostility from several fronts at once: Debbie (resenting my lack of commitment to our relationship), my fellow orthopods (annoyed with my growing success), and my own simmering resentment of Paul (for repeatedly reneging on our financial agreement). But I continue to plod along, working my ass off, going to the gym, and dating "freely."

As my operating room case load increases, so does my arrogance. I develop the philosophy that "the only thing that should determine the outcome of surgery is the patient's pathology and my level of skill to correct it." This makes me short on tolerance for substandard care by the operating room staff, whether it involves a broken instrument, lack of the proper equipment, or what I consider a nurse or technician's ineptitude. Before long I am acting out in the O.R.; raising my voice or standing like a child in the corner to keep from blowing my top, when I perceive incompetence.

The day I throw Laurie, a demure assistant-head nurse,

out of my room for trying to help calm me down, the reality of my actions finally hits home. After the case she tells me through her tears that she will no longer stand up for me when none of the staff wants to be assigned to my room. She says she knows that I am a good surgeon, but my childish actions have ruined my reputation. Still a bit soft for me, she takes me into one of the empty operating rooms and shows me a substantial hole in the wall. I had seen that hole before and always wondered why it was never fixed. "That came from a mallet that Dr. Paul threw in a fit of rage more than ten years ago," she says. "He won't let anyone fix it because it reminds him of how callow he acted that day."

Okay. Alright. I get it. I've been acting like an asshole! From here on in, I make it a point to pause and say a mantra before entering the operating room: *I know that things beyond my control will go wrong today, but I will weather the storm and act like a man instead of an asshole.*

DOCTOR SCHULTZ...they are waiting for you in O.R. 8!

Huh?... Right...Of course. I am shaken back to reality.

As I gown, the patient jokingly asks if I purposely got lost and would rather be playing golf.

"Ha. You've kept your sense of humor," I counter. "And you said you'd be scared out of your wits to be awake inside the operating room."

"Shitless," she replies. "I said I'd be scared shitless...but it would be worse if you decided not to come back to fix my knee."

The case goes well. All the instruments work, including the laser. The medial meniscus has a parrot beak tear that is amenable to partial excision. There is no other pathology. The patient will be happy.

After dictating the op report and completing the orders I am delighted to see that the operating room is turned over quickly and the next patient is already on the table. This is when the operating room routine becomes robotically repetitive; aside from the idiosyncrasies of the patient, the pathology, and the music being played.

Back at the scrub sink I watch through the O.R. window as the circulator carefully tucks the scrub tech's rather long hair up under his cap to prevent contamination…

CHAPTER 23

Breaking the Glass

When a gaunt, less than tidy young man with serpentine shoulder length hair is led into my consultation room and introduced as Johnny Landau I am starkly shaken out of my narrowly focused, deep doctor reflections. *Oh my God, it's Johnny!* This is the very same boy about whom I gave council to two very troubled parents, years ago. Never did I expect, back then, that this man, now in his mid thirties, would remain a translator and ardent disciple of the Dali Lama. Not so bold as to show up in the orange robes of a holy aesthetic monk, he nevertheless is dressed much like the "road people" from my travels in the early '70s.

Now more than ten years removed from those "drop-out" days of exploration and adventure, I am drawn back to thoughts of peace, free love, rebellion, revolution, and the belief that Nirvana is attainable. Talking with Johnny (whose front is to see me for his sprained ankle, but secretly is honoring the wishes of his parents who are hoping that my own "prodigal son" story will somehow rub off on their brainwashed boy) makes me introspective and somehow a bit ashamed that I did not stand my ground like Johnny. But as we talk (and I ask my staff to give me extra time with this special patient) I sense that he is lost between two very different worlds and, despite his calm demeanor, will certainly not be influenced to change his commitments by spending thirty minutes with me.

Once Johnny leaves and I complete my patient load for the day, I am left to contemplate what might have been had I not met Bill Daut whose mesmerizing mystique and psychic energy held me from using that return trip ticket to Bombay. Stepping back for a moment, I find the hassles with my girlfriend, partner, and colleagues to be not so much after all.

For some time now Mom has been speaking to me about settling down, getting married, and changing my diet so I gain weight. She dislikes that I am still eating primarily vegetables (including coleslaw mixed with Brewer's Yeast) and "junk" from the health food store. She likes Debbie who is Jewish and sane.

"If anyone can get Bobby to eat right and stop his nonsense it is you," she tells her right in front of me. "He likes you. He will listen to you."

A Jewish mother is both a gift and a curse. The love, the caring, the worry about your health and well-being is precious, but the smothering can be oppressive. Swayed by forces far greater than I, I agree to let Debbie move her clothes into "our" condo in Washington Commons. Nevertheless, she continues to share the lease at Quail Heights with her "roommate" Becky.

By 1986 my patient load is finally substantial thanks to my dedication to taking Emergency Room call, my notoriety as "The Newspaper Doc," and my general level of competence that translates into patient word-of-mouth referrals. The mounting pressure from my peers for using the dirty tactic of "advertising" causes me to give up *The Doctor's Office* column, but my rapid rise to competitive status has made my colleague's wrath unforgiving. The first thing they do is create a rule that no single orthopaedist can take more than four E.R. calls per month in order to prevent monopolization of the E.R. personnel. In other words, because I am in the emergency room so often (and providing good service) the staff often refers patients to me for follow-up even if my name is not up on the "On-Call Board." Despite the new rule, however, there is enough complacency among the older members of the orthopaedic department (who abhor taking call) that I am still offered coverage slots several times a week.

It becomes routine for me to leave the office about 6:00 PM (on my on-call days), head over to Renaldo's Pizza Parlor, where I have a couple of slices and BS with Bill the owner, before heading to the hospital to hang out in the E.R. Bill is a sweetheart of a guy who more often than not wins the argument when it comes to me paying for my order.

"I love talking with you, Doc," he says between hiccup-type eruptions due to his low grade Tourette's syndrome, "you break up my day and let me brag about my son. I can't let you pay." Bill's son, Billy, is a natural child actor without any formal training who has a ton of credits including a recent run on the sitcom *Punky Brewster*.

Once in the E.R., I am usually busy until about 11:00 PM

(reducing broken bones and admitting hip fractures to the hospital) and then make sure it is quiet enough so I can slip out and head back to my condo (always keeping my pager on).

At this stage Debbie has essentially moved in, but is still sharing the QH apartment rent with Becky; which is becoming more and more of a sore point in our relationship. My never-ending workday and reluctance to commit fully to our relationship (which, quite frankly, means marriage) brings me home one night to find Debbie and all her stuff gone. While this has happened before, this time seems different. After all, she will be turning twenty-nine years old and the thought of approaching thirty for a woman may well be a biologic time bomb. I am now thirty-nine and well aware that my youth is also waving good-bye. It is the first time I can appreciate why Jack Benny kept on turning thirty-nine each birthday (how ridiculously old that used to seem).

The following day I am sitting in a hospital committee meeting next to Dr. Bernie Sklar, a family practitioner, perhaps ten years my senior. *I'm not getting any younger and, although I'm not a woman, I still want to have kids at a reasonable age. It wouldn't be fair to them if I am an old fart when they want to play catch, or have to explain that I am really their father not grandpa.* Bernie passes me the attendance sheet and then shoves me gently when I don't respond.

"You okay, my friend?" he whispers. "If you need time by yourself, take it. The meeting can go on without you right now, Bob." Snapping out of it, I tell him that my girlfriend (whom he had met at a couple of hospital functions) is fed up and just moved out. "Do you love her?" he asks softly.

"Yeah, but the problem is," I sigh "I just don't know if I can spend the rest of my life with her."

"Can you spend the rest of your life without her?" he responds matter-of-factly.

Bingo! It all instantly falls into place somehow. I never thought of looking at it that way. Bernie later tells me he went through the same thing twenty years ago.

Despite knowing that I do not want to spend the rest of my life without her, I still have time to mull it over because my one week vacation is coming up and I scheduled a solo trip to the Club Med in Martinique. The scene is exciting with some of the guests taking advantage of the nude beach (although it is far tamer than the action nearly fifteen years earlier on Formentera and the beaches of Goa). The all-inclusive holiday makes for excessive eating and drinking. Although I do not hook-up with any knock-outs, I manage to have a good time, but definitely miss Debbie. Bingo, again! I realize that part of me has already committed.

Upon my return, I find a jeweler who specializes in diamond engagement rings and make the purchase of a stunning 2.14 carat round solitaire (after all I am a doctor). As afraid as I am of giving up my freedom after thirty-nine years of bachelorhood, I somehow feel elated to have finally made the decision. Debbie, meanwhile, is playing the wounded soul and not easily swayed into coming over to the condo. *Just Bob being horny* she, no doubt, thinks. But then again, girls get horny too, so she gives in.

To say that nerves don't get the better of me is pure denial because dropping the ring and having it roll under the couch kind of blows the romantic surprise; especially when I yell, "Shit, where's that damn ring? It's expensive."

But Debbie is all aglow as she helps me move the couch and then giggles as my hands shake while I slip the ring on her finger and ask her to marry me.

Putting the ring on first, I guess, was kind of presumptuous, but I was not really thinking. Although I forget the specifics, I do know that she accepted because it is not long before she is vying with her brother David (four years her junior) for a fall wedding date since he, too, is getting married around the same time. He and Susan get November leaving the enchanting month of December for our union.

On December 14th the Crystal Plaza in Livingston, NJ is decorated tastefully; the one hundred thirty-five guests look elegant in their gowns and monkey suits; and Rabbi Glustrom (who performed my bris and Bar Mitzvah, and married my sister) is ready to go. Escorted by her mother Betty, Debbie comes down the isle looking positively radiant and gorgeous. I am at peace and grateful for Bernie Sklar's wisdom. The ceremony is concluded with breaking of the glass (a Jewish tradition in which the groom steps on a wine glass signifying that the marriage will last as long at the glass is broken). The shattering sound beneath my heel is trumped by cries of "Mazel Tov!"

For Debbie, our honeymoon destination is a surprise. Little do I know that she is afraid of flying, especially in small planes. So when our six-seater aircraft from Puerto Rico lands on the dirt airstrip in Virgin Gorda and my bride jumps in my arms with tears in her eyes, I mistake her relief of being on the ground for the excitement of being at Little Dix Bay, an exclusive Rock Resort.

No TVs, radios, or phones. Bicycles are the only available

transportation. We are taken to our very own luxurious Neepa hut up on stilts above the sand overlooking the private bay. Sumptuous culinary spreads are everywhere and the warm tropical air is filled with steel band island music. With nothing to do but enjoy each other in Paradise, we feel blessed to have our whole lives together to look forward to.

After a couple of days on the beach I talk Debbie into taking a ride on a whaler (she is a good sport, because she doesn't like small boats either). Given gourmet lunch baskets, we are dropped off on our own secluded island to do as we please without disturbance. I do my best to indoctrinate her in Formentera beach scene customs.

The night before our departure from Paradise is perfectly clear with a balmy breeze tickling our hair and soft island music dancing in our ears. As we stand barefoot in the sand I am struck by my old friend and reference point, the full moon which has followed me all this way from Hamilton College to Formentera, to Afghanistan, to Goa, and here to Virgin Gorda. Different places, different times, and yet that globe up there seems never to change; always a constant, reminding me that my life is a series of chapters that inexorably unfold before my eyes. This night is very special and I try to make it last forever.

CHAPTER 24

"Alone" at Last, Again

My New Year resolutions of 1987 include getting a handle on my relationship with Paul. I am in my fourth year of practice with him and although Paul calls me his partner the financial inequity between us remains. He explains that although the gross revenues have doubled since my arrival it is actually the result of our mutual efforts and cannot be solely attributed to my hard work and long hours. Besides, he plans to retire "soon" and that means that the entire thirty-year-old practice will be mine.

Never wanting anything more than a handshake before, he now asks me to sign a contract which turns out to be nothing more than a buy-out agreement. When he decides to ride off into the sunset I will have to pay him a multiple of the practice's yearly earnings in order to secure the telephone number and referral base. My dad and other advisors are shocked by his proposal (which, no doubt, comes from Paul's brother-in-law attorney who pumps him up by telling him that I could never have been so successful without him).

Over the course of the next several months our relationship becomes further strained by my not signing the contract. This, along with the contentious bickering of my jealous colleagues at the hospital, is temporarily interrupted by a surprise party Debbie throws at our condo for my 40th birthday. My good friend and "financial advisor" Mark acts as the decoy by taking me out that evening for sushi. We get a bit loaded on Saki and then drift back to my place about 8:00 PM where I am absolutely shocked to find my house filled with the enemy (as well as some friends). Paul and his wife along with several of my detractors yell "surprise" and then make out like they are my good buddies all night long.

It sort of reminds me of the surprise birthday party for me (and Norm) in my parent's basement back in '62; full of deception. Debbie explains that she had to invite them all for fear of throwing fuel on the fire. So they eat my food and pretend to celebrate with me as if we are all at a bipartisan congressional affair. Politically correct, but irritating.

I manage to get Debbie back with a surprise party for her 30th birthday on October 30th. Good-bye twenties. It coincides beautifully with the new TV series *Thirty Something* that premiered on ABC on September 29th.

***

It is a Saturday morning when the phone rings. Debbie and I are lounging around in bed. I am surprised that it is Paul on the phone because he seldom calls on a weekend and pretty much hates talking on the phone anyway. The conversation is quick. He asks point blank if I intend to sign the contract or not. When I once again explain why

I have a problem with its verbiage the line abruptly goes dead. Debbie asks me what is wrong and I tell her, quite dumbfounded, that Paul just hung up on me. After talking it over and then discussing things with my dad I decide to let things cool off over the weekend and sit down with Paul on Monday in the office.

On Monday morning I arrive early, as is my custom, and as I put the key in the door am surprised to see Jeanne (the office manager) pull up to the curb and hurriedly open her car door. But it is too late. My key does not work. He had her change the locks over the weekend and she felt so badly that she wanted to head me off before I got the full impact of humiliation.

"I'm so sorry," she gasps. "He was angry and felt you were ungrateful," she says in his defense.

"Just help me get the charts of the patients who are mine," I respond in a fog of indignation. "I am entitled to that, at least."

I storm out of Paterson and back to Fair Lawn where I find my dad in his office. He has a way of remaining calm despite his sympathy for my obvious despair. "This is your office," he smiles warmly. "It always has been, since the day you were born. I am so proud to work with you. I will see my few patients when you are in surgery. My practice will not interfere with your busy schedule, son. Everything will be fine. Fair Lawn is where you belong."

What can I say? I am looking at a man who loves me to death despite my putting him through the wringer for four years. I acted completely in my own interest and yet, because of him my education was paid for and I am free of debt. Now he invites me to crowd him out of the office and profession that defines him. As he hands me his life I am in awe of him. We begin renovations to meet the demands of a fulltime, busy orthopaedic practice. Without hesitation, Debbie quits her sales job with Capezio in New York and asks her girlfriend Michelle (of the couple Sonny and Michelle from the gym) to help us out since she has some familiarity with Medicare insurance forms.

I manage to get a couple of part-time x-ray techs from the hospitals to work for us; and, remarkably, Jeanne brings me a slew of charts from the Paterson office of patients that have seen only me (never Paul) in the past. With my makeshift, but very motivated crew, we manage to piece things together. The limiting factor, of course, is finding a full-time x-ray tech since x-rays are needed on most patients in order to make proper diagnoses. So begins the hunt. Unfortunately, good techs are hard to find.

And then along comes John. The guy simply answers an ad that we had been running in a local paper. His credentials are solid having worked for years at Columbia Presbyterian Hospital in New York. Getting past the tattoos, one saying TURK on his upper arm, and the cross dangling from his ear lobe are easy for me considering my years on the road where brandings were commonplace. The fact that he is looking for a job as a cover to his numbers racket is unbeknownst to me. After seeing how adept he is with our x-ray equipment and hearing that his working hours are flexible, I give him the job. So now we are off and running.

Within six months of being solo I net more money than I did in my three plus years with Paul! So when my old partner calls me up and asks if I can make time to join him for lunch I say, "Sure, why not?"

As we sit across from one another at the Fireplace Restaurant in Paterson, he uncharacteristically puts his hand on mine and apologizes for pressuring me to sign the contract. "Let's get back together and start afresh; we are stronger as a team," he explains. Somehow saddened by his obsequious plea I simply say, "We'll see."

As the year goes on it becomes obvious that we need a dedicated and committed office manager who can oversee the day-to-day operation. Debbie is the obvious choice, but after talking with her mother and friends, she is apprehensive about taking on in that position for fear of putting a dagger in our marriage. The more peripheral (and important) role of submitting claims and collecting money for my work is her real focus of attention. So another hunt begins.

We go through David, Gwen, and Sonya (who somehow keeps hitting her head on filing cabinet drawers and misses several days of work tending to her sister who incredulously glued her eyes shut when she mistook Krazy Glue for eye drops) until we find Irene. With no previous medical office experience she is initially hired as a receptionist, but soon becomes a rising star, mastering each administrative facet of the business right before our eyes. Her honesty and integrity makes putting her in charge a no-brainer.

CHAPTER 25

Oh, Baby!

With the practice in gear and our finances looking good, Debbie and I buy a charming old house in Franklin Lakes, an upper-middle-class town out in the country. The primary section of the house was built in 1899 and it is set well back off the road. Excited to renovate the place, I ask Sonny (the other member of the Sonny and Michelle team from the gym), who is a stone mason and knows local builders, for help. He recommends Pete, who owns a construction company. Before long we are knee deep in demolition. It is at this time that Debbie informs me, "We are pregnant!"

I am going to be a father! Excited, frightened, and very relieved (Debbie and I had been trying for awhile and even began talking about getting medical help) I have trouble thinking about anything else. While it signals another chapter that will round out my book of life, it also enshrouds me with a new layer of responsibility and steals another chunk of my independence. *This demands ultimate commitment; the Full Monty!*

Fortunately, I have little time for ambivalence because I am up to my neck in work and the in-your-face home renovation. It is a huge project because we are completely redoing the house, part of which is solid stone constructed in 1899. Add to this the unnerving fact that Pete, our general contractor, turns out to be far more concerned with his own welfare than ours (surprise, surprise).

But it is not just "renovating-your-house-with-a-general-contractor-that-doesn't-give-a-shit-about-you" tension that I am under: we are pregnant for the first time and the summer of 1988 is beyond hot! The heat wave is so severe that between 4,800 and 17,000 deaths around the country are attributed to it.

With nearly the entire house uninhabitable, save the old section with a small bedroom above the kitchen, I come home one night (after 11:00 PM as usual) from the hospital and find robustly pregnant Debbie hugging the sole window A/C unit upstairs in the bedroom. Despite it being almost midnight the temperature is still over 90 degrees outside. Debbie kisses me hello, but is not ready to relinquish her embrace of the air conditioner. Dog tired, I lie down on the bed, loosen my tie and try not to move a muscle for fear of drowning in sweat.

Before long, it becomes all to clear that Debbie and her belly cannot continue to stay in this dusty inferno. So she bites the bullet and moves in with my parents in Fair Lawn for the remainder of her third trimester. I elect to tough it out in the house in order to have a presence there and keep it secure.

Having saved the renovation of the old section for

last, I explain to Pete that the bedroom above the kitchen needs to be cleaned up at the end of each workday because it is the only place I have left to sleep. "No problemo!" Pete reassures. His son is doing the trim work and understands the situation. Unfortunately, I am unaware that Pete, Jr. has a cocaine habit and is completely irresponsible. So when I come in after 11:00 PM dog tired (knowing that I may actually get some sleep because Debbie will not be blocking the A/C unit) I am totally freaked out to find sawdust, pieces of trim, and nails on the bed and everywhere else! Without hesitation I leave Pete a voice message telling him, in no uncertain terms, that he is fired and to not even think about returning to the job site! I then spend the next hour cleaning off the bed while trying not to step on nails or letting my rant awaken the neighbors.

Eric or Erica is due on 8/8/88, an interesting date; one that Chinese culture treasures because the number "8" in Mandarin sounds like "prosper" or "wealth," and in Cantonese sounds like "fortune." In any event, Eric is born on 8/12/88 by C-section. Debbie is a trooper and even allows me to bring my camcorder into the delivery room as long as I keep it tasteful.

"It's a boy, oh boy!" I shout remembering my dad telling me that he said those exact words when I was born. Of course, Dad is right there; actually scrubbed in on the case (Dr. Gartner, our obstetrician, would have it no other way). That night Sonny takes me and all who will come (Debbie, of course, is sleeping it off in the hospital) to his gumba's ristorante in Paramus. As I walk in, there is a huge sign saying "It's a Boy!" slung across the back wall. Turns out, his pizan also had a boy that week.

After discharge from the hospital, Debbie and Eric stay another two months with my parents while I somehow manage to continue working with Pete in order to complete the house renovation (Debbie fears retaliation from Pete, Jr. so I take a deep breath and finish the deal).

Finally, we have a brand "new" house and a brand new baby. Now I really have something to work hard for and something new to play with when I come home. Unfortunately, Eric is more into spitting up than playing. I amuse myself by taking pictures and videos, simply biding my time until he is old enough to pay me some recognition.

Debbie, on the other hand, is totally into motherhood and only gets freaked out in the very beginning when our Eric would not "take to the breast." Wanting so much to breast feed, she is not at all pleased when my mother offers her opinion that "Breast feeding is overrated. I never breast fed Bobby and look how healthy and strong he turned out!" "Of course she never breast fed you," Debbie says to me in private. "You had that blood disorder and were put in the intensive care unit...and if she had had the opportunity to breast feed you; maybe you wouldn't have run off for four years!"

Perhaps?!

It is amazing to me that women can complain about how sore their breasts are from breast feeding and still do it— for months! In June we make the pilgrimage up to Clinton, New York for my twentieth Hamilton College reunion. We leave ten month old Eric with my parents and mother-in-law, with little regard for Dad who is left to mediate the two ladies' fight over the baby. By this time Debbie has been breast feeding the kid for ten months—enough already! She agrees that the trip up to Hamilton will break the feeding frenzy and get her back on the wagon. The problem, of course, is that her breasts are not cooperating. The ongoing production of milk is brutal and requires ingenuity since we are caught by surprise and have no breast pump.

All in all, we have a great time despite missing little Eric. Staying in one of the old Kirkland College dorms is freaky for me, but somehow kind of erotic remembering my exploits there twenty years ago. Playing basketball with the guys, getting loaded and talking jive is just what this forty-one year old needs. At night I look for that full moon from two decades ago, but one can't have everything; so I settle for a crescent.

***

It worked! Eric is off the breast and Debbie is accepting of it. She is also pregnant again! She gives me the news on August 12th, Eric's first birthday; just before the party. Even though we had some difficulty getting pregnant with Eric, Debbie tells me that she thought this might happen as soon as she stopped breastfeeding (she reads a lot about stuff like that). So now I have a son that toddles and a baby on the way. This is the chapter where I am getting waist deep in the whole family thing. Independence and self-indulgence are things of the past. Am I ready? Did I have my fill somewhere between Formentera and Goa?

Knowing that I need to start planning for the future so that my family will be financially secure, I realize that my pal Marc (best man at my wedding) is not equipped to be my (or anyone else's) financial planner. Not only has he gotten me into several 2:1 and 3:1 tax write-off limited partnerships, but the restaurant investment in Harmon Cove and the brownstone renovation project in Weehawken are not panning out. He smokes too much weed and is into blow.

Fortunately, my dad attends an estate planning seminar at the hospital and likes what he hears from a guy named Chris Stanziale who runs a company called Access in Clifton, New Jersey. At our very first meeting (prompted by my close questioning of his background) I learn that the guy is a Vietnam vet, with no formal college education, who has developed unique computer software that tracks investment portfolios and systematically updates each client's financial status so that adjustments can easily be made based on current and long term data. Impressed with his honesty, ingenuity, and straight forward approach I decide to give him a try; but, because of my disappointment with Marc, it will take all of his street smarts and integrity to keep me as a client. It is only much later that I learn that this man has been raising three children on his own while dealing with a wife suffering from severe alcoholism. My respect for him increases as I get to know him.

It is not long before Chris suggests that I consider getting a partner to help share the patient load of my busy practice. I make him aware of my distrust of partnerships after my experience with Paul and how proud my dad has been all these years to be able to say that every dime he has made he earned with his own hands. "Your Dad grew out of the Depression. He is proud not to have a mortgage or any debt. He pays for everything in cash and has no credit. This is a different era. You are not your dad," Chris explains.

The seed is planted, but does not grow until I take a rare vacation and find myself riding up a ski lift with a total stranger. He is crude and arrogant and blows cigar smoke right in my face.

"What do you do, son?" he says condescendingly.

"I'm a doctor," I respond knowing there is no escape.

"Solo or do you have partners?" he says between puffs on the huge Cohiba.

"Solo," I say looking for the dismount station.

"Well, I own a textile business," he brags. "Runs 24/7 and only closes for Christmas and New Years." I have no response. "You know, son. When we get to the top of this mountain I'll be worth more and you'll be worth less than when we got on this damn lift," he goes on to say with a shit-assed grin on his face.

There was a time, not long ago, when making money was not even on my list of priorities; when existentialism and self-evolution was all that mattered. At the bottom of the mountain I hurriedly put a call into Chris, telling him that I am ready to take on a partner.

CHAPTER 26

The Gray '90s

As we jump into the '90s I am looking to gear up the practice by hiring a young orthopaedist who will eventually become my partner. Besides advertising for candidates I plan to use the search services at the annual meeting of the AAOS (American Academy of Orthopaedic Surgeons) being held in February in New Orleans. Four years ago, at the 53rd Annual Meeting, also held in the Town of Jazz, Debbie came with me and we had a blast. We weren't married then and had no kids. This time, however, she is pregnant and elects to stay home with little Eric.

As soon as I get down there I hook up with Jay, my old friend from Nebraska (that's "Mag Citrate" Jay). His wife, Marilyn, is home taking care of their kids so he is also solo. Aside from a little carousing on Bourbon Street we manage to keep each other out of trouble.

On February 11th we are enjoying New York strip steaks at the Hilton restaurant and hear crazy cheering from the bar. We gobble down our food and arrive just in time to watch James "Buster" Douglas, in the ninth inning, jabbing the hell out of heavyweight boxing champion Mike Tyson over in Tokyo, Japan. He has us all cheering and, in the tenth round, puts "Iron Mike" on the canvas for the first time in his career. Not making it up before the count Tyson loses his crown to a 42-1 underdog (who had sadly lost his mother to a stroke twenty-three days before the fight). Everyone is high-fiving each other and one ecstatic patron buys drinks for the house. I take a jab at Jay by telling the bar tender that my friend will have Mag Citrate on the rocks. I'll never let it go.

Despite interviewing several graduating orthopaedic residents and one guy in his fellowship I find no one of interest who seems likely to move out to New Jersey to join my practice. Although the search goes on over the next several months, it crosses my mind that perhaps I am my father's son and meant make a living with just my own two hands.

***

When my Stephanie Paige is born on April 24th, it is no surprise to Debbie that I am on call for the hospital emergency room. Fortunately, I do not get called down to the E.R. until well after the delivery. With camcorder in hand I dutifully and tastefully record the event. Blessed with a healthy girl we now have the perfect American family! This is our decade, filled with joy and expectations of the best to come. 1990 is quite the year.

With Reagan's hard-line diplomacy and Gorbachev's perestroika (economic reform), glasnost (government transparency), and fall of the Berlin Wall, the Cold War is now an old war without much steam. It makes me think back to Junior High School when our teachers were strongly recommending that we learn Russian in order to be best prepared for life with the powerful Soviet Union. Of course, I'm glad I took French (which at least helped me out with Virginie and travel in Morocco) rather than struggle to learn a language with a funky alphabet that now belongs to a defunct empire.

The John Gotti murder and racketeering trial is good drama, but becomes personally interesting when I see Gotti's lawyer on TV. He may be more stout and balding, but he's just as energetic and hard driving as the Bruce Cutler I knew as a DKE fraternity brother at Hamilton College in the late '60s. A one time muscular Adonis type in college, he is intriguing in his new enigmatic roll as a Mafioso defender. He looks so serious in court; a marked contrast to my wild memories of him at the DKE House.

My own weight lifting efforts are definitely catching up with me. Sure, I'd like to look like Bruce (back in the day). Though six feet tall I have never weighed more than 175 pounds, but recently have been working out hard with "Dr." John who is all muscle. Having won several body-building competitions, the guy is totally into diet and work-out technique. He does no drugs (other than a squirt of steroid now and then, I suspect) and does not drink. With John (a confirmed bachelor) it is all about packing on muscle in order to get the babes.

Going heavy and doing fewer reps supposedly is the formula for adding mass and bulking up. The upright lateral dumbbell raises that John says are essential to getting big "delts" are brutal and begin to hurt my shoulders, especially my left. But I am seeing the results (forget that I am an orthopaedist) so I figure "no pain, no gain," right? After all, who wouldn't like to have John's size?

So one day I pull into the parking lot of EPAC (Elmwood Park Athletic Club) and reach behind me into the back seat of my car to grab my gym bag. The burning pain that shoots through the subacromial region of my shoulder is so exquisite that I feel nauseous. I literally have to leave my arm there while I gingerly twist the rest of my body around to it in order to wrest it free.

From that point on my left shoulder is a constant source of pain, causing me to have to prop it up on a sterile mayo stand while I operate and figure out ways to sleep at night in order to avoid rolling over on it. I already know that I probably have a torn rotator cuff. For confirmation I get an arthrogram-MRI. This test involves putting dye with Novocain into the glenohumeral ("ball and socket") joint of the shoulder using a large needle. Moments after the fluid is injected I shout "Damn!" which startles the radiologist who thought he hit a nerve. "Are you all right?" he cries. "The pain is gone," I respond. Unfortunately, this means I must have a large tear in my rotator cuff because the hole allowed the numbing medicine to leak up quickly into the bursa area where I have been having the pain. This is not good; I need to have my rotator cuff tendons repaired.

In just weeks I clear my office and surgical schedules for three months so I can have surgery of my own. Now more than ever I wish I had a partner to carry on the practice in my absence.

The rotator cuff repair is done at Columbia Presbyterian Hospital under regional block so that I am awake during the surgery. My surgeon happens to be the head of the shoulder service and an occasional tennis partner of mine. During the procedure, he and I discuss the findings. He tells me that I am lucky; the tear is not very large and I should do well.

Strange, I think. *The arthrogram-MRI showed a large delaminated tear.*

Unfortunately, I am right and will require a second operation (when I get up the guts) to fix the major portion of the tear that is missed on this day. Recovery is a bitch— longer and more arduous than I could have imagined, but it gives me profound insight into what my patients go through after I cut into *their* shoulders.

CHAPTER 27

Upside-Down Turk

Within a few months it is almost as if I never missed a beat and I am back to the routine of leaving the house by 7:00 AM, working my ass off, and coming home no earlier than 11:00 at night. While I am still having no luck finding the right guy to join me, all in all, things are going well (although my shoulder still hurts). I have two healthy kids; one of each gender and Debbie is playing mother perfectly (as I always knew she would). My practice is booming and the heat from the other orthopaedists is off now that I am an established player. The Dow goes over 3,000 for the first time. It is all good, until "Turk" gets busted!

John (aka Turk), my Irish-Italian x-ray technician is skilled at his job and takes pride in his work. He is excellent with the patients with a knack for making them laugh and feel at ease. He also handles the office inventory of braces and medical supplies and removes sutures and casts as well as any doctor. But John has an inclination to pick up extra dough on the side by running numbers. I sort of knew about his pastime, but our agreement had always been for him to keep it away from the office. To my knowledge he had complied one hundred percent. Then, out of the blue, he gets busted for recreational cocaine use in his house. Unfortunately, he lives within a "drug free" zone near one of the schools in town. A conviction is a felony and carries a mandatory one year prison sentence.

Although he has been with me for less than four years our relationship is solid and one of loyalty and mutual respect, not to mention a whole lot of fun (he is a warm-hearted character). He seems most distraught over having let me down, but the fact is that he is likely going to jail and his presence cannot easily be replaced.

Bummer!

I try to pull strings, but John is heading to the clinker and suddenly both our worlds are turned upside-down.

***

On January 27th, 1992, Dad turns 80! To celebrate this milestone Helaine and I arrange for a surprise party at Pete's restaurant in Boca Raton. Our parents are snowbirds, spending the winters in South Florida, although the old man still takes the "red-eye" back and forth to Jersey each month to see his steadily dwindling patient population (after all, at 80 he was forced to forfeit his hospital operating privileges and he gave up his large obstetrical practice years ago because of my mother's nagging that he was too old to work such late hours).

It is a miracle that Mom is able to keep her mouth shut about the party around Dad and, at the same time, pressure all of the relatives and friends to also keep it secret. Then, too, Dad is a typical man, oblivious to most small talk and gossip, and deeply caught up in his daily routine of playing cards, golf, and thinking about his patients.

The day before the event, while flying down to Boca (Debbie stays at home to take care of the kids), I find myself sitting next to a woman on the plane who tells me of her elderly uncle who had a heart attack at his surprise 80th birthday party. *Bitch! Thanks for the heads-up!*. But that gets me thinking...*you never know?* Thank goodness for Helaine's pragmatism. "Nah, he's Mr. Calm. He'll just smile and probably cry a little." I go along with her intuition, but can't help remember how my whole Bar Mitzvah suit shook as Dad's hands trembled on my shoulders while he had to recite a blessing in Hebrew before a packed house. *He's more emotional than he let's on*, I keep thinking.

"SURPRISE!" Dad is absolutely stunned when he walks into the back party room at Pete's, but does not have a myocardial infarction. He does smile and cry a bit. I am profoundly relieved and also cry a bit.

***

Back home, my office is in duress because John, my x-ray tech extraordinaire, is doing time. He'll be in the slammer for a whole year, despite my best attempts to get his sentence commuted. Several attorney friends of mine try to work the system, but to no avail. I assure the judge, in writing, that John has a full time job to return to when he gets out and that his service to my patients has always been meritorious. John has a tough exterior, but it is heart-breaking to see him and his family suffer. His indiscretion took place in his own home and hurt no one. Sometimes laws with mandatory sentences are simply unjust; an overreach that leave no room for reasonable punishment. A good man in this case is shamed and branded. Were I not his employer he may not have been able to survive a future background check.

For the time being I decide to put my hunt for a partner on hold until the office milieu is stabilized with a replacement who can take quality x-rays and help out in other areas. To say that the search is difficult does not do justice to the seemingly endless revolving door of candidates. The whole gestalt is not only emotionally torturous; it paralyzes the office.

In an attempt to get our minds off the trauma at work Debbie and I start looking at houses on the weekends. We are serious shoppers, but in no rush. The house on Stonewall Road with the red brick, perfect interior layout, pool, and tennis court on two acres in Saddle River ("where Richard Nixon lives," as they say) is the one Debbie falls in love with. Thing is, I don't realize that she is actually in *love* so I pass on raising my asking price despite knowing that there is another bid out there. (I am also of the mind that one never falls in love with an inanimate object, especially a big-ticket item like a house.) That evening I learn that Debbie bumped into our realtor at the Market Basket in Franklin Lakes and was told that the other offer was accepted by the seller. The copious flow of tears indicates to me that Debbie is pissed— big-time!

After about a week of regret (not only because of Debbie, but because I also really liked the house despite the red brick) I call the agent who tells me that it is another doctor (a cardiologist whom I know) who has the contract on the house. He and his family are so excited. *Great! That means there is no second chance in hell, on this one.* So I ask Debbie (and myself) to move on. It's just hard to know that you had the perfect house (*sans* the red brick) in your hands and…*oh well…I'm a f***in' idiot!*

About a month later, seemingly out of the blue, the sweet little realtor calls informing me that the Stonewall contract has been terminated and asks if I am still interested? I tell her absolutely, but at the same price that I offered originally (knowing that the seller is from South Korea and, believing that his original deal was solid, has already made plans to return to his country). She brings the offer to the seller and that very same day we become the official buyer. It is an absolutely beautiful story for us until we learn that the reason the first deal went bad is that the doctor's young son developed aplastic anemia, a potentially fatal disease of the bone marrow, causing them to put everything else in their lives on hold.

So, let me see, the house I refused to fall in love with and then wind up agonizing over comes back to me at my original asking price, but at the expense of an innocent child whose potentially fatal illness is the reason why I go from being totally bummed to absolutely groovy. Of course, the real reason I can allow myself to feel so good is that the boy is treated successfully with a bone marrow transplant in Seattle—all guilt is absolved.

Naturally, the house needs a new interior paint job before we move in so I hire one of my patients who seems competent and willing to please. While he goes to work on our Saddle River digs we are still living in our old house (the one we painstakingly renovated), which we now have up for sale. I get an offer (just below my asking price) within a day of it going on the market, but turn it down believing that there is certainly a better deal out there.

Meanwhile, the patient/painter I hired inexeplicably decides to take a flashlight to each wall in the house meticulously looking for nail pops and other irregularities so that he can correct them perfectly before applying primer and a new coat of paint. His obsession makes the house look like it is riddled with machine gun bullets where he has replaced each nail with a screw every few inches.

"You have got to be kidding!" the McEnroe in me shouts.

"You have a magnificent house here, Doc. I think the walls should be perfect," he responds with a straight face.

"Nothing is perfect, you idiot! I contracted you to paint my walls not make them flawless. Get out of my house, now!" I scream, despite the fact that I am relatively harmless because my left arm is again in a sling from my recent revision rotator cuff surgery. Not for one second does my higher self, the one that should have evolved so well on the four year pilgrimage to Nirvana, take over to calm my hostile mind.

Luckily, the guy is so sufficiently freaked by my rage that he simply leaves. Unfortunately, I find out later that he took all of my paint. In her usual rational manner, Debbie puts on the restraints and persuades me not to pursue the jerk.

Once the house is finally made ready by workers that I wisely hire outside of my patient population, we joyously move into our swanky Saddle River abode a few months after selling our Franklin Lakes house (for, you guessed it, less than the first offer and far less money than we had into it). Live and learn.

But it is all worth it. The kids love the new back yard, especially skating and riding tricycles on the tennis court. Debbie sees to it that the pool and all the cabinets are professionally childproofed.

It is an exciting, fairytale-like time for my family and me—a stark contrast from my sister's household scenario. In early spring Helaine drives up from Hershey, Pennsylvania and sits Dad and me down in the kitchen to give us the news that she and Cliff are getting divorced. Being more surprised than Dad, I realize that she must have been discussing her marital problems with him for some time.

"Have you told your mother?" he asks tenderly. "No, I can't," she laments. And suddenly I remember all the times that Mom spoke harshly of Aunt Annette for having been a divorcee even though she remarried and raised three of our cousins (one from the previous marriage) with a wonderful man, Uncle Maurice.

Eventually, Helaine gets up the courage to do the inevitable—she tells Mom about her failed marriage, despite believing that she would be blamed for not being able to hold onto her man. But when it comes to her own daughter, Mom rises to the occasion; she is not callous or close-minded. Instead, she gives comfort and, of course accuses her miserable, soon-to-be ex-son-in-law of being a heartless pig.

Having known Cliff as long as anyone in our family, including Helaine (he was one of my counselors at Camp Ta-Ri-Go in 1955), I am heartbroken to hear of the split. The only time I stick my nose in is when I hear that he is vehemently disputing the monetary settlement since he is the one opting out after twenty-seven years of marriage.

"I understand that falling out of love happens," I explain to him on the phone. "But I expect that after all these years and two children you will treat my sister fairly." It is unclear to me whether my conversation has any impact at all on the financial outcome.

On March 28th Debbie gives me the traditional surprise birthday party to celebrate my 45th year on earth. While I deeply appreciate the love, I am silently distraught over the fact that I am missing the Duke vs. Kentucky basketball game that determines who will go to the Final Four. As it turns out, Mike Krzyzewski and Rick Pitino watch their teams play "the greatest college basketball game ever played" with the Blue Devils beating the Wildcats 104-103 in overtime on "The Shot" by Christian Laetner as time expires. While I dutifully open presents, I am unknowingly deprived of the climactic excitement of every sports fanatic's fantasy. Seeing the game highlights the next day helps little since I already know the outcome of the contest. Duke goes on to get by Bobby Knight's Indiana Hoosiers and then wallops Michigan 71-51 at the Hubert H. Humphrey Metrodome in Minneapolis, Minnesota to win their second consecutive national title.

By the end of the year three marvelous things happen to me: my shoulder seems to be improving; Turk is released from prison; and my brother-in-law David (just having completed his orthopaedic hand fellowship) tells me that he thinks a guy with whom he trained would make a perfect partner for me.

***

The next year, 1993, starts out with a reality check. I am

nearly the same age as the newly inaugurated President of the United States, Bill Clinton. He and his Vice President, Al Gore (a year my junior) are the first baby boomers in the White House. The impact is huge—much like going to a Yankees game and being struck by the fact that the athletes are kids half my age!

Face to face with the passage of time is chilling. I allow myself to consider that this is "middle-age." I am half way there (or through, depending on your point of view). Were it not for my years on the road and late start with raising a family I might have a mid-life crisis right this minute! Perhaps those extraordinary years of freedom and self-indulgence were extremely productive?

Now that John has done his time and is back in the fold, the office starts to return to normal. All I have to do is trust that when he is on the phone it is John doing office business and not Turk taking "action." He swears that he is clean and would never jeopardize the practice or our relationship ever again. I decide to drink the Kool-Aid and return my attention to finding a partner.

The tip from my brother-in-law, David, seems promising since he has had personal experience with the new candidate during their orthopaedic training. Ken's curriculum vita is solid (undergrad at University of Delaware, medical school and residency at Tufts, and presently completing a foot and ankle fellowship at Thomas Jefferson University Hospital in Pennsylvania). He graduated with honors in each place he trained. Our conversation on the phone is pleasant and we look forward to meeting one another, but the blizzard of '93 (March 12-15) drops so much snow on the east coast (New England gets up to forty inches and even Georgia gets eight inches) that our tête-à-tête gets postponed until late spring; no big deal to Eric and Stephanie who love throwing snow balls, building snowmen and crawling through snow tunnels.

When finally we meet, Ken turns out to be better than expected. His genuine warmth and friendliness is an absolute turn-on. I show him my hot-shot house in exclusive Saddle River and the meager office I share with my Dad in middle class Fair Lawn. He seems perfectly in balance with each and hits it off well with the office staff (including Turk who gives me his thumbs up on the new doc), but is most taken with my family and my vision of the practice. North Jersey is right in between New York (his wife Sharon's home) and his home state of Delaware. His two young boys can grow up with a nice back yard in suburbia. So we agree to draw up a contract and not allow lawyers to get in the way of what we hope will be a beautiful relationship.

He finishes his fellowship in May and starts working for me in July. Getting him patients is a bit harder at first than I expected. My patients do not want to see the "new guy" and getting Ken emergency room call (in order to drum up business of his own) at the hospitals takes awhile. In his spare time Ken becomes almost as quick at finishing a crossword puzzle as Turk.

And then it happens. I notice the staff is starting to put a fair number of overflow patients onto Ken's schedule. I recognize many of the names and am a bit startled by how comfortable these patients (*my patients!*) seem to be with the "new guy." It kind of freaks me out so I tell Ken that I'm having a tough time with it. "Bob, why the hell did you bring me on board; to get good at crossword puzzles or to help you with the patient load?" His pragmatic outburst and serene smile sets me straight, despite being thirteen years his senior.

I do my damndest to get used to another fish in the pond, but here we go again. I get back to the office from the hospital; hurriedly put on my white coat to start office hours and walk into an exam room. "You're not Dr. Levitsky," the patient says. "Sorry, miss," is all I can muster as I back out of the room. *Damn. This patient doesn't even know who I am. She wants Levitsky, and no part of me.* Another heart-to-heart discussion with Ken gets me another "What-the-hell-did-you-bring-me-on-board-for?" session. It is a lot like learning to meditate all over again—not allowing wasteful thoughts to rise and feed the ravenous ego. This time, however, the reward is not about finding Nirvana, but all about making money without having to do it with my hands alone.

Eventually, I embrace the concept that Ken being busy is good for the practice, covers his salary, and puts money in my pocket. Before long we are outgrowing my dad's small office (which I purchased from him the year before so he could feel more comfortable with easing into retirement).

The search for more space begins amid an insulting malpractice lawsuit that comes across my small desk accusing me and my tech John of manhandling an IME patient some months before. IME stands for independent medical evaluation. It is work that I do primarily as a favor (though I do get reimbursed) for certain workers' compensation carriers that refer patients to me on a regular basis. In these cases I am asked to evaluate a patient's condition and report my findings without proceeding to treat the individual (much like a second opinion).

Mr. "Slimeball" was seen briefly in my office at the request of the New Jersey Turnpike Authority for an IME over claims that his chronic back condition was exacerbated when the rear wheel of the car he was driving rolled over a pothole on the highway. Our encounter was so brief and uneventful that I cannot even recall what he looked like. The only thing I manage to remember is that he came in wearing a plastic lumbar brace that did not appear to fit all that well. In any event, he claims that John, following doctor's orders, forced him out of the brace and onto the x-ray table against his will. Suffice it to say that our office policy clearly avoids taking x-rays or performing any procedure without absolute permission from the patient whom we are serving.

As I sit in my insurance carrier's lawyers' office (incredibly pissed to high hell that this nonsense is causing me to miss a day's work) undergoing interrogatories from the plaintiff's attorney, I am asked if I know about my x-ray tech's prison history. Just short of blowing out one of my temporal arteries I counter with, "Of course! What has that to do with your client's deception and your complicity?" My lawyers artfully make the peace and gingerly guide me back to my chair before I can exit the "bullshit room." Now get this: at the end of the session my interrogator (who characterized me as "flippant") actually has the nerve to ask me what I think about his painful knee that is screwing up his golf game. "Take two weeks off and quit playing," is my trite but final parry.

As it turns out, the slime-ball plaintiff has six personal injury/malpractice cases going on all at once including with the Turnpike Authority, a private citizen with whom he was in a motor vehicle accident, the spine surgeon who operated on his back and the brace manufacturer for faulty orthotic construction. In a matter of a month the case against me is dropped, but it takes us nearly six months to get John off the hook.

CHAPTER 28

The Material Boy

Even before Ken came on board, I was enticed by the idea of constructing a new medical building in Mahwah, an upscale middle class town twelve miles north of Fair Lawn, near the upstate New York boarder. Several docs had attempted to buy a piece of property that the hospital had appropriated (for the building of an adjunct medical center) but had to abandon because of conflict with its medical staff participation.

Much work had gone into the site so some of us felt that a concerted private effort might produce a 35,000 square foot center housing about twenty subspecialty physicians who could provide one-stop "shopping" to its patient clientele. Supplies would be bought in bulk at a discount and in-house referrals would be great for business.

After carefully choosing private practices, each of a different subspecialty (such as ortho, pediatrics, OB-GYN, general practice, GI, etc.) in order to avoid internal competition, we begin having organizational meetings.

The initial harmony and enthusiasm is inspiring, but the lack of business acumen (among our myopic doctor board) soon becomes painfully obvious. Decisions, like hiring knowledgeable, well-connected attorneys and building contractors are dangerously flavored by personal interest and global distrust. By the end of the year our semi-monthly meetings starting at 9:00 PM are ending in shouting matches at 1:00 in the morning.

Of the original twenty-two members only eight of us tenaciously survive, with the other fourteen slots entirely made up of newcomers. Nevertheless, somehow through attrition and sheer determination, a well-constructed building emerges for dedication in the New Year. While I am pleased with the new medical center (which means that Ken and I will have to rotate our office hours between two towns) I am skeptical that there will be economic harmony within the building's practices as originally planned.

Although consumed in business strategies I somehow reunite by phone with J.G. who now has a wife and two kids of his own. He is on the straight and narrow, apparently working for his father-in-law. In August I manage to slip away with the family and drive down to central Jersey to visit him. I am excited for the reunion and the introduction of our families, but Debbie is mortified when we walk out into their back yard and our kids unabashedly shout, "Hey, where's the pool?" "Not everyone has a pool," she whispers. J.G. and I think it is hysterical; I can't speak for his wife. Over a few beers we reminisce about another life long ago, while our wives roll their eyes and the kids find something to do besides swimming. We promise to get back together soon (but life's a busy place and "soon" is a long way off).

Before long our Eric starts kindergarten at Wandell School in Saddle River and little Stephanie begins pre-school at Early Enrichment. With the two of them out of the house during the day Debbie's wheels start spinning: it is time to expand the family.

Simply stopping contraception does not work as easily as stopping Eric's breastfeeding did. But while spending a week down in Boca Raton with my parents (as we have come to do routinely during school's winter break) the magic reappears. Debbie swears she knew she was pregnant the night of inception, but I don't find out until two weeks after our return from Florida. The news just so happens to coincide with the availability of ten thousand square feet of office space just across the street from Dad's (I mean my) office. We sorely need more room for our ever-expanding patient load. So "expansion" becomes the working theme of my life.

Fortunately, I do not have to find a bigger house (which will be over nine thousand square feet once we finish off the basement), but I will have to sell the old office in order to have funds to renovate the new one. With my head spinning from these new financial and strategic demands, I am suddenly brought back to earth when my daughter narrowly escapes tragedy that would definitely have rendered the house and office issues meaningless.

While walking in our dusty, partially renovated basement with little Stephanie at my side (marveling at the construction tools and equipment) I suddenly hear her screaming bloody murder and find her on the ground holding her face. The laceration just above her right eye, from the sharp metal edging suspended on two saw horses that she unknowingly walked into, is ugly. Were she one inch taller it most certainly would have taken her eye out.

After tending to her wound I allow myself to tremble and think *what if?* Unlike a near car accident when instinct tells me to send up a prayer of thanks and then is quickly forgotten, I know that this near catastrophe is sealed in my memory vault. As a physician, I am constantly reminded of the saying "I cried because I had no shoes, until I saw the man who had no feet," when I treat a patient with severe rheumatoid arthritis, amputation, stroke, or multiple sclerosis (diseases that will never go away). But recalling what almost happened to my precious Stephanie that day in our basement makes me grateful for my family's health and shames me when I lose site of the blessing.

While Debbie is full with our third baby (and thoroughly enjoying it) it is also a time of plethora for me professionally. I have reached my critical mass of patients, to the point where I need Ken to handle the overflow or lose patients that I am just not physically able to see. I see as many as sixty patients in a day and perform over five hundred surgeries per year. Surgical fees are high across the country, but especially in the New York and greater metropolitan area. So I am driving a Porsche 928 to the office and a Mercedes S500 in the evening. When Debbie and I go shopping we seldom look at the price tags. I am the "material boy" and digging it.

When a young athletic woman comes to see me for her knee, I make the diagnosis of ACL deficiency (the knee is unstable because the anterior cruciate ligament is not holding it together properly).

"But how can that be?" she cries. "I had it fixed last year by Dr. B." In response to her frustration I suggest that she return to him for his opinion and possible revision surgery. "No," she answers quickly; then asks if I will perform the operation so she can get back to sports. After I agree she thanks me and leaves.

At the end of office hours, Irene tells me that she has scheduled our young lady for revision ACL surgery, but adds, "You know, when I told her that your surgical fee is $7,500 she started to cry. I told her that this is revision (redo) surgery, which is much more difficult than the primary operation because of altered anatomy and scar tissue. 'That is why our fee is so high,' I told her. I mentioned that her insurance would pick up most of it and that she could pay the balance over time. Dr. Schultz, through her tears she managed to tell me that Dr. B charged her $16,500 for the primary knee reconstruction and when her insurance paid $12,000 he still balance billed her $4,500. Despite paying him $2,000 out of pocket, three months later his office put her in collection for the rest. She was actually crying for joy that our fee is lower than that thief's."

I have always kept track of the fee schedule for orthopaedic care in our area and maintained billing for my services somewhere in the middle range. That being said, I still appreciate that there are two sides to the argument: getting paid thousands of dollars for less than two hours work (and a few office visits of follow-up care) is robbery; while, on the other hand, comparing the correction of a bum knee for say $10,000 is a bargain compared with spending $30,000 for a car that will last perhaps 3-5 years. And then, of course, there is the fact that becoming a surgeon requires up to ten years of training *after* college and great financial expense (while one's peers are already out in the work force making a living). In addition, there is the lifestyle sacrifice of being on call at all hours of the day and night for one's patients, along with the ever-present danger of exposure to bodily fluids (that can carry life-threatening infectious diseases like hepatitis and HIV).

Nevertheless, the young lady's story carries great impact for me as I recognize the level of greed that we physicians portray to our patients and the public. *We are killing the golden goose* is all I can think. But just as I am not willing to call out Dr. H down the street who is putting total knee and hip replacements in just about everyone who walks in his office, I am not ready to demand fee regulation of Dr. B. Policing our own is not a strong suit of my profession, and although I do not personally cheat my patients, I am craven in my lack of denouncement of those who do. I also recognize that the ever-growing business of managed care is partly a consequence of doctors' own self-absorption and avarice. Healthcare is a multibillion-dollar industry that businessmen and government bureaucrats are sinking their teeth into because the public is becoming convinced that doctors and hospitals need regulating.

✳✳✳

The move into the large new office is awesome and deflating at the same time. Selling the old office (my dad's for over fifty years; my first home and the place where my bris was performed) is emotional for both Dad and me though we never openly mourn about it or belabor the inevitable. Mom sheds tears and, at the same time, tells me how proud she is that I need a bigger office and have surpassed Dad's and her expectations for me. As she reflects on the agony that they went through when I turned my back on them (and medicine) to search the world for something better, Mom tells me that those years of tribulation did not simply end when I returned from India; they continued through my gradual transformation from their gaunt, barely recognizable child back to the once self-determined young man who handed them his Cornell University Medical College ID at the front door when they returned from their trip to Portugal in 1974. "Every day I pinch myself to make sure I am not dreaming and that my Bobby is really back home and safe," she swoons.

Dad spends hours in the cellar of the old office (before it is sold) going through files of patients he has not seen in years. Finding him sitting there late at night under a single hanging light bulb reading every word of a chart discolored by age moves me nearly as much as the moment he looks up with glassy eyes that speak of the lifetime of fulfillment he enjoyed from being a doctor. It breaks my heart to rip out from under him this monument to his dedicated life. All at once I forgive him for being too tired to play catch with me when he came home from office hours in the summers, or for having to cancel a trip to Yankee Stadium because one of his patients decided to go into labor.

Once the office is sold (to an insurance agent who rents out the small back room to a dentist) Dad officially retires and spends the entire winter in Boca Lago (the small golf course community in Boca Raton, Florida) with Mom. Being a practical man he decides to ignore emotion and sell the house he built brick by brick (in which he and Edna raised two children and shared a lifetime of dreams) to move into a high rise apartment in Hackensack. "The house is just too big for the two of us to handle anymore and our friends are very happy on Prospect Avenue" (aka, Rue de Upscale High-rise Living). "We will even have a doorman," Mom says confidently. But the cleaning out of memories at the house on Berdan Avenue is poignant and oh so sad. Out of self-defense I beg out of helping any more than necessary. Mom understands my sensitivity. Helaine would certainly have pitched in, but her divorce is becoming finalized and her head is in a far off place.

While Helaine's '50s TV-style family life comes to a screeching halt mine is still growing (interestingly, 1994 is designated the "International Year of the Family" by the United Nations). On October 14th at 5:00 in the evening Morgan Rebecca comes into our lives, healthy as can be. She is instantly fought over by Eric and Stephanie who see her as a totally functioning toy whose batteries never run down. It will not be long before "Her Toyness" morphs into a gremlin that steals Mom's attention and must be outperformed. Naturally, I leave those family dynamics up to Debbie to deal with.

Having successfully taught Eric to ride a bicycle last year by running alongside him up and down our very quiet street while surreptitiously letting go of him until he miraculously found his balance point, I am now confident that I can do the same for Stephanie. She so wants to be grown-up and not need those embarrassing training wheels, the stigmata of still being little. This teaching session, however, is longer and more grueling than last year's, either because Eric's boyhood made him more daring or Stephanie's awareness of my grasp (or lack of it) is much keener than was his. In any case, I am committed to the training process and getting it done in one session, no matter how many times I must run up and down the block.

Despite difficulty finding that elusive balance point, Stephanie is having a blast (between screams of "Dad, don't let go! Please don't let go!"). At the very moment I inevitably "hit the wall" my little girl finds the zone and grows up right before my eyes. "Whee! I can do it, Daddy! I'm riding by myself!"

Although Debbie is fully immersed in our house full of little kids I manage to convince her to leave them in the capable hands of Grandma Betty and come away with me to Scottsdale, Arizona for a few days. After all, Betty "The Bookie," as she is known in Long Island for managing an OTB (Off Track Betting) facility, is very cool under fire. When her parlor was robbed at gun point not long ago, it was Betty who got the hero write-up in the papers for having the wherewithal to talk the gunman down and get him to leave the cowering staff and patrons, prone on the floor, alone. She gave him some reserve money, ushered him out the door and coolly called the cops. Certainly she can handle our three little angels.

My gig in Scottsdale is arranged by an attorney friend and neighbor Chris who asks me to present a talk on "upper extremity injuries in the work place" at a symposium for personal injury lawyers. With my expenses paid by the PIP organization, the minimal cost of bringing Deb along is a no brainer. We can finally take a mini vacation *sans enfants*. All my effort goes into convincing her that Betty is competent and that the airplane we are taking out to Arizona is not going to crash (leaving our kids orphaned).

Once there we get to relax between numerous check-up

phone calls back to the house (done strategically without the use of a cell phone) to be certain that the kids are okay and Grandma is still in control.

My talk to the attorneys is well received despite several of the slides being out of order in the carousel after the AV guy had an embarrassing mishap (years before Power Point). The rest of the vacation is spent eating and talking about the "Trial of the Century;" with everyone, including the "good 'ol boy" lawyers, expecting O.J. to be found guilty. Chris, a member of Arcola Golf Club (which he uses principally for networking, not being a golfer), loves telling the story of rubbing elbows with Simpson, a Club member due to the benevolence of the CEO of Hertz (himself a board-member of the Club). My mind replays the Hertz TV commercial with O.J. dashing through the airport terminal dodging and hurdling passengers in his way. Now, of course, their only black member (they don't take Jews either) was forced to resign for being such a naughty boy.

The cast of characters: Judge Lance Ito, prosecutors: Marcia Clark, Christopher Darden, Gil Garcetti: William Hodgman; defense attorneys: F. Lee Bailey, Johnnie Cochran, Alan Dershowitz, Robert Kardashian, Barry Scheck, Robert Shapiro, and Gerald Uelman; witnesses: Kato Kaelin, Mark Furman, Rosa Lopez, and Paula Barbieri are all household names and faces as the court room drama is played out like a daily soap opera on live TV. The fact that this is a true story about a black football superstar accused of killing his beautiful blond ex-wife and her unfortunate young handsome white male companion makes the media inundation too juicy to ignore. The only question most of us have is will he get life in prison or the death sentence?

Another news story saddens me as it does millions of baseball fans nationwide who revere Mickey Mantle as a genuine sports hero. The iconic character known for his athletic prowess, boy-like quality and outlandish carousing is back in the papers and on TV because he is dying of liver failure. The once handsome, powerful looking "Mick," whom I saw a few short years ago peddling the anti-inflammatory medicine Voltaren at an AAOS meeting in San Francisco, now appears emaciated and frightened as he faces liver transplant surgery. Naturally, the press has to publically opine that Mantle must have been moved to the top of the transplant list because of his celebrity. Regardless of the far left media's anger, the Mick gets a new liver but dies anyway. It is a very sad day for this diehard Yankees fan.

The Arizona trip is over in a heartbeat. Back home we find that Betty survived the kids and the kids survived Betty; and O.J. is still on trial. It is also nearly two years since Ken joined my practice as an employee and it is now time for us to talk about partnership.

Since business is good (with two very productive offices running full blast) and both Ken and I like and respect one another, it seems a no-brainer that we agree on a buy-in formula and sign the contract. Simple, until the wife, parents, friends, and lawyers are thrown into the mix. My promise that Ken will become a rich man as my partner is born out by the books, but he will have to write me a substantial check for the opportunity; sweat equity is simply not enough. "If you want to join any old practice you may get in on sweat equity, but we have something special here, like the Yankees—and if you want to join the Yankees you have to pay the price," I say unabashedly.

During the ensuing weeks I become acutely aware of two important things: Ken is more than hesitant to commit and I am really getting fed up with the way the operating room at the hospital is treating me. If my surgery is not the first case on the morning schedule it is common for the charge nurse to tell me, when I arrive for my scheduled time, that the surgeon ahead of me is running slower than planned and that I will simply have to wait for him to finish. This, of course, means that when the guy is finally done, the room still has to get turned over (cleaned) and my patient seen by the anesthesiologist before being brought into the O.R. The fact that I have several cases and the rest of the day booked with patients in the office is of no consequence to her (or to the hospital administration). And should I arrive even a minute tardy to the hospital I can expect to get angry glares and threats that my case was "almost bumped, so next time be on time!" The fact that as an individual I bring in the most surgical work in the entire department of orthopaedics (not to mention that I routinely have to deal with broken equipment) gives me no clout or sympathy whatsoever.

The light goes on! I decide to build my own ambulatory surgical center (attached to my new office); run by my own handpicked staff. No longer will I have to be at the mercy of others not on my payroll or spend precious time in the car traveling between my office and the hospital. Just as importantly, Ken will also have the same luxury should he choose to sign our partnership agreement. The $1 million price tag to build such a facility will be entirely on me.

Before I have a chance to spill my dream to Ken he asks that we meet in the hospital library for a private discussion about our deal. I sense that he is looking for neutral territory in which to break the news to me that he has decided to part ways.

Our talk is emotional and I can see how hard it is for Ken to tell me that his advisors think him an idiot to shell out big bucks to become my partner. I tell him that I understand; that we will remain friends and I will refer foot cases (his specialty) to him when I can. Despite having to run two offices and being firmly committed to my plan of building a surgical center, I somehow have no fear of the future (a feeling much akin to that of running off to India). Outside in the parking lot, just after we make a quick departure hug, I mention my intentions of building a surgical center. Though his eyes momentarily get big, nothing further is said.

The plan is for Ken to leave the practice and go out on his own after three more weeks in my office so that all loose ends are cleaned up and patients are not blindsided. But a few days later, while we are both seeing patients, our eyes somehow lock and we decide to sit down for another discussion.

That evening, after office hours Ken tells me that the surgical center idea sparked his interest and that he and Sharon (his wife) are reconsidering their gamble on me. I make it clear that the cost of building the ambulatory care center is entirely on my shoulders and we will make oodles of money; most of all, I promise that he will never regret his decision to stay. I also affirm the need for us to find another orthopaedist to help out with the patient load and give Ken someone who will eventually buy into the practice and support his equity.

Being a man of my word, we aggressively advertise for a new orthopaedist and quickly find Bill, a Princeton man, who signs an employment contract with us before the year is out.

***

The blizzard of '96 pummels the northeast. Philly gets over 30 inches of snow and it is similar in North Jersey. The kids miss more school than I remember missing in all my youth. Naturally they are ecstatic even though they are too young to be burdened with any real homework. They focus on making snowmen, snow forts, and having serious snowball fights. There is so much snow that the plow guys can't even make out where our driveway begins (and although they come several times during the night, I still have trouble getting out in the morning). I am happy for the kids, but hate the blasted white stuff to death.

It is all put into perspective, however, when a couple we know loses the younger of their two boys when he is run over by a snowplow right in front of their house. The driver apparently did not see the child playing in a snow drift. The gruesome story blindsides the entire community hard and both Debbie and I are deeply saddened for the family (who supposedly maintain the little one's room for years to come just as it was on the day of his passing) while, at the same time, feeling grateful that it is not our own personal tragedy. The loss of a child is not understandable or forgotten by those nearby and fills our dreams with the unthinkable: *it could happen to one of our own.*

Life goes on for the living. The surgical center is being constructed in a section of the building adjoining our office so that, once completed, Ken, Bill and I can easily walk between facilities to operate or see patients during office hours. No more driving to the hospital to be told that my case is delayed or to be treated indignantly by the O.R. staff if I show up a few minutes late. No more busted instruments that have no backups (the idea that a really good surgeon can operate with a knife and fork, like one of my arrogant colleagues often says, is total BS).

The intricacies of the practice are expanding quickly (three docs, two offices and soon a surgical center) so I know it is time to hire an administrator. The days of an office manager running the show are history. Maureen, an articulate outgoing woman working in the administrative office at the hospital becomes my target. She has been looking for advancement and, despite her boss warning me that she is just a glorified secretary, I give her the opportunity to join the "Yankees."

The build-out of the center involves a cast of characters starting with Harry the chain smoking, coffee-guzzling architect who is so demure that his recommendations are always suggestions and his bills are always presented with apologies. Big Bill Fink (who somehow reminds me of Big Mike Fink "King of the River" who battled Davy Crockett on the Walt Disney Show back in '55) is the general contractor. Despite his size he is gentle as a teddy bear, but still manages to piss off Art the plumber because of his lack of neatness. Art has worked for my dad for years and has been my plumber through several residential renovations including my first house in Franklin Lakes, my basement in Saddle River, and my house in Sea Girt on the Jersey Shore. He is looking out for me almost too well and can go on talking about almost anything (especially my mom's fruit salad flavored with the grenadine syrup). Danny the electrician is a reserved, cool dude who seems not to answer his pages unless I call personally. His obvious respect for me goes a long way towards keeping him on the job.

The actual construction takes less than six months, but the acquiring of building permits and eventual state certification takes almost as long. During all of this I am working hard at convincing Dolly, the nurse in charge of operating room supplies at the hospital, to join me and run my surgical center. Over the years she has been the only consistently reliable member of the hospital operating room hierarchy who has the magic to turn disaster into triumph. She is dedicated and well networked. If she takes the job of my O.R. supervisor I am confident that my worries about staffing, equipment, and daily operation will instantly evaporate.

I offer her double her present salary, but she is concerned about the survival of my new facility. I make it clear that we as a team cannot possibly fail. Originally from the Philippines, and not into baseball, she still gets my analogy to the New York Yankees and (with some convincing from her husband Albert) decides to take the plunge. And so Garden State Surgical Center is born.

Opening day is grand. All our staff and family members, local dignitaries, representatives from Chase who financed the project, the contractors, and referring docs wander through the shining new state-of-the-art center munching on hors d'oeuvres and sipping wine. While my kids run around the place I give a speech acknowledging all those who helped make this day possible. And then my eighty-four year old dad asks to be heard. He is not comfortable speaking in front of a crowd, but is so moved by my success that he needs to tell everyone who will listen. It is a moment that I will always cherish; to see my father bursting with pride because of my accomplishment is more fulfilling than any adventure I managed to survive. I am positively overcome by the moment (which will be even more meaningful to me several months later when he suddenly passes away). He mentions the time I ran off, leaving medical school behind and how worried he and Mom were for me. "Had we only known at the time that this day would come…" suddenly choking back the tears, overcome with emotion, he simply comes over to me with a big hug while his audience applauds.

Paul, my first partner, is not there. Although many of my orthopaedic colleagues were invited to the opening, few show (not surprisingly). Paul has an excuse other than jealousy; he is terminally ill with lung cancer, diagnosed months ago. Although he stopped smoking (to my knowledge) back in 1983 when he took ill with his lung infection, the big "C" finally caught up with him. After hearing of his plight I make an effort to visit with him at his home and during his radiation treatments in the hospital. As always, we talk of the Yankees and the great season they are having. We are both skeptical of the new manager, Joe Torre, who does not come with a great managerial resume. But somehow the club is winning despite their superstar Don Mattingly having retired at the end of last season with a chronic back injury. In a dark moment Paul says he hopes to live to see our team make it to the World Series. My encouragement apparently falls on deaf ears; Paul does not make it to October.

At the first World Series game my son Eric and I are sitting in the upper deck along the first base line at Yankee

Stadium. Andy Pettitte is getting rocked and as a misty rain starts to fall, with the Yanks down 7-0 in the seventh, I suggest that we go home. "Come on Dad," Eric pleads, "they're going to pull it out. It's not over 'til it's over." With most of the 56,000+ fans emptying out the stands we make our way down to the box seats just behind the Atlanta Braves dugout. My eight-year-old son is right; we can't bail on our beloved Yankees. So we make it to the end of the game and leave to Frank Sinatra's *New York, New York*. The final score is 12-1.

Even after losing the second game 4-0 and having to play the next three at Atlanta-Fulton County Stadium, the Bronx Bombers somehow win the next four in a row and become World Champs for the first time since 1978. Watching a teary-eyed Torre on the post-game interview on TV I think of Paul and wonder if his spirit is thinking that we both should have had more faith in old Joe than we did.

Sports-wise my big regret during 1996 is not having taken the family down to Atlanta, Georgia for the Games of the XXVI Olympiad where Muhammad Ali lit the Olympic torch to open the Games; and Americans Michael Johnson, Carl Lewis, and Andre Agassi won gold along with the U.S. women's soccer team. But then, on July 27th a bomb went off in the Centennial Olympic Park injuring 111 and killing one; so Debbie trumps my regret by being utterly grateful that we did not attend.

CHAPTER 29

A Gentle Man

By the start of 1997 the family is healthy, my marriage is sound, the practice is rolling along, and the new surgical center looks like it will pay for itself in no time. Just when things can't be better I get blind-sided by a late night telephone call from Harvey, a dear longtime friend of my parents.

It is nearly midnight on January 21st, Debbie and I are tucked away under the covers when the phone rings. Deb is always the designated answerer so she picks up and after a brief interlude hands me the phone. I know I am not on call, but the life of a busy doctor is filled with off-hour emergencies so I assume this is one more until Deb says with concern, "It's Harvey in Florida. Is there something wrong?"

"Bobby," Harvey says in a morose voice, "I am so sorry to tell you that Dad has just passed away."

Exploding with anger I leap out of bed and scream, "No way! This is bullshit! He is not dead!" Debbie is speechless (a rare occurrence, but she knows I am talking about my dad and she feels every bit of my pain). Harvey quietly waits for me to regain some semblance of composure and then gently proceeds to tell me what happened.

Dad had been busy all day driving Aunt Marsha, his younger sister, to Miami from Boca to visit a doctor for treatment of a sarcoma (soft tissue cancer) in her leg. As a physician and responsible sibling Dad accompanied her in order to help her better understand her diagnosis and treatment options. After a long emotional day, he drove her back up to Boca and discussed things with her husband Harold. By evening Dad was exhausted (though he never complained) and changed into pajamas for an early night. While sitting on the bed he mentioned to Mom that he did not feel well and was going to get checked out in the local emergency room. Hearing this (from such a stoic guy) and noticing that he had wet the bed made her rush to call an ambulance. But Dad, always calm in the face of disaster, insisted that he was going to drive there himself. Incredulously, Mom gave in and allowed him to drive them both to the E.R.

At the Boca Raton Community Hospital this elderly man presents to the triage nurse with a complaint that he doesn't feel well. He is changed into a gown, placed on a stretcher and wheeled away from my mother who is directed to sit in the waiting room. Completely out of character, Mom actually does what she is told and does not raise a fuss. This is a woman who cannot go to a restaurant and wait for seating without standing over the hostess to expedite the readiness of her table. As the time goes by she simply sits (in what I believe was a stupor) before hearing a code called and personnel rushing down the hall in the direction Dad was taken. At 11:45 PM she becomes a widow and is being consoled by Harvey and Esther Schoenfeld.

Throughout this acrimonious story I am wedged between the wall and floor completely drained and unable to overcome gravity. When Mom and I speak we are both heartbroken over our loss so there is little coherence to our conversation. I cry that I did not have a chance to say good-bye and she simply responds by saying, "Irving, oh Irving, how could you leave me?"

Calling my sister to tell her of Dad's passing gives me some momentary direction; and her commiseration and pragmatism gives me the desire to emulate our father and stare down the tragedy. Breaking the news to my kids is hard because they have never seen me cry before. Eric asks who will take him golfing if Pop-Pop is no longer around. Stephanie wonders if Nana will still come to watch her dance without Pop-Pop. And my dear Morgan, who is only three, cries hysterically because she can't really remember her Pop-Pop.

In the Jewish faith we make every effort to bury our dead without delay. So it is my task to see to it that Dad's remains are brought back up to New Jersey and funeral arrangements made promptly. All the while I am seething about the circumstances of my dad's death and anxious to find out more details. Even the cause of death is simply listed as "probable acute myocardial infarction" (heart attack) and the fact that he entered the E.R. *hours* before the unsuccessful code was called is very disturbing.

So after I bury the man responsible for my becoming a doctor (a gift that gave me the knowledge of the human body, how to treat its ills, the joy of ministering to people, and the ability to make a good living) I set off for Florida to investigate his death.

On the plane I cannot help thinking about how fortunate it was that my dad, a Great Depression survivor, got to see my economic success, which, to him, meant that his Bobby achieved security. He taught me to be frugal (to the point of eating a yogurt all the way down to the bottom of the container, and respecting others who did likewise) and to put my money into my house because that is where my family and I spend most of our time here on earth. His pragmatism rubbed off on Helaine and me, but drove Mom crazy. She always fancied herself the bohemian type who wanted to splurge and be adventurous. No doubt it was her gene pool (along with drugs) that was responsible for my rebellious/exploratory years.

The fact that Dad was a doctor, who wore a jacket and tie just about everywhere, was well-respected in the community and, along with his fellow physicians, seemed to enjoy a certain level of affluence (security) made me want to be a doctor more than anything else. Of course TV shows like *Ben Casey* (Vince Edwards) and *Dr. Kildare* (Richard Chamberlain) had some influence on me. But emulating, and yes, surpassing Dad's accomplishments have always been my driving force. Now he is gone; so abruptly that I did not have the chance to say good-bye, and I am furious!

Even before I go to our newly constructed house in Woodfield Country Club in Boca, I head to the Boca Raton Community Hospital and find the Administrator in Charge. The fact that I am a physician helps expedite my obtaining records of Dad's emergency room visit on the night of January 21st, just six days before his 85th birthday.

Going through them word by word is agonizing, especially as I begin to realize that he was not actually seen by a physician until the code was called some two hours after he was checked in. Since our religion frowns on any desecration of bodily remains no autopsy was permitted. Therefore I have to piece together Dad's previous medical history with what Mom remembers were his complaints on the eve of his passing. The hospital medical records are of no help in this regard because aside from his chief complaint of "not feeling well" and the recording of near normal vital signs for his age little else was entered until the code began.

Believing that he died of a dissecting aortic aneurysm rather than a heart attack and furious over the lack of attention he received until it was too late; I discuss the case with an attorney friend of mine down there. Although nothing will bring Dad back (and I am loath to bring a medical malpractice suit against "my own kind") my anger drives me to force those, who saw his death as just another elderly part-time Floridian dying of natural causes, to know that he was someone's father, husband, and a fellow health care provider. I want them to remember that night—and worrying over a lawsuit might just get their attention.

What I find out on the legal end is that the death of an octogenarian does not garner the same level of interest as that of a more viable human being (with the death of a child bringing the most attention). After weeks of investigation, accusations, and threats I come to the realization that I have done all that I prudently can to make my feelings heard and bring closure to my agonizing loss. Helaine wisely reminds me that being energetic and productive on the day that you die is not all that bad. She remembers how Grandpa

Phil, Dad's father, died at age eighty-one while playing Gin Rummy at his country club. We always said that was a great way to leave this earth (rather than being infirmed and causing misery for everyone at the end). "So you didn't get a chance to say good-bye," she counsels "he spared you *both* that torment." There it is again; that pragmatism she inherited from Dad, making total sense.

The next job is seeing that Mom gets by without her mate of 60+ years. Sure she can cook and take care of the house, but not knowing how to write a check or put gas in the car is not good. So the process of being certain that she can get by begins. Luckily she has friends who have gone through this before. You cannot reach your eighties without knowing others who have become widowed and can empathize with your grief. Edna C., Esther, Harvey, Mina, and Louise all look in on her down in Florida and later when she and they return to New Jersey for the summer. Everyone puts up with her near constant sighs and incessant, "Irving, oh Irving, why did you leave me?" mantra.

I am struck by my mother's guilt for having often asked (demanded, at times) Dad to be different than the guy he was. "Come on, Irv, you move so slowly." "Why do you spend so much time in the bathroom?" "You have to be more ambitious." "Let's take more trips; we're not going to live forever." "It's time to retire; you've practiced long enough."

Now that he is no longer here she has no one to nudge; no one who simply replies, "Edna, please." The sweet, gentle, handsome man with whom she eloped, well over half a century ago, is now just a bunch of memories; some of which break her heart because she did not always appreciate his subdued, tender manner. The fact that he was such a good guy; that he was her only lover, makes coping with her sudden loss daunting. Aware of the high mortality rate for the elderly who suffer the loss of a longtime spouse, I fear that Mom might pad that statistic.

With my mind easily wandering, I am ready fodder for another one of Debbie's surprise parties; this time for my fiftieth birthday. Staged at our house I am happily ambushed and grateful to find that my mother (who has come up from Florida a couple of weeks early) is in on the celebration. She looks good and breaks a smile for the first time in months. In just ten days she will turn eighty-four and saves me the trip of flying down to surprise her.

While turning forty and forty-five seemed like proud middle-age milestones, fifty has an ominous feel. The number in terms of years connotes the beginning of old age; or at least it always had. I remember my dad's fiftieth birthday party (when I was fifteen) and associate it with him asking me to pull out a gray hair he found on the top of his head.

My fear that fifty is indeed the start of being old is eventually borne out by my first episode of (what will become intermittent, though chronic) low back pain when I awkwardly lift a heavy house plant to move it outside for watering. But by far the biggest sign that I am entering a more precarious stage of life comes with the sudden passing of J.G.

He, too, turned fifty this year, but just six days after his birthday dropped dead. Though he had certainly gained weight and had a family history of heart disease, I always thought of him (and myself) as a youngster, exploring the world and having a blast. His passing is excruciating for me;

I hardly know how to express my sadness to his wife and two young children. I arrive at the wake shortly after J.G.'s old college roommate Al (and his full secret service posse) departs. Sorry to have missed him, it means a lot to me that Al took the time out of his governmental duties to pay tribute to his old friend, who was a really great guy.

***

Mom decides to spend the winter with her snowbird friends down in Boca Raton. She keeps the villa that she and Dad had so meticulously decorated, proudly entertained guests in, and, of course, where she and he spent their last days together. Our visit during the holidays finds her lonely, but actually better than I expected. Not much of a golfer, she manages to fill up her day with socializing, playing cards, and shopping.

The lake out in the backyard is stocked with fish and she always has fishing poles and bait (pieces of hot dog) for the kids. Eric is particularly distraught by the fact that Pop-Pop, who got him interested in golf a couple of years before, is no longer around to take him to the course. Having consistently said that I would never waste my time with such a goofy game, I consent to take him to the club's course as long as he promises to play some tennis with me afterwards. Up north the kid plays all the "manly" sports (football, baseball and basketball) that I grew up with and, despite my joining Edgewood Country Club (at a discount under my father's old membership) I am confident that my son's fascination with golf will be fleeting.

We make two trips down to Florida this year. The second is in February during school's winter break. We love our house in Woodfield, but spend most of our time visiting Nana (Mom) who just beams when she is around the kids. I only wish she wouldn't encourage Eric's golf game so much. I am, however, really happy (and relieved) to see that my mother is getting along so well on her own. The discussions I have with Helaine and Debbie about moving Mom into an assisted living facility seem moot.

In March my comfort level is completely upended by the phone call from (you guessed it) Harvey who tells me that Mom hurt her hip when she was getting out of her friend Mina's car. Apparently, the car rolled just enough for her to lose her balance and fall. She sustained a subcapital hip fracture and will need surgery. Because this is a routine operation I simply tell the orthopaedist (a guy with a good reputation) to proceed, and that I will be down as soon as I can get a flight.

When I arrive in the morning, Mom and her post-operative hip x-rays look fine. But now comes the arduous aftercare: transfer to a rehab facility; finding a permanent assisted living home for her; and, sadly, selling the villa. This makes all my other worldly projects fall well down on the priority list. It is positively startling the way this incident has suddenly put the brakes on my entrepreneurship freight train. With Helaine and Debbie's efforts we manage to wend our way through the myriad extended care, independent living, and assisted living centers in South Florida. After several weeks we get Mom situated in Brighton Gardens while I sell the villa. It angers me to no end when a prospective buyer criticizes the décor. I tell the realtor to get rid of him; no way will he get my folks place—whatever the offer!

Unfortunately, once her ties to Boca Lago (her Florida community) are broken Mom loses interest in making new friends. So we move her back up to Jersey hoping to ignite some sort of spark.

The Classic Residence by Hyatt in Teaneck is billed as a high-end facility with both independent and assisted-living accommodations. It is physically much better than anything we found in Florida. Mom unabashedly points out that she is surrounded by "old people," many of whom are well into their nineties. Fortunately several are acquaintances of hers from Fair Lawn and Paterson, who after many, many years of living have suffered a similar fate—old age and widowhood.

This final chapter, though not in a dreaded nursing home so reviled by many—especially Mom—is still a major loss of independence. Meals are served at specific times, the rooms are all similar, and there are rules that each resident is expected to follow. She still has her car (a Lincoln Continental that I helped her pick out last year down in Boca), but when we celebrate her eighty-fifth birthday on April 7th, I can't help but think that in the not too distant future, that last link to self-sufficiency, too, will be taken from her.

I, as well, am losing the independence that is inherent with autonomous parents. My level of responsibility to my mother is no longer one of performance for admiration, but is now that of caretaker and "parent." I am reminded of the way I saw those in the orient interact with their elderly parents and grandparents; a profound reverence that seemed so foreign to me then and now still does, because as much as I try to embrace old age, I have been taught that it is a stage of deterioration rather than liberation. Very sad, but something I know is a major failing of our western culture.

The good news is that Mom ambulates well with just a cane, is still extremely alert, and, for the present, even goes shopping in her Lincoln for the other, less mobile "girls." As a new comer, with more energy (and better handwriting) than most, she is elected secretary of the Residents' Advisory Board. For the time being, organized activities like bingo are beneath her; a sign that she intends to hold onto her independence for a while.

CHAPTER 30

Take My Breath Away

With Mom squared away, I put my entrepreneurial hat back on and recruit a new orthopaedist who just completed his hand fellowship with Dr. Malone, a heavy-hitter in New York City. Steve is excellent and because of his recent association with Malone gets thrown some B celebrity patients.

Shannon "The Cannon" Briggs is a heavyweight boxing contender who has a painful wrist. His up coming fight at Trump Casino in Atlantic City against the ageless George Foreman is for the Linear Heavyweight Championship of the World. Steve gets ringside seats because he must tend to Brigg's bum wrist. He asks if I would like to bring my son Eric and sit ringside with him. Youbetcha!

The plan is to stay overnight at Steve's condo in Brigantine, a suburb of A.C. because the main event won't get going until around midnight. With Debbie's approval and strict admonition to "WATCH THE BOY!" we drive down.

The night is packed with stars, including The Donald himself. My ten-year-old Eric is absolutely fascinated, especially with all the famous boxers around. He is a sports freak and did his homework. He gets autographs from Ernie Shavers, Roy Jones, Jr., and a picture with Larry Holmes. After the second preliminary fight is over I turn to Eric to see if he wants something to eat. He is not beside me!

As my pulse quickens I feel sickening warmth overtake my body. I frantically go up and down the aisle calling "Eric!" "Eric!" I slip while climbing up to the top of bleachers, to survey the area, as my sweaty hands give way. The stain on my pants from my bloody shin means nothing. Near the point of dehydration and full blown panic, I find the ring announcer and plead with him to page my son. The announcement is barely audible above the din of the massive crowd. I want to die because of my stupidity and fear that Debbie will make death seem enjoyable if she ever finds out.

The nearly fifteen minutes of cataclysmic fright seems like days. Then, "Dad," accompanied by a tug on my pants, "Look what I got." In one inexplicable motion I pick the boy up and pin him against the side of the bleachers. "Eric, where the hell were you?! Don't ever do that again; you hear me?!" And as I smother him in a hug he mutters, "I was just in the fighters' locker room getting autographs—see?"

I don't remember anything about the championship, but I am told that Briggs defeated Foreman. I am too preoccupied with trying to figure out whether to tell Debbie what happened or maybe to just keep my mouth shut. The latter seems best.

Meanwhile, Dr. Malone has a falling out with his partner in the City and decides to make Steve a "once in a lifetime" job offer helping him treat "A" level celebrities like Patrick Ewing of the Knicks. So, facing the inevitable, we elect not to enforce the two year employment contract Steve signed with us and simply wish him the best, dancing with the stars.

Under duress, we manage rather quickly to sign another hand surgeon, and move on to address the partnership buy-in of our young Dr. Bill who has already successfully put in his two years of employment. He is given the same option as Dr. Ken—to pay a fair price for shares in the practice. The only difference is that he will also have to buy shares in the surgical center if he wishes to own part of that entity as well. Ken, of course, did not have that condition because the surgical center was not yet built when he was up for partnership. Although this had all been discussed with Bill when he signed the employment contract he is not pleased, so the discussions drag on for several months. The numbers never change and are exactly the same dollar amount as Ken's buy-in, with exception of the very productive surgical center.

After far too many long, wearisome meetings going over the same numbers ad nauseam, I find myself sitting with Bill and Ken very late one night after office hours. My mind wanders to the mindless quibbling that went on between doctors during the planning stages of the Mahwah medical center; the distrust, avarice, and pugnacious bickering that made it a miracle that we actually got around to putting up a building. At that moment I lose my patience with Bill's impertinence. "Enough!" I moan, rising from my chair. "Go off on your own if you think you can do better." I apologize to Ken, knowing that to him Bill represents security, and I leave the office.

Before reaching home my car phone rings. It is Bill who is now apologizing. He wants back in and is sorry for pushing us too hard. "I only wanted to get the best deal I could," he squeals. *Exactly! What happened to appreciating a good business opportunity and to being a team player?* I tell him I'll confer with Ken in the morning and inform him of our decision then. The next day Bill, as is Ken, is relieved to know that he has just joined the "Yankees."

Speaking of the Yankees, 1998 is a miracle year. Not only does Mark McGwire break Roger Maris' thirty-seven year old single season home run record (by cracking number 62 off of Cubs' Steve Trachsel at Busch Stadium on September 8th), the buffed freak of nature goes on to hit an absurd 70 round trippers (all the while nearly being matched by another pumped up Adonis, Sammy Sosa). In the meantime, the Bronx Bombers are cleaning up the American League with 114 regular season wins and go on to streak through the post season finishing (by sweeping the San Diego Padres in the World Series) with the best record in the 123 years of Major League Baseball history, 125-50. Although it is an exasperating year for the Schultz family matriarch and her loved ones, it is a miracle year for our Yankees. The juxtaposition of personal strife and my elation as a die-hard sports fan makes me re-evaluate the notion that professional athletes are overpaid. *What price escapism?*

The end of the year is football season. On the way to a tailgate party at Giant Stadium with my son, I get a call from Debbie who asks if I read the newspaper before I left. "Only the sports section," I reply, so she reads an article to me about a doctor who is being accused of criminal sexual contact with a female patient. Of course, this is never good to hear, but then she says, "And do you know who the doctor is?" I tell her, "No clue;" and then she hits me with, "Ray—." *No way!* I am flabbergasted.

Ray is a physiatrist who is a consultant for the Giants football team. He is a good friend and refers plenty of patients to me. He is good looking, charming and married to a beautiful woman. They have two lovely little girls. There must be a mistake or maybe he is being set-up by a forlorn patient. I realize that such dreadful accusations could happen to any of us, so from this point on I make sure I have a woman staff member with me in the exam room every time I see a female patient. It is a burden, but if this can happen to Ray, it can happen to anyone. I can't take any chances.

***

In 1984 the book *Computers in Crisis* written by Jerome and Marilyn Murray raised the "Year 2000 Problem" or "Millennium Bug" issue. Since computers store years with only two digit numbers, what on earth will happen when 97, 98, 99 becomes 00? Will the software interpret it to mean the year 1900 instead of 2000? Incorrect date comparisons could produce incorrect data, incorrect conclusions, and incorrect results leading to failure in utilities, telecommunications and other crucial infrastructure technologies. According to John Hamre, Deputy Secretary of Defense, "The Y2K problem is the electronic equivalent of the El Nino and there will be nasty surprises around the globe."

The acronym "Y2K," attributed to David Eddy, a Massachusetts programmer who sent an email on June 12, 1995 regarding what was then being called CDC (Century

Date Change) or FADL (Faulty Date Logic), is catchy and really takes off. McGraw-Hill reissued *Computer Crisis* under the name *The Year 2000 Computing Crisis* in 1996 and by 1999 even my little kids are refusing to come out from under the covers. Me, personally, I'm just figuring out how to send an email so, *why should I worry about something I have absolutely no handle on?*

Debbie, on the other hand, is totally freaked out since we will be coming back from our annual holiday vacation in Boca Raton on New Year's Day. She has completely bought into the media hype (and for all I know, she and they may be right), but what can I do? She won't take drugs and or accept my logic (to "relax and go with the flow") so the question remains whether or not we should skip the vacation. I am already paying for upkeep on the house in Woodfield Country Club, along with full golf membership dues (so Eric and I can be treated like kings when we go to the course). The club's New Year's Eve celebration is like no other; and I love the warm weather smack in the middle of winter. Debbie knows how I feel. I know how she feels. We spend most of 1999 "discussing" our options.

As the year unfolds the newspapers are filled with daily updates on the doctor accused of sexually assaulting his female patients. At first there was one patient; now they are coming out of the woodwork with several apparently stepping forward to press charges. The female prosecutor is very explicit in her descriptions of the goings on in Dr. Ray's office. At some point she even makes it public that one of the victims was wired and that the doctor is heard saying, "I know this is wrong, but I just can't help myself." As the tide turns against Ray I learn that he has agreed to temporarily stop seeing patients. His two partners will run the practice while he tends to his legal woes.

As more concrete evidence is brought to light I am absolutely dumbfounded by the story and find it incomprehensible that an educated guy like Ray, who has it all, can harbor such demons. During several telephone conversations, initiated by Ray (as the referring physician of patients he is still sending my way), he never sounds contrite. Only once does he say that things are not looking good for him and that he apologizes for "letting me down." There is no further clarification.

On December 3rd Ray is arrested and agrees to give up his license to practice medicine in New Jersey and New York. He is about to be sentenced to prison for up to one year!

The good news is that the economy is doing great (or so it seems). The Dow Jones Industrial Average has risen more than 10% this year, closing over 10,000 at the end of March and above 11,000 on May 3rd. Guys in the surgeons' lounge brag about making 30% on their investments while others counter that even a chimpanzee can do that by throwing darts at the stock listings and buying the equities above and below where the darts land. The economic boom, together with my state of high productivity (coupled with monetary rewards from the surgical center and partnership buy-ins), puts me in the annual income bracket of an NFL quarterback. Not ready to sit back and relax, or chance becoming a pawn in the storm of managed care control over medical practitioners' reimbursement, I forge ahead with expansion.

We open a physical therapy center in the suite next to our surgical center in order to capture income from some of those patients we have been sending for therapy elsewhere. When our three year contract with the group of anesthesiologists who have been staffing our surgical center is up, I hit them with an entirely new proposal: we will pay them a set annual fee for their services, but we are taking over the billing and collection for anesthesia services. In other words, we are creating a new entity, Fair Lawn Anesthesia; take it or leave it. They leave it, so we find another qualified anesthesia group that is happy to collect $325,000 per year with no overhead for staffing our center from 7:30 AM to 4:30 PM, five days a week. It turns out to be a homerun! Fair Lawn Anesthesia collections prove to be solidly in seven figures annually.

And then there is the wooing from several internal medicine and general practice groups in Hoboken, New Jersey for us to open up a satellite office down there. We have been told for the past couple of years that the area is sorely in need of an up-to-date high powered orthopaedic group to serve its growing community. Ken and I figure, why not? So we make several trips down there and find a gentrified yuppie town of historical significance (beyond Frank Sinatra's roots), overlooking New York's financial district and jam packed with extraordinary restaurants. Being just thirty minutes by train or car (depending on traffic) from the Fair Lawn office, what's not to like? So after several months of due diligence we find (and open) an office across the street from the Clam Broth House just around the corner from the tram.

We are on a roll. With three offices and several ancillary medical services to keep us busy we are again in need of more orthopaedists and health care providers. Ah growth!

Only in America!

While tasting the American Dream I also feast on another fabric of our culture: organized activities for kids from affluence. Eleven year old Eric plays on the Saddle River / Allendale towns' baseball, basketball, and football teams. Nine year old Stephanie dances six days a week at Robin Horneff's Performing Arts Center in Waldwick. (Robin was the leader of the "Golddiggers" who danced around Dean on the old Dean Martin Variety Show back in the late '60s and early '70s, so how bad could she be, right?) Five year old Morgan doesn't know what she wants and hasn't shown any prodigious talent as yet, but piano and dance lessons seem like good starting points for now.

Debbie and I are really into the organized, competitive sports scene with Eric. Sitting in the bleachers with the other kids' parents and whooping it up is awesome. My only regret is that my son is the youngest in his grade and still a bit smaller than his teammates. Our decision to have him start kindergarten at Wandell Elementary School just two weeks after his fifth birthday was based primarily on his intellect, with little concern given to his maturity level. I take full responsibility for that one. (The lack of physical maturity on the athletic field is one thing, but hanging out with older boys in high school and college will be quite another issue.)

In any event, Eric is athletic (thank God!) and holds his own. His eye-hand coordination is good so he excels at baseball. He pitches and plays short stop and can hit. While Debbie cowers in the stands when he is on the mound or at the plate, I remain cool and confident (even when he walks the first two batters in an inning). He is really good at my favorite sport, so I am devastated when he tells me that hitting a baseball is interfering with his golf swing.

Joining Edgewood Country Club was supposed to give the Schultz family that social pizzazz; swimming, tennis, dining, and yes, some golf for Eric; but the kid really got into golf. How many times did he beg me to take him out on the course? I'd get in a cart to make him happy, and read a journal or the sports section of the paper, while he tore up the turf. "Come on Dad, hit the ball with me," he would plead. And when I tried, I looked like a fool running the ball along the ground while he would howl with laughter. Enough humiliation; I finally signed up for swing lessons. *Damned if I am going to be mocked by that little punk!*

Meanwhile, Debbie is into Eric's golfing thing (what with Tiger Woods on the scene) and gets him regular lessons. By the end of the summer she starts booking him into junior golf tournaments. All I can do at this point is work on my own game (or at least get one).

We converted over to a minivan four years ago when baby Morgan came along (making a car with less than five separate seats and little room for junk impractical). My Porsche and S500, being off limits to the wrecking crew, keep my personal suave, dashing self-image intact. Debbie's absorption into motherhood and her exclusive world of "Ericstephaniemorgan" has absolutely no adverse effect on me (the other human being in the house). How on earth could it? I who have lived more than half a century, traveled around the world, experienced exotic cultures, operate on broken bones, and sowed my oats many times before succumbing to marriage and fatherhood am clearly above such mundane egotism.

Being convinced about all the above, I am grateful that

being the other human being in the house is my cart blanche for sitting back and doing my own thing. My own thing, of course, is working my ass off and growing the empire.

The vague memory of having become a doctor to get "M.D." after my name in order to facilitate getting my writings published is rekindled when Ben, a young patient of mine from Fair Lawn, gives me a screenplay to read that he wrote called *Boiler Room*. This well-written script is so reminiscent of the 1987 movie blockbuster *Wall Street* (written and directed by Oliver Stone, starring Michael Douglas and Charlie Sheen) that I doubt it will make it to the silver screen. I certainly recognize Ben's talent and congratulate him on his effort. He tells me that he has been working on it for the past couple of years and is in the process of peddling the script. I wish him luck, realizing that the big bad world of Hollywood is not easily broken into.

CHAPTER 31

The New Millennium: A Spacey Odyssey

Yes. Yes, I know that "The New Millennium" should begin with the year 2001, but I do not want to throw off those who simply associate the words "New Millennium" with the number "2000."

The first day of the last year of the second millennium A.D. (after all, being Jewish I could be calling it the middle of the fifth millennium based on The Old Testament) begins with Debbie actually taking a Xanax. Yes, we made the trip down to Boca the day before Christmas and are risking "all-hell-breaking-loose" by flying back to New Jersey on Y2K!

The New Year's Eve celebration, as billed, was not to be missed. All ten different venues at Woodfield Country Club (known for its high-end food and entertainment) were well worth whatever angst the next day's air travel might bring. Just sitting there watching the outdoor laser show and describing the food (including the rotating suckling pig on a spit) to my dear friend Ari back in Jersey, who called to exchange New Year best wishes, made whatever happens when 2000 pops up on the calendar (including a major computer glitch) superfluous as far as I'm concerned.

The good news is that the Y2K disaster never happens (either because enough attention to computer upgrading around the world was accomplished in advance or computers are smarter than we give them credit...Hal from *2001: A Space Odyssey* (1968) certainly was). Debbie sleeps the whole way home.

***

In early February I receive a hand delivered invitation for Debbie and me to attend the exclusive, premier screening of the new feature film *Boiler Room at* the Ziegfeld Theater in New York City. Apparently Ben and his agent not only succeeded in selling the movie to Hollywood, but my young screenwriter friend actually got to direct the film as well. To say the least, this smooth talking, talented dude is making history in a very tough arena. We all recognize that writing and directing one's first feature film is monumental. His appearance on the front page of the theater and leisure section of the *New York Times* is a testimony to his instant success. The movie itself is drop dead and proves me wrong when I read the screenplay and wrote it off as simply being a redo of *Wall Street*. It makes me hungry to rekindle my own creative writing efforts.

But with a booming practice and three offices to cover, I see no time for writing until we hire at least another orthopaedist. Unfortunately, Tobena, our new hand surgeon who replaced Steve, is turning out to be a scatterbrain who can't even manage to show up on time for office hours or surgery. After a zillion attempts to right the guy, we conclude that he is incorrigible and decide not to offer him partnership.

The search for another hand surgeon begins, but in the meantime we find Ron who has just completed a pediatric orthopaedic fellowship in Florida. Though a pleasant, unintimidating chap (who fits the role of a kiddies' doctor to a tee) Ron does not exude confidence and, quite honestly, makes me concerned that he may not have the chutzpah to hold up his end of the bargain. And who knew that when the cold, dark days of winter in New Jersey strike, Ron would get bummed out without his Florida sunshine? Nevertheless we tolerate his moodiness, anticipating remission of his depression come spring.

Mom is tiring of the Classic Residence and being around so many old people. It is clearly aging her spirit and I can see that she is losing her edginess. Helaine agrees, but accepts the apparent slow demise much better than I. I give my sister a lot of credit: she drives four hours each way from Bethesda, Maryland to see mother every other weekend (missing only because of inclement weather).

After noticing Mom's slowing reflexes behind the wheel of her Lincoln, we painfully decide that it is best for her to give up driving. Mom barely puts up a fight and sadly relinquishes her last bit of independence. I feel like an ogre—a mean parent punishing a naughty child for not being more than she can be. Helaine sees it as preventing our mother from doing damage herself or someone else on the road.

The spring brings a mixed bag. Moody Ron is indeed in

better spirits and has found himself a girlfriend. Good news. On the other hand, my son Eric tells me that he simply can no longer play both baseball and tournament golf. The plane for hitting a baseball is so different from his golf swing that it is ruining both sports for him. The little eleven-year-old pipsqueak informs me that this will be his last season playing baseball.

Prophetically, it is actually a Godsend for his coach that Eric is willing to play through the season. I make it a point to attend all the ball games and as many practices as I can because I love the game (and especially enjoy watching Eric play). So during one of the practices I notice that Paul, his coach, is popping Tums like they are M&Ms. Not having seen him do that before I ask if he feels all right. His pallor is evident and his pulse feels thready, so I insist that we go to the hospital, which is just down the street from the playing field. Initially he is reluctant but minutes later loses his machismo and comes with me.

I call ahead to the E.R. and arrange for a cardiac consult. It turns out that thirty-something, athletic Paul is having a heart attack. He is cathed that very hour and the coronary artery blockage is opened with balloon dilatation right there on the table. Paul's heart damage is kept to a minimum and Eric is rewarded with more pitching time than ever before.

But after a lovely spring and summer in the stands with the rest of the Saddle River/Allendale parents I watch my boy pitch his very last game. It is only seven innings long, and each and every out brings me closer to the truth: Eric is a golfer not a baseball player. Debbie will miss cutting up oranges into slices and bringing them to the games. She will miss the hooting and hollering from the stands with the other fanatic parents, but she will not miss the game of baseball because it is boring. She finds the more dignified game of golf with its preppy clothes and prudent rules preferable. Besides, she doesn't have to watch her precious boy slide into home with that big, bad, heavily armored catcher blocking the plate.

Of course, Eric is a huge sports' fan. I raise all my kids to root for the Yankees, Giants, and Knicks. But somehow things go terribly wrong one day when my son starts screaming for John Elway to throw a touchdown pass against the Giants while we are sitting in the stands at Giant Stadium in the Meadowlands. During my horror the guy sitting next to me says, "Hey buddy, can you shut that kid up?" "It's a free country," I fire back, nevertheless fully appreciating a fellow Giant fan's angst at my kid's blasphemous indiscretion. Frustrated, the guy pulls out a twenty and says, "Here, tell the kid to go get something to eat… and take his sweet time." This positive reinforcement for rooting against the Giants no doubt seals the deal. But just how the kid becomes a die-hard J-E-T-S, Jets, Jets, Jets fan is beyond my understanding. (Must be some sort of masochistic trait he inherited from Deb's side of the gene pool.)

The evening of October 21st is a dream come true. It is game one of the World Series between the New York Yankees and the New York Mets (the first Subway Series since 1956). Eric (a deeply committed Yankee fan, *praise be*) and I are in fabulous seats under the net behind home plate. This makes it the fourth in five years that we have been in Yankee Stadium to watch our Bronx Bombers in the Fall Classic. All the pomp and majesty never gets old, especially this year with our cross-town rivals as the enemy and Andy

Pettitte pitching against Al Leiter.

The game goes into extra innings when the Mets closer (Armando Benitez) gives up a one run lead in the bottom of the ninth. By the time the Yankees push the winning run across the plate in the 12th inning the place finally shoots its load, erupting like the entire series had just been won. No one wants to leave, especially Eric, but as we file out with the raucous crowd, our brains dancing to Sinatra singing *New York, New York*, a Newsday reporter asks Eric for an interview. "It doesn't get any better than this. We're going to win every game," he is quoted as saying. Well almost; the Mets do manage to take game three, with the Yanks winning their 26th World Championship right in the Mets fans' faces at Shea Stadium in game five.

***

Before the year is out, our practice administrator, Maureen, decides to run off with her new boyfriend forcing us to hustle to find a replacement. The interview process is intense and furious, but I am determined to hire a new administrator before the holidays. All the candidates remaining on the short list have previous experience managing a medical practice. Alex is the most computer savvy of the lot and the only male left. He has held the second spot on the list from the start, with one or two others leap-frogging over him for various reasons. When the dust clears, my partners and I decide to go with the guy (primarily because of his computer skills) despite concerns from women staffers that he may not be able to relate to our nearly all-female staff of over forty people. We shall see (it's all about living on the edge).

The true beginning of the 3rd millennium and the 21st century, 2001, for me is the title, in part, of my favorite movie of all time, *2001: A Space Odyssey.* Written by Stanley Kubrick and Arthur C. Clarke and directed by Kubrick this 1968 prescient epic was spectacular on and off acid. In 1991 the movie was deemed "culturally, historically, or aesthetically significant" by the United States Library of Congress and selected for preservation in their National Film Library. The flick somehow makes me more excited to have reached 2001 than I might otherwise have been.

Perhaps subconsciously, because I saw the film so many times, I envisioned the culmination of man's evolution to be in this year. Thank God it doesn't end here because clearly we still have a very long way to go. While computer HAL 9000 is now a wireless laptop, available in all colors, and has relatives that run everything from our cars to our phones, I like to think that it is still human intellect that controls our lives. Unfortunately, intelligence is often difficult to define as the year 2001 clearly demonstrates.

Ron (our pediatric orthopaedist) is again on shaky ground come the New Year with its cold short days and long frigid nights. His girlfriend has been a stabilizing factor and there are whispers of possible engagement the night of the Super Bowl party at Ron's apartment in Hackensack. The New York Giants have made a spectacular run (winning seven in a row after being 7-4) to surpass head coach Jim Fassel's guarantee to reach the playoffs. So despite Vegas heavily favoring the Baltimore Ravens, with the best defense in football, we dutifully sit around Ron's TV, munching on anything salty and praying for a miracle. Of course, as fate would have it, there is no divine intervention (Ravens 34,

Giants 7) and time would prove the same for Ron joining our partnership; no dice.

So having worked our way through Tobenna, Steve, and Ron we sorely need manpower to handle the patient load. Still enraptured with the concept that we should pursue docs with subspecialties other than our own we even consider David, an excellent hand surgeon with several years of experience in private practice down in Richmond, Virginia. He is actually the one who hooked me up with Ken (with whom he did some training in the past). David's wife is sick of Richmond and looking to move back up north. There is just one small catch: David is my brother-in-law, i.e. Debbie's brother.

Now, talent-wise David is top notch. What I am not sure about, however, is whether or not he, or any hand specialist for that matter, will be accepting of taking general orthopaedic call on a regular basis, as we all must do in the practice. Subspecialists concentrate on one part of the anatomy for a reason; they like it and feel comfortable treating that specific body part. What will happen after a year or two of having to see some people with back pain, or having to admit patients to the hospital with broken hips (even if the subsequent care is taken over by one of us later)? If the hand surgeon is unhappy then we simply won't take him on as a partner. But what if the guy is David, my brother-in-law? *Hmmm*…it could mean big trouble—family trouble!

So far, miraculously, Debbie and I have been able to work closely together in the office without any real blow-ups. Of course, her paramount job is and always has been raising the kids; but she is, nevertheless, very tied into the office.

After much thought, sleepless nights, and gut wrenching conversations we (Deb, Ken, and I) elect to pass on David (despite my strong feeling that he would aggressively help to grow the practice and is a cool guy to be around). Ross, who is just completing the prestigious Indiana Hand Fellowship, gets the nod instead. David, thankfully, is scooped up by a very successful hand practice in Philadelphia. A very touchy, personal interlude mercifully comes to closure.

Not willing to rely on Ross getting through two years of employment and then wanting partnership (after all, he is a hand surgeon and very much married to that part of the anatomy) we dutifully work on recruiting another doc as well. Doug is a dentist who reinvents himself by going through medical school, orthopaedic residency, and a total joint replacement fellowship. He is married to a dentist and already has two little kids when we sign him up for the two-year employment deal. Now we have five orthopaedic surgeons in all; a number that should work well with call coverage and handling our patient load.

It is all good at the practice. Alex turns out to be a competent administrator. He makes us paperless (which is essential to the integration of three offices) and builds a capable staff able to handle the extra burden of the ever-expanding managed care and government regulations. Debbie seems grateful that her office demands are diminished so she can give more time to the children.

Morgan is seven and still very much into piano and dance. She is absolutely captivated by any artistic challenge (like knitting which she picks up from a stranger whom she sees poolside making a scarf during one of our trips down to

Florida). To be honest, there is something about this child that attracts attention. She has magnatism. I'm not sure if it's her smile, her genuine curiosity, or just pure charisma, but I love her *je ne se quoi* star quality. At times she catches me staring at her while at the dinner table and asks, "What?" "Just looking," is all I can come up with.

Stephanie is eleven and hooked on ballet. When I discover that she is a really fast sprinter, blowing her brother and his friends (nearly two years older than she) away, I try desperately to get her to consider track and field. I line her up next to the older boys doing wind sprints for football and show her that she has unbelievable speed. I enter her in races at the hospital picnic against teenagers and she wins easily without even running in a straight line. Unfortunately, she has no interest in any of this, other than Dad's fascination. She is a dancer. All the other stuff is crude.

Eric is barely a teenager, but good at everything, including school. He is (as was I at that age) grateful to finish up Hebrew school which prepares a Jewish boy to become a man or, as we say, a Bar Mitzvah. The event (though certainly not as elaborate as back in my day, with a full piece band and MC) is a blast. Debbie puts in countless hours making the guest list, hiring entertainment, booking Edgewood Country Club, ruminating over the décor, menu, and place seating. The theme, of course, is golf and each table goes by the name of a famous player. Once the religious ceremony is over in the morning everyone takes a breather and gets ready for the evening celebration. Nearly 230 people gluttonize, dance the horah, wear goofy neon party favors, listen to toasts and get through the candle lighting ceremony and video montage of Eric's first thirteen years on earth. It is the first of three such events that comes with the territory of raising three Jewish kids.

In May (my favorite time of year) the weather is warming; the days are getting longer, and I have a whole summer to look forward to. Early one Monday evening, while I still have at least another hour or two of patients to see, I notice that Bill (my number two partner) is done with his office hours and is just standing in the hall waiting to catch me in a lull. So I turn to him and ask "What's up?" He mumbles something, hands me an envelope and mutters, "That's it."

As he heads out the door I open the letter which states that he can "no longer be a part of the deception" and is "quitting effective today." Momentarily stunned, knowing that the man has surgery scheduled in our surgical center in the morning and the rest of the week solidly booked with patients, I force myself to snap into action. I ask our surgical coordinator, Irene, how many cases Bill has on the schedule for tomorrow and to get each patient on the phone for me to speak with. Next, I call Ken and inform him of the bad news and the need for him to give up his day off during the week in order to help see the patients that "Big Bad Bill" has cravenly abandoned by abruptly running off. Fortunately, all three patients on his surgical schedule for tomorrow have known me for quite some time and prefer having me do their surgery rather than cancelling. I see two of them at the end of hours and the third in the morning for proper preoperative counseling.

The next several weeks are filled with legal action taken to answer BBB's accusations that we treated him dishonestly and to make certain that the restrictive covenant he signed (preventing him from practicing in our area) is upheld. Our corporate lawyer Frank, who is slicker than baby oil on a newborn's butt and as legally wise as a biblical prophet, tells us to lay low; "keep out of the way," and let him handle things.

As it turns out, Triple B has been planning his escape for sometime (no doubt prompted by his wife who felt he could do better on his own). Part of his plan is to alert all of our patients that he is leaving the practice and solicit them to see him at his new address for future orthopaedic care. The A-hole actually enlists his parents in Florida to send out a mass mailing to all those on the list he mendaciously extracted from our computer data base. Each day several loyal, outraged patients (and even some of our own employees) produce the audacious solicitation letter mailed from Florida on BBB's behalf.

The accusations of illegal and unfair monetary distributions among the partners is, of course, a scare tactic employed to make us back off and allow him to violate his restrictive covenant (thus allowing him to practice locally in the area).

By the time Frank gets through, he has turned Big Bad Bill into Wimpy Whining Will who not only loses all his accounts receivable, but has to pay a handsome fee to properly buy out his restrictive covenant. For the next couple of years Bill, whom I see at the hospital, is unable to get his voice to work when around me. But the year 2001 is about to dramatically trivialize my noxious experience with Dr. Bill.

My early morning drive from home in Saddle River down Route 17 to Fair Lawn has always been a bit awe-inspiring especially on a clear day. Straight before me, for about seven miles, lays the majestic New York City skyline. I can't help but remember when the Empire State Building, during my youth, was the tallest building in the World. For years now I marvel at how easily the twin towers of the World Trade Center take over the horizon despite standing well in the background. Each tower reminds me of the monolith in *2001: A Space Odyssey*. This double tribute to man's ingenuity and technologic skill fills me with pride and a quiet kind of gratefulness for having been born an American.

Enough...my next scrub will be short or I'll have no more skin left on my arms. Office hours at noon; I'm ahead of schedule...sweet. I only wish these patients' insurance plans allowed me to do their operations in my surgical center instead of here at the hospital.

I back into the O.R. protecting my hands from contamination. A sterile blue towel is draped across my arms by the scrub nurse and I dutifully dry them.

"All set, Mr. Shilling?" I say to the patient once I'm properly gowned and gloved. He is not a particularly talkative guy so I take his grunt as a "yes." "Okay then, Sir... here we go."

As I insert the arthroscope into the knee I hear some noise (*probably horsing around*) outside in the hall, not typical for this rather conservative facility.

I find some low-grade chondromalcia of the patellofemoral region and medial compartment in Mr. Shilling's knee...not much I can do for that other than show him the pathology and make him aware of the need to lose weight, keep his quads strong, and take glucosamine. The meniscus tear, however, I can rectify.

Absorbed in the case my attention is momentarily diverted when the music is lowered so Dr. Blady can hear what the nurse at the door is saying. Apparently a Cessna flown by some clown just hit the World Trade Center. Someone makes a joke about taking bets on which floor the Piper Cub struck.

It is not until I finish the case that word spreads rapidly through the O.R. that two planes have hit the towers and explosive panic ensues—we are under terrorist attack! The rest of the day is a blur of horrific television shots—people leaping from windows, the towers crumbling, panicked citizens and firefighters covered in soot; man-made devastation never before experienced on American soil! I remember the outrage with which Dad used to describe the 1941 Japanese attack on Pearl Harbor. But that was an attack on our military and occurred thousands of miles away from where he called home. This one is deeply personal.

For the next many weeks I see the continual plume of smoke still rising from the ghostly void that used to be the twin towers as I drive south on Route 17. My sadness is immense though balanced to some degree by the overwhelming display of patriotism and civility that everyone on the road shares.

At the Hoboken office, just a scant mile from Ground Zero, my senses are further assaulted by the smell of ash and sporadic cries of anger from people on the street who get no respite from the memory of that fateful clear, bright Tuesday morning. Here American flags are sold on every corner and memorials to friends and relatives who tragically perished are seen in windows and on doorsteps. Even back in Bergen County my kids have friends who lost parents in those collapsing infernos. My dear friend Ganey (a general surgeon) is blessed to have his only child escape without injury from the fifty-first floor where she worked in her very first job since graduating from college. All at once, things like sports and making money and planning vacations seem so very base and unimportant.

After more than ten days of mourning, however, it becomes clear that we must rally and get on with our lives. President Bush addresses the joint session of Congress and the American people telling us "to live your lives, and hug your children… uphold the values of America, and remember why so many have come here… it is my hope that in the months and years ahead, life will return to normal. We'll go back to our lives and routines, and that is good… But our resolve must not pass. Each of us will remember what happened that day, and to whom it happened. We'll remember the moment the news came—where we were and what we were doing. Some will remember an image of a fire, or a story of rescue. Some will carry memories of a face and a voice gone forever." Not willing to succumb to terrorism we reopen our stock markets and our ballparks. Shea Stadium, a staging area for rescuers (with its parking lot filled with food, water, and medical supplies) resumes being a field of play on September 21st when sports return to New York.

The World Series, delayed by nearly two weeks, runs into November. Our President throws a strike for the ceremonial first pitch. Derek Jeter becomes "Mr. November" with a walk-off homerun hit just after midnight to tie the series at 2-2. He is the first Major League Baseball player to hit a round tripper in the month of November. Unfortunately, the sentimental favorite New York ballclub loses the Series on November 4th when Arizona scores the tying and winning runs in the bottom of the ninth inning; *almost* a storybook ending.

CHAPTER 32

Nothin' Could Be Fina'

Despite my booming practice, 2002 does not begin well fiscally. The bear stock market is a bit of a shocker (though understandable after 9/11) and the negative returns make me think that I can put my money to safer use than in the equities market. I am also uneasy because I am turning fifty-five years old, an age I always associated with retirement, and have not yet made any concrete plans. I know that when I do "hang it up," I must get out of New Jersey. Everyone here knows me as Dr. Schultz and no day goes by without my being asked for medical advice—if I'm putting out, I might as well get paid for it, in which case I am not retired. Though Debbie is not big on change, she is a good sport and willing to explore greener pastures. My theory is to find desirable property and build a house with the money I am otherwise burning in these down financial markets. It will be our retirement home one day.

Having family on the east coast, we are not willing to move out west. Florida is out of the question because of the monotonous (often hot, humid) weather, which is particularly brutal in summer. So we choose to explore the Triangle area of North Carolina that is said to be replete with the nation's highest concentration of M.D./PhDs; and on the top of almost everyone's list of most desirable places to live. The fact that Eric and, now, I are extremely into golf makes NC, the eastern capitol of the sport, all that more attractive. Eric is also a Duke Basketball fan and I fantasize that I can get a part time orthopaedic teaching gig at Duke University Medical Center (just to stay in the game and give something back to a profession that has given me so much).

On our first trip down south we visit the Governor's Club (a new development, well advertised up north and complete with a championship golf course designed by Jack Nicholas) in Chapel Hill. The experience is a turn-on. Not because of the community (which is extremely hilly and makes us fear that our daredevil kids would take some serious headers there), but because the southern hospitality blows us crude northerners away. Arriving late at night and starving, we manage to find a Food Lion supermarket with the lights still on. It is just after 11:00 PM and the store is actually closed, but the clean-up staff sees us outside and graciously opens the door.

"We just flew in and want to get a few things to eat. We'll be real quick. Thank you so much," we say in unison.

"Take your time, Ma'am. No problem, Sir," the clerk pushing the mop says with a broad smile.

No need to be in a rush… hmmm… something very different is happening here. Deb and I are flabbergasted as we run around the place grabbing produce and granola bars. Have we really found the land of the laid-back and polite?

"Thank you. Thank you so much," we repeat again and again when the porter insists on taking our grocery bags out to the car for us.

With the hilly Governor's Club crossed off our list, the realtor brings us to Treyburn in the suburbs of Durham (one of the three towns along with Chapel Hill and Raleigh known as the "Triangle") where "all the Duke medical docs live." It, too, has a golf course (designed by Tom Fazio) and is absolutely lovely. In no time I find a piece of property just off the ninth tee box and agree to put down a deposit. I envision building a house that looks right down the fairway. But within the next two weeks Debbie informs me that her investigation into the Durham school system reveals that the only acceptable place for our kids to go to school is Durham Academy. *Swell, they'll go there* I figure; but I figure wrong. There is apparently no guarantee that this popular educational choice will have an opening for a child, much less three from one family. Besides, Debbie does not like the fact that Treyburn is located way out in the country; a significant drive from shopping and other amenities of civilization. My deposit offer is (from my perspective) sadly taken off the table and we plan another trip down to the Triangle.

Prestonwood Country Club, owned by the richest man in North Carolina, multibillionaire and SAS CEO Dr. James Goodnight in Cary, is another community high on most lists of places to consider for relocation. Despite its fifty-four holes of golf and established neighborhood, we cannot find any vacant lots on which to build or homes for sale suitable to our taste. On a lark, we run up to a new development called Wakefield Plantation in North Raleigh. With plenty of vacant lots from which to choose, I find the perfect site overlooking the par three 14th hole of the Hale Irwin designed TPC course. Again a deposit promise is made, but this time Debbie finds nothing prohibitive about the place. So I hook up with the builder who comes with the lot (the developer sells to builders who then build spec homes or find pre-sale customers) and proceed to get the show on the road. No more money burned in this terrible bear market; instead I will build a magnificent house on gorgeous property in highly desirable North Carolina. If for some reason my family opts out of the move, I will at least have a valuable piece of real-estate to sell.

The design of the new house is similar to that of our comfortable Saddle River home because my family loves it, and I want them to feel the same about the new one. I work through emails with Kim the designer (who makes a trip up to our home in Jersey) and Chris the independent architect who will oversee the project during the construction phase. Much of the building cost will be reduced because I agree to have the house be part of the annual "Parade of Homes" held each year during three consecutive weekends in October. This state-wide event gives builders and home suppliers the opportunity to show off their wares to the public who are encouraged to walk through the participating Parade homes. The houses, in various categories, are judged and the award winners publicized. Suppliers pay for the publicity by passing along substantial discounts to the builders and homeowners. I have absolutely no problem with thousands of people passing through the house since my family and I are comfortably five hundred miles north of the scene.

My creativity spills into a screenplay I decide to write

with my old college roommate Carl (a professional writer who makes a living by doing commissioned trade books and writing for T.V. shows like *Miami Vice*). I can't help but think that if Ben can bring an idea like *Boiler Room* to the big screen, so can I. Call me a dreamer, but I figure this quest is far more reasonable (and safer) than attaining Nirvana. My fascination with creative writing remains strong; it was what motivated me to go back to medical school. So *Malpractice*, the story about a young orthopaedic surgeon whose ambition overrides his longtime friendship with an NBA star, and leads them both down a treacherous path, slowly comes to life. When completed I plan to ask Ben and Bobby Newmeyer, head of Outlaw Productions (*Training Day, The Santa Clause*), whom I know through Ben, to critique the manuscript. Carl and I are both excited that we have real moviemakers to whom we can show our work.

And there is more excitement outside of my Hollywood dream world. Debbie calls me in the car on my way home from the office. She ran into a neighbor, the wife of an NBA superstar who is struggling with a bum knee. He is apparently frustrated with the care he has been getting and wants another opinion. Would I consider stopping by his house on my way home? Because of this player's elite celebrity I consent without hesitation.

Jason is a lot bigger than he looks out on the court. His left knee is a lot bigger than the right one. The swelling, he says, always occurs when he plays back-to-back games. In addition, his knee exam shows quadriceps atrophy and patellofemoral crepitus, indicating kneecap problems. He apologizes for not coming to the office, but does not want any publicity about the injury. I appreciate his position and make recommendations for restoring his thigh strength and minimizing his symptoms. We agree that I will return later in the week to tap his knee and send the fluid for lab analysis. When I arrive home, Eric is still awake and bouncing off the walls because his mother told him who I was seeing. I agree to take him with me when I make the next house call.

On that special day, my usually vocal Eric is so in awe of Jason that he is barely able to say "Hi." He sits quietly in the living room while I drain the star's knee as he lays supine on the kitchen counter. The aspirate (fluid) analysis turns out to show nothing unusual and Jason makes it through the remainder of the season through shear toughness. The Schultz family is rewarded with courtside seats. Eric can't believe his good fortune and tells all his peeps to look for him on the tube.

At about this time my buddy Ari (the spine surgeon whom I met through my brother-in-law David) suggests I interview Sam, a local orthopaedist who has been in practice for over ten years. He is very unhappy with his present group and wants out. Ari says he is a great guy who is in a bad situation. As it turns out, Ari is dead on. Sam is well trained (a graduate of my alma mater Cornell University Medical College) and warm, like a big huggable teddy bear. His partners are not at all business savvy and poor Sam is literally poor despite being an orthopaedic surgeon who works his ass off. Ken and Doug both agree that Sam is likely to be a team player; and since Ross (our hand surgeon) has already expressed his desire to do only hand (surprise, surprise) and join another practice, specializing in hand, in central Jersey, we certainly have need for another doc. So Sam is welcomed aboard and joins us full time in June.

Working my usual long hours, building a house, writing a screenplay, and husbanding/parenting seem like plenty, but they all suddenly take a back seat to my mother's painful right hip; the one she broke two years ago. It has developed advanced osteoarthritis to the point where she has pain with every movement. I try medicines by mouth, by injection, and physiotherapy without any sustained relief for her. When she refuses to get out of bed because of the pain I realize we have no choice. Despite her being ninety years old she will need to have hip replacement surgery or surely die in bed. I ask Joe and Doug, two of my colleagues with expertise in this procedure, to be her surgical team.

After medical clearance, Mom undergoes the operation without a hitch. It is around post-operative day two, however, when she begins to deteriorate mentally. It starts with simple "sun downing" as we call it when elderly patients become disoriented at night because of their unfamiliar surroundings. We stop all of her narcotic pain meds and anything else that may be contributing to her obtundation. Because I am on the hospital medical staff and she is my mother, a myriad of tests and consultations (including psychiatry) are performed. This process, of course, keeps her in "house" for ten rather than the customary three days for hip replacement surgery. Not surprisingly, every day in hospital she seems to become more disoriented. So I take matters into my own hands and insist that she be transferred to the Kessler Institute, an in-patient rehabilitation facility in Saddle Brook. Although she does not meet the criteria (being able to follow verbal and visual cues) for admission to the center, I use my influence and get her in (thank you, Dr. Parikh). I know this is our only chance to keep her out of a nursing home where I fear she will never recover her faculties.

Knowing that she needs fulltime assistance and motivation, I hire Joanne who works as a health aid for a local agency. Joanne is my age, a baby boomer who recently lost her own mother, and had two sons which she raised as a single parent until one of them was killed by gunshot. This dedicated woman miraculously adopts my mom as her own. She treats her with tough love and refuses to allow Mom to quit. "Miss Edna," she says repeatedly, "you are going to keep your eyes open and walk. If you don't I will tell Bobby and he will be very angry with you." Somehow, after weeks of this, and my coming regularly to her therapy sessions to coax, implore, cheer, and yell, Mom seems to rally. Just seeing her regain some of her obstinate, ornery personality gives me hope. Helaine, still making the four-hour drive up from Maryland on a regular basis, is also relieved, but more prepared than I to accept the likelihood that Mom will not make full recovery.

After a few weeks (longer than most patients stay at Kessler after hip replacement surgery) we finally get Mom back to the Classic Residence in Teaneck. They welcome her return with a little party. It is there I notice that she *is* one of the "old people" that she so much hated to be around.

***

It is well after 7:00 PM and, as usual, I've been working for nearly twelve hours today. *Enough already!* There is a chart on the door of each of my three exam rooms and none on the counter at the front desk. That means when I am done with these three patients I get to do my end-of-day callbacks (phone calls to patients who left messages during the day) and then go home. With my "its-nearly-over" spirit I enter room number one, take a history, do an exam, and send the patient down the hall for an x-ray. As I exit the exam room, my eye catches the counter at the front desk. THERE ARE FIVE MORE PATIENT CHARTS ON IT! *I'M NOT CLOSE TO BEING DONE!* The only thing that keeps the top of my head from blowing right off is the thought that next year I am retiring while I still have my health and sanity.

I think back to early '84 when I had been going nonstop through most of the weekend: taking call at the hospital; operating at all hours of the day and night. I was dog-tired. It was Monday and I believed that once I got through office hours I would go home and sleep it off. Then Jeanne, our office manager, told me that she put a case on the add-on surgical schedule at the hospital for me. "No, Jeanne," I pleaded. "I've worked all weekend and have nothing left in the tank." Her response? "Well, *you* wanted to be a doctor!" No sympathy there. How many times over the last two decades have I heard my family and friends tell me that I will burn myself out working so hard?

It is not just the long hours, but the kind of work and level of responsibility that is involved in doctoring. Eating, drinking, and sleeping orthopaedics has been the foundation of my last twenty years. *Did I pull the drain out of that patient's knee too soon; make the right diagnosis; reef up the shoulder capsule too tight?* Questions I fall asleep to; dreams filled with second-guessing. A colleague of mine used to describe it as "trying to fall asleep with my patients on the foot of my bed". There comes a point at which, when the fun is gone and only drudgery is left, change is the only recourse. That is why the new house down in Raleigh (that I frequently visit by trip or email pictures) keeps me holding on, knowing I will soon be there on my permanent "spring break."

I am fifty-six years old. Reverse the numbers and you have the usual retirement age. Even though I am nine years early, I had for years envisioned my retirement to come at fifty-five. My Stephanie's plea to allow her to finish 8th grade at Brookside School in Allendale, and my own sense that the office needed another year or two out of me to achieve stability before I bolt, stalled me a couple of years past my mark.

All of this personal stuff is going on under the backdrop of a war with terrorism and our country's impending invasion of Iraq. The heated controversy over sending our boys over to eradicate weapons of mass destruction and a renegade dictator in a country that is not directly responsible for the 9/11 attacks on our soil is monumental. We all anxiously watch TV as Secretary of State Colin Powell makes the case before the U.N. Security Council about a desert country that must be brought to its knees. He shows aerial views of cargo trucks moving WMDs in the middle of the night and documents the lack of cooperation by Saddam Hussein with U.N. inspectors and other world authorities over the last twelve years. Congress has already given its approval for the Commander-in-Chief to take necessary and appropriate action in dealing with the uncooperative nation of Iraq. Then, just six weeks later, we and the rest of the world watch the bombing of Bagdad, which falls twenty-one days later to U.S. ground troops.

Shortly, thereafter our newest partner, Doug (who

helped pay for his education by joining the Army Reserve) is unexpectedly called up to serve our country in Iraq, leaving us temporarily short-handed. We are fortunate to bring Adam (who just finished an orthopaedic sports' medicine fellowship at Lenox Hill Hospital in New York) into the fold. But the patient load remains excessive, so we decide to take a chance on hiring a PA (physician's assistant).

I am fearful that our patients and referring docs will feel slighted by our use of a PA to see the patient overflow, but fortunately Mr. Thomson (our new PA) turns out to be special. He is not only experienced (having worked for years in an emergency room), but has a warm, caring personality that is absolutely contagious. Before long patients are asking for him as readily as any of us doctors. It is almost as if we never missed a beat by the time Doug returns after several months' duty at the military hospital in Bagdad. He (who has always demanded and expected that everything in the O.R. be "just so") describes the experience as "surreal;" especially given the fact that he treated far more Iraqis with war injuries than Americans.

At my daughter Stephanie's Bat Mitzvah in the spring, we drink a toast to Doug's service and his safe return. Mom makes it to the affair (with Joanne her caregiver who is always by her side), but is looking old and sadly overwhelmed.

While Stephanie's affair in April was high-end, I and my family attend a *super* high-end Bar Mitzvah on October 25th. It takes place at the Waldorf Astoria. The black tie event, complete with a twelve piece band, magnificent food to titillate all 300+ palates, unearthly party favors, and fresh Krispy Kream donuts served with the *New York Times* (hot off the press) after midnight, makes my recollection of the Bar Mitzvah wars (between the Levys and Schultzs) of my youth seem like child's play. The Bar Mitzvah boy is Mathew, my partner Ken's oldest kid. The extravagant affair is testimony to the promise I made him ten years ago that he would become stinking rich if he joined my practice.

The only dark and sickening moment of the luxurious evening comes just after 11:00 PM when I witness, on one of the hotel bar's TVs, the final out of Josh Beckett's complete game shutout of my New York Yankees in the sixth and final game of the world series against the lowly Florida Marlins. I ask Ken how the hell he could let this happen on such a glorious night of celebration. He stairs back at me through martini glazed eyes and mutters something about being "sorry," as he tries to figure out how to do the damn Electric Slide.

***

It is here, 2004: the year of my retirement! Arrangements for extrication from New Jersey have been made. The Saddle River house is under contract for $1.3 million more than I paid for it twelve years ago. Not bad; making the fact that I had to dump fifty grand into a new septic field more tolerable. Debbie and I promise each other that we will never again live without public sewer and water (septic waste back up will do that to you).

The new house is ready despite a disaster over last December when a leak in one of the tiled outside decks over the family room caused water damage requiring repair of two ceilings and a floor, not to mention remediation for mold. It turned out that the subcontractor who laid the porcelain tile on the deck managed to staple the supportive mesh to the impermeable membrane beneath. Brilliant! There was never a chance that the rooms below would stay dry. It costs the builder over $200,000 to fix everything. Miraculously, I and my insurance carrier are spared any expense.

My plan is to work in the office and surgical center right up until the day before our departure for North Carolina. I say my good-byes to patients each and every day. Some tears are shed, but never do I feel remorse for looking forward to a new, less regimented life. Will I miss the routine, the patient "thank-you's," the majesty of "being the man"? Don't know and don't care. The excitement of opening a new chapter in my life (and owning each day) is inebriating.

I am not so self-indulgent that I am willing to let all my hard earned knowledge and surgical skills decay and go to waste. Through contacts, I arrange to take a position in the Orthopaedic Department at the Duke University Medical Center in Durham, thirty-five minutes from our new house in North Raleigh. I will work two days per week teaching residents (with my malpractice coverage, continuing medical education costs and family health insurance covered), but receive no direct monetary compensation. It is all about giving back to a profession that has been very good to me (and, of course, keeping my orthopaedic skills intact). The rest of the week I will dedicate to my family, writing, staying fit, and lowering my golf handicap. As Jackie Gleeson used to say, "How sweet it is."

The family, naturally, is apprehensive about the big move. In anticipation of this I have brought them down to Raleigh several times. The new house, with its high ceilings, walk-out basement to a pool with waterfall and built-in slide, movie theater, spacious bedrooms (each with its own private bathroom), and manicured property on a championship golf course is the peace-de-resistance. The mild weather, lack of traffic, and laid back lifestyle, hopefully, will also ease the pain of leaving familiar surroundings and friends.

While caught up in the family ambivalence of moving and the final months of preparation, tragedy strikes Garden State Surgical Center. Our gentle, highly competent anesthesiologist, Tommy Chen, has been suffering for some time with radicular (radiating) pain down his arm from a herniated disc in his neck. So he asks one of our physiatrists, who specializes in pain management, to perform an epidural steroid injection (nerve block) on him. But Tommy has an irregular heart beat for which he takes warfarin (a blood thinner) to prevent clot formation that could result in a stroke. Unfortunately, an epidural injection is contraindicated (should not be done) in a patient on blood thinners because it can potentially lead to bleeding around the spinal cord. Without consulting anyone, Tommy elects to stop the warfarin for a few days so his blood viscosity can return to normal and he can have the injection.

It is Wednesday, my morning to operate, but there is no sign of Tommy who usually comes in by 7:00 AM to prepare the first patient for the 7:30 "dropping of the knife." Dolly, our surgical supervisor, tells me that she has been trying to reach him by phone without success—most unusual. And then Tommy's wife calls. She apologizes; he couldn't get out of bed this morning so she called an ambulance. He is in the hospital with a severe stroke!

Over the next several days we watch Tommy deteriorate.

Unable to speak, he somehow manages to communicate, in his sweet sensitive way, through hand squeezing and facial expressions (even though he struggles to open his eyes). It is the saddest thing to watch this once vibrant doctor (whom I used to see often at the gym on a stepper or treadmill) being moved out of bed in a Hoyer lift for cleaning and decubitus care. The attending neurologist offers little encouragement regarding Tommy's prognosis. "We do not like to stop anticoagulation (blood thinners) in patients with atrial fibrillation (Tommy's irregular heart beat) for any reason," he says. "This is why."

When I think of how many times one of my own patients with the same condition was reluctantly taken off their blood thinners so surgery could be performed, without dire consequences, I can only think of how lucky we all were.

Tommy passes away in June; just two months prior to my retirement. Although he had me by several years, I always felt like his contemporary. Much like when J.G. died shortly after we both turned fifty, Tommy's death impacts me with a serious look at my own mortality. One never knows when the game is up so any guilt that may have been creeping in with my "early" retirement is shot full of holes.

In midsummer Ken invites Ari, David, and me to play golf at his club. Of course, we have a blast despite some ugly shots. The 18th hole is a par three over water with the two-tiered green lying just below the clubhouse balcony. Ari hits one in the water and I am surprised to hear the crowd gathered on the balcony groan with displeasure. *Their party must be boring if they are all watching us,* I think. Then it is my turn and I manage to hit the green. The place erupts with applause and shouts. Still mystified as to why the crowd is so locked into us I wait until the other two have hit and then slowly make my way down to the green. It is not until I cross the bridge that I start recognizing faces on the balcony: Debbie, the kids, my mother, our entire office staff and docs from the hospital. Just like my fiftieth surprise birthday party, I am totally bushwhacked—an easy mark, that's me.

The retirement party is touching and were it not for the obvious absence of Tommy Chen (representing the tenuousness of life) I would be fraught with ambivalence. One of the going away gifts presented to me is a picture of Ken, Chris, Ari, and me on a golf course with New Jersey Governor James McGreevey. The event was a political (PAC) fundraiser, but who knew then that the Governor would come out of the closet, publically declare that he is gay and resign from office a couple of years later. As always, in poor taste, we make fun of Chris standing there next to the chief executive who nonchalantly has his arm on Chris' shoulder. Aside from Mom looking frail, the farewell celebration is a beautiful bow on the end of this present chapter.

The actual move, on August 10th, comes after an emotional week that includes a tag sale of just about all our furniture and "unwanted" stuff. Of course, Morgan refuses to give up anything, so we fill one of our three cars with stuffed animals, games, and her replica miniature shoe collection. Driving out of the driveway is slow and painful, much like a funeral procession with our family members and Margaret ("Debbie's wife," as I like to call our live-in housekeeper) divided up between cars. While Eric seems oblivious, the girls are in tears, including Debbie who pretends to be adult about the whole maudlin exodus.

The eight-hour drive is made in relative silence and the

abundance of Baptist churches seen as we hit the North Carolina border doesn't loosen any tongues. But once we arrive in Wakefield Plantation, the awesome house on Billings Gate Lane buoys our spirits. Eric runs out back to play the 14th hole, while the girls pretty up their rooms. Debbie and I temporarily exhale believing that the trauma of leaving Jersey is now behind us. All three start school at Ravenscroft in less than three weeks and it is our hope that new friends will usher in a new beginning.

The adjustment to living in the South is a bit convoluted. Rumors about who built the big house on the 14th hole lead curiosity seekers to befriend me and offer up a slew of sure-fire business deals. Debbie tries to be tolerant of the frequent (well meaning) suggestions that she slow down, "After all sugar, you're in God's country now. Relax, we're on Southern time." The kids can't get over the cotillion bred manners and southern accents; while Eric is the first in our family to learn what barbecue really means down here. Bo, already seventeen and driving, asks Eric if he likes barbecue. Expecting burgers and dogs, Eric jumps in the car excited to be going off campus for lunch. My Yankee son's reaction when he bites into the vinegar soaked pulled pork in a bun is just what the local boys hope for. Welcome to Carolina, dude!

CHAPTER 33

Duke, Duke, Duke...
Duke of ...

In October my New York Yankees are back in stride tearing up the Boston Red Sox in the American League Championship Series. Up 3-0 in games and ahead by a run in the ninth inning of game four with Mariano Rivera on the mound it seems unlikely that Boston can avoid the sweep. The "Curse of the Bambino" is in full force until, somehow, Mariano blows the save (and the Red Sox win in the 12th inning). It is all a blur after that. No team in Major League Baseball history (and only two teams in North American professional sports history; the '42 Toronto Maple Leafs, and the '75 New York Islanders NHL teams) has ever come back to win a seven game series after losing the first three games. Why on earth it has to be the f***ing Red Sox making history over my Yankees is unclear (I don't want to get into "the law of averages" or karma), but "The Comeback" (as it will no doubt be referred to in the future) is excruciating; only made worse by Boston subsequently sweeping St. Louis in the (100th) Fall Classic to win their first World Series since 1918. Although I avoid the sports section of the newspaper and Sports Center on TV for weeks I manage to reconcile the humiliation by dredging up some appreciation (as a true sports fan) for the unprecedented accomplishment.

We spend our last Christmas/Hanukah holiday in our Florida house (which I sell next summer because of the exorbitant upkeep for a place we have come to use only one week per year) and have the time of our lives. During the vacation a massive earthquake registering 9.3 on the Richter scale erupts just off the west coast of Indonesia. The result is an enormous tsunami that crashes into Thailand, Indonesia, India, Bangladesh, Sri Lanka, Malaysia, Myanmar, and the Maldives killing 186,983 with another 40,000 people missing. The television footage is absolutely shocking. I later find out that Sayuri, the daughter (and only child) of my dear surgeon friend Ganey and his wife Manel, was visiting the coast of Thailand at the time and narrowly escaped injury. She is the same young lady who three years earlier was working on the fifty-first floor of the World Trade Center when the commandeered planes struck, but managed to survive the 9/11 inferno. The family is Buddhist and fatalistically takes the second near miss in stride.

The buy-out agreement I have with my orthopaedic practice in New Jersey involves paying me two times earnings for my share over seven years. Because of the extended timetable of payment and my commitment to helping them thrive without me, I schedule trips back to Jersey for each quarterly business meeting. Between meetings I make interim visits up there to see Mom who is still living at the Classic Residence in Teaneck with her caregiver Joanne. Helaine and I consider moving mother south to be closer to us (a residence in either Raleigh or Bethesda), but we conclude that such a move might be too disorienting for her. So every six weeks I make the pilgrimage on Continental Airlines to Newark Airport. Helaine is still driving up from Maryland every two weeks, as she has been doing for the last many years. Aside from an episode of aspiration pneumonia (an unfortunately common occurrence in the elderly) that lands Mom in the hospital for a week, she seems to be making out all right.

"Bobby," she whispers frequently to me, "don't grow old. It's not good. You'll see." Although I surely understand what she means (the boredom and compromised mobility look absolutely frightening), I joust back saying, "But Ma, think of the alternative." She seems to deeply consider my question, but does not respond. *Hmmm, could it be that bad?*

When I come up, I try to get into the City to see Carl who makes regular trips down from Cherry Valley in upstate New York to tend to his brownstone on MacDougal Street in Greenwich Village (left to him and his sister Anne by their parents). We go over our screenplay and reminisce. Out of the blue one day, he surprises me by reuniting Elliott (my bro from college and Formentera/Morocco days) and me. Totally dynamite!

Elliott looks healthy and suave as ever; except that a shaved head has replaced the afro with the pick in it. I ask him where he keeps his comb these days. Despite more than thirty years of noncontact we fill in the gap quickly and find our old friendship to be timeless. After a "J" for old time sake, Elliott and I head to the upper eastside.

Finding it frustrating to hale a cab, my black brother says, "Watch this," as he steps back off the curb leaving me waving alone. Immediately, two cabs appear for my service. Choosing the first, I jump in while Elliott quickly follows. "Just coincidence," I tell him. He laughs at my naivety and says, "We'll see on the way back."

The trip back to the Village is a repeat, with the addition that even a couple of black cabbies won't stop when Elliott is by my side. I'm starting to get the picture. Elliott is nicely dressed and groomed; looking certainly more proper than I in my jeans and baggy coat. It is all about his blackness; no doubt about it. But how do you figure the black cabbies passing him by?

"Profiling and fear," my old friend says. "I've put up with it all my life. Nothing's changed."

"Good thing they can't see my Jewishness," I respond. "Otherwise we'd still be standing on the first street corner."

We laugh; another bonding moment. But the truth is that Elliott's poignant demonstration of what a black man goes through on a regular basis is a real eye-opener for me.

My job at Duke is also an eye-opener. I am the new boy on the block and working only two days per week makes me no more than an afterthought to my colleagues and staff. The clout and respect I have become accustom to in my field are history. Assigned mostly to the VA (veterans administration) hospital across the street also carries an obsequious flavor. Despite the last twenty years of being "the man," I remind myself that most of my life has been a ride up and down the totem pole: from elementary school, to junior high, to high school, to college, to medical school, to the second class citizenry of a hippy, back to medical school, to residency, to junior partner, to "the man", and now back to an "afterthought". The bouncing around between neophyte and senior status is nothing new. It keeps things in proper perspective, allowing me to find security in who I am rather than in what people perceive me to be.

Unfortunately, the ego battle can be brutal when it comes to overseeing residents in the clinic or operating room. The task of teaching (even with compliant students) is far more challenging than simply taking over patient care and doing operations myself. The first and second year residents are far more malleable (and pleasant) than the smug, arrogant senior and chief residents who are a year or less from completing their training. Knowing that I too suffered from similar delusions back in the day helps me cope—a little.

My biggest support comes from Tyson, a silver-haired senatorial looking physician with a stately southern countenance that immediately commands respect (unless you are a self-absorbed chief resident). Doc is retired from his successful orthopaedic practice of more than thirty-five years and, like me, does not want to simply turn his back on his profession. An alumnus of Duke University and once president of just about every medical society in North Carolina, he actually has a football field named after him in his hometown of Wilson. Yet he is assigned to the VA and, like me, struggles with the obeisance of his new position; especially when demeaned by young'uns.

Our friendship is immediate despite his anticipation of meeting an arrogant "young" whippersnapper from New Jersey (home of the "hired guns" who testify for money against other doctors who are being sued for malpractice).

Between commiserations we have fun talking about the world now and how it was back in each of our day. He is a renaissance man; a raconteur and historian from a military family who, despite being well into his seventies, has a myriad of obscure facts at his fingertips. I watch as he learns, over the next several months, to use the computer, and, like a kid at Christmas, starts to explore the world of "Google." Despite having two total knee replacements, bilateral carotid endarterectomies (to prevent a stroke), and a thoracotomy, the guy continues to play competitive tennis and snow ski along with his wife "Mama" (aka, Peggy; "a pretty lil' thang," he met on the Duke campus back in the '50s).

A few months later Tally (who recently left private practice to spend more time with his three kids after his wife died of cancer) joins us as chief of the VA orthopaedic department. He was a medical student at Harvard when I was an orthopaedic resident up there. Although our paths hadn't crossed we knew many of the same people. Our instant bond is a good thing.

My part-time job, though menial, is fulfilling and enjoyable. Having been accepted into the Duke community, I invest in season tickets to watch Duke Basketball in the legendary Cameron Indoor Arena. No one is more excited about this move than Eric, my little sports' fanatic.

He's a great kid, with excellent grades and a splendid golfer. All my kids are good, so it is a shocker when we get the call that our sixteen-year-old is having a party at our house while we are at the Grove Park Inn in Asheville, four hours away. Of course there is booze (and God knows what else) involved. Our girls are with us and it becomes very clear that we made a major mistake leaving Eric for the weekend to stay with his golf coach and young family. The stark realization that trust and expectations do not necessarily have a place in dealing with teenagers is sobering. My first inclination is to rush back home and wring the kid's neck. Debbie almost has to tackle me, as I run down the hotel corridor. "It is nearly midnight, the mountain roads are dark and we are over four hours away," she pleads. "You weren't any better, you know." *Hmmm…got me there.*

Early next morning, after cutting our long weekend short, we race back home to hear the excuse that the festivities started out with just a couple of buddies, but quickly escalated into something just short of a bacchanalia. Trying not to be hypocritical, I am nevertheless upset that he is starting these things at such a young age (for which I blame the internet and cell phones for giving kids the facility for instant communication and lascivious knowledge they certainly can do without). My biggest concern is the liability I face should something untoward occur out of my home. I am smacked in the mouth with profound fear that my mother's curse, for what I did to her when I left medical school and ran off to see the world, might come true: *May his offspring teach him the true angst of parenthood* (or something like that).

Despite Eric's various indiscretions (no doubt partly our fault for starting him in grade school at too early an age) he winds up matriculating in the class of 2010 at Duke University as a member of the golf team (1520 on his SATs didn't hurt). College golf is a big commitment and should keep him busy and out of trouble. When he elects to pledge a fraternity Deb and I think he is biting off more than he can chew. He throws back at us the fact that I was in DKE at

Hamilton and played basketball. "Yeah, but that was division III and life was simpler back then," I counter in my best Socratic tone. He doesn't buy it. No surprise.

Now I have two reasons to root for Duke; my son goes there and I am on faculty at the medical center. So it offends me when I hear many of the students boo Richard Brodhead at one of the late March basketball games at Cameron Indoor. After all, he is the new university president from Yale and deserves some respect. It is not until the news of the prior weeks unfold that I begin to understand the story behind the students' avarice.

The top ranked Duke Lacrosse team had an off campus party and foolishly hired two strippers for entertainment. When one of them claimed she was raped the news media, of course, got all over the story. The fact that the stripper was black and all the players present that night were white helped fuel the story and gave muckrakers like Nancy Grace and Al Sharpton fodder for their bloviating. Unfortunately, Brodhead made the decision to fire the coach, Mike Pressler, early on without proper investigation. He also went on to cancel the lacrosse season and throw the players under the bus. It is for these cowardly acts that the student body at Cameron booed him.

As the year unfolds, even before publication of *It's Not About the Truth* by Don Yeager and Mike Pressler; and *Until Proven Innocent* by Stuart Taylor, Jr. and KC Johnson, it becomes clear to me that the university cares more about its name than the students it is chartered to educate and nurture. Even iconic basketball coach Mike Krzyzewski's silence suggests that the boys are guilty. The school's lack of due process is not only disappointing, it sickens me. I work there, am a committed supporter of Duke Athletics, a member of the Iron Dukes booster club, and above all, have a child being educated by Duke Faculty. What is he learning? That "privileged" white guys don't stand a fair chance on today's far left college campuses? That telling the truth sometimes doesn't matter?

When I voice my concerns to several honchos on staff and in the administration I am met with craven apathy and the suggestion that my concerns are blown out of proportion. The good news is that my son, like many jocks on campus, supports the denigrated lacrosse players and is angered by their vilification. All I know is that while I still enjoy going to Duke Basketball games and rooting for the team, I no longer have the same heartfelt respect for the coach or passion for the university that I once had. Indeed, as more facts about the character of the plaintiff and prosecutor are brought to light, and the radical left-wing "Group of 88" faculty members publicly call for the "hoodlums'" heads to roll, I realize that the students' booing of their school president was way too soft. He is letting the faculty ideologues pursue their bigoted agendas unchecked and unabashed. Shameful!

Meanwhile, my recent visits up to Jersey hit me hard with sadness as I watch Mom deteriorate both mentally and physically. My most difficult moment comes when I hand her a picture I found (and framed) of her and Dad as a present on what would have been their 72nd wedding anniversary. After struggling to unwrap the gift she looks tentatively at the picture. A good while passes before she innocently asks, "Bobby, who is this man in the picture?" No longer the sigh, "My Irving; my lovely Irving." She has gone to a far off place protective of memories of better times—times to which she no longer has access.

CHAPTER 34

Lil' Orphan Bobby

om is somnolent most of the day despite Joanne working hard to stimulate her. She no longer wants to play bingo or do crossword puzzles. She falls asleep reading the newspaper or watching TV. Her preference of keeping her eyes closed even during a conversation concerns me to no end and leads me to order lab tests (including an MRI of her brain) through her geriatrician. Aside from the commonly found cerebral atrophy and minor lacunar infarcts seen in the elderly, her tests show nothing wrong. We stop her medications (primarily consisting of antidepressants and a memory stimulant), but her lethargy persists. I begin to conclude that she is fed up with her boring, restricted life and closes her eyes in hopes that it will all simply go away. I plead with her to act alert when she is downstairs socializing and at meals. I have already been warned by the operations manager that my mother may have to find other residence or be moved over to the nursing section of the facility since she no longer appears independent. Helaine and I do everything possible to delay the inevitable.

While up in Jersey, I attend my Fair Lawn High School 41st reunion. We never had a 40th because Liz Blum Powers, our supreme class organizer (who published our quarterly newsletter for decades and handled all past reunions), became very sick with multiple sclerosis. Fortunately, other wonderfully nostalgic classmates took over and put the night together. Debbie stays down in North Carolina with the kids and does not come to this one with me (she had enjoyed sharing my high school past with me at several earlier reunions).

I am surprised and pleased to see a turnout of a couple of hundred (although we did have about 740 graduates in the class of '65, and the turnout does include some spouses). Despite the significant passage of time I am impressed with how good everyone looks. They say that only those who are in shape and successful attend school reunions, but I believe that curiosity and nostalgia also play big rolls in who shows up. Facial expressions and mannerisms help with recognition of old friends, while the blessed name tags sure help thaw brain freeze and prevent embarrassment.

Drinking beer and laughing with the guys about how Mother Nature sure has bitch slapped some of the hot girls in our class is priceless. Of course, I'm sure the other gender has its own laughs about us, but that's too painful to think about. Bob Wolfe, one of the organizers, is a great MC and aside from some silver gray hair still looks like a teenager (must have taken a chapter out of *The Picture of Dorian Gray* or swallowed some Dick Clark Kool-Aid).

I really don't want the night to end, and I get the

impression that I am not the only one. A few hours reliving my youth and seeing what the years have done to some is both fascinating and thought provoking. Artie (aka, "Pebbles"), his wife from high school Tina, Lee and his wife MaryAnn (a grade below us) and I keep on reminiscing until the place shuts down well after midnight. Reunions (especially high school) help momentarily slow down the gallop of passing years and provide me with subsequent days of rewarding introspection.

While I do not regret retirement I can only play just so much golf. Getting my handicap down is challenging, but low on my list of fulfilling endeavors. Teaching at Duke certainly has its rewarding moments, and having a lifestyle that allows me to spend time with my family is something my dad never had. But writing the book *Street Smarts* gives me a sense of purpose to which I have become accustomed over the years. Working towards a goal that brings praise or money is the driving force of the American Dream. It is something I learned as a child and fervently feed on as an adult. Only during my traveling years did I abandon the force in hopes of finding a dimension even more powerful and fulfilling. Now, as I approach sixty, I still feel the need for producing something that will be helpful to others and ultimately bring me a pat on the back. Perhaps the time will come when I will be so secure in my own skin that simply living each day will be all the reward I need.

Street Smarts for the Practicing Physician and Surgeon is a guide to the nuances of private medical practice and is published at the end of the year by Data Trace in Maryland. Based on the premise of the book my associate Tally and I begin a series of dinner lectures (called "Leaving the Duke

Nest") at various local restaurants for the residents and fellows. We and guest speakers provide insight into what lies ahead in the real world for these young docs: choosing a practice, negotiating contracts, avoiding malpractice suits, marketing yourself, dealing with difficult patients, etc. How sweet it is to be productive! I really need that.

***

Every day Morgan, my youngest, comes home from school and tells us how much she hates it. The kids are "spoiled;" they "make fun" of anyone they don't like and the teachers just "don't care." Strange stuff coming from someone so blessed with charisma and sensitivity for others.

Hey, I'm paying fifteen grand a year for private school, just like I've done for my other two. They didn't complain and seemed to like Ravenscroft; although both were in the upper school. Maybe it's just a phase; Morgan is only in middle school and that is a hard time for young girls socially, we are told. She is also upset that Ravenscroft has no girls' golf team (that's right, she's really into golf after befriending a tomboy classmate who loves the game); another reason she wants to go to public school next year. "So make the boys' team," I challenge (a daunting task since the team wins "States" most years and the players are long off the tee). I try to reason that kids are kids, people are people, and no matter where you are, getting along with others requires effort. Besides, switching schools just so you can play on a golf team is a bit much.

Since Debbie is the one picking Morgan up from school most days, she gets the brunt of the griping. Not wanting to see her baby so unhappy she begins the process of looking into other schools. As it turns out, the switch we ambivalently make to Wakefield Public School the following year solves the entire problem. Morgan absolutely loves going there and comes home each day happy. I can only think back to 1961 when my parents tried to send me to private school at Montclair Academy (an all boys' prep school). After passing the entrance exam, I freaked out at the interview when the Headmaster criticized my dad for showing up "unshaven" (he had been up all night with a difficult delivery). "My dad's a doctor! What's your degree? How many years of school did you go to?" I ranted. The bottom line: no way was I going to be subjected to the pomposity of private school. Dad, looking mortified, ushered me out, but later told me how proud he was that I stuck up for him. He told Mom that he thought it cruel and unusual punishment for a young boy to miss out on socializing with the opposite sex. She wondered why he hadn't spoken up about that concern before they had me apply.

My dear, sensitive Morgan is also worried about her Nana after hearing me tell Debbie how my mother seems to be deteriorating a bit more each time I visit. She begs to go up to New Jersey and play piano for Nana and her lady friends. It is remarkable to see how joyously the residents smile and clap for each song she plays; blissfully oblivious to any mistakes or breaks in the concert. The piano sunroom fills up quickly with nonagenarians and some centenarians, almost from the first note. They can't get enough of a child at play. Clearly, the magnetism of youth becomes stronger with age (as long as there is no responsibility attached to it).

Morgie wonders how Nana will be able to make it down to North Carolina for her upcoming Bat Mitzvah in

October. She is not alone in her concern. Of course, Joanne (her caregiver) will have to accompany her, just as she does everywhere Mom goes. I can only imagine the difficulty they will have getting on and off the plane, making their way through the airport, and keeping Mom awake for the Bat Mitzvah ceremony and celebration.

On May 13th I get a call from Joanne that Mom is having labored breathing and that she called an ambulance to take her to the hospital. After alerting Helaine I call the emergency room and ask for the E.R. doctor to call me when she arrives. The diagnosis is pneumonia (which she had once in the past and fortunately made full recovery). After being reassured that her vital signs are stable, I book a flight up to Jersey for the next day.

A few hours before takeoff Helaine, who drove up from Bethesda early in the morning, calls me and says, "I just walked in and I think Mom is dying. I am holding the phone up to her ear. Say good-bye." Through the tears I manage to say, "This is Bobby, Ma. I love you." Helaine graciously says, "She heard you and smiled."

The funeral two days later is harrowing because Debbie, her mother and the kids, elect to drive eight hours early the same day and just make it in time. Everyone is sad. I am struck by who turns out to pay their respects. Very few of Mom's contemporaries make it because they are infirmed or in graves themselves. Estelle, a few years older than Helaine and our housekeeper back in the day, sobs about how well Mrs. Schultz always treated her; "Like I was her own daughter." Art the plumber talks about how tasty my mother's fruit salad was; "the grenadine syrup was a great touch." Harvey and Esther (who were with Mom in Boca

Community Hospital the night Dad passed away in '97) seem to miss her as much as I do. And there are many friends of mine, office staff, and fellow physicians who only knew of her because she was my mother.

As a new orphan I eulogize both my parents for having had a sixty-two year marriage and a sixty-five year romance here on earth. It started in Bradley Beach on the Jersey Shore and continues on in heaven now that they are reunited. How did I get so lucky to have such traditional parents? They were *Ozzie and Harriet, Ward and June Cleaver, Jim and Margaret Anderson.* As I look at my own children I can only hope they feel the same warmth and security with which my parents blessed me. Thirty-seven years ago I left medical school and ran off to see the world at the expense of these wonderful parents of mine. I know my father has forgiven me (it is just the kind of man he was) and I know my mother never will. I love them both the same and am grateful that they were able to see their son finally make something of himself. We will miss them at Morgan's Bat Mitzvah, but know that their spirits will be embracing us.

Rabbi Glustrom, who presided over my Bar Mitzvah, my sister's marriage, my marriage, my son's bris, and my father's funeral, now lays my mother to rest. His half-century of service to my family comforts me with a sense of continuity that gives special meaning to the spirit of family roots. It is at this moment that I contemplate writing *Autobiography of a Baby Boomer.*

Morgan's Bat Mitzvah is beautiful. Though just thirteen, I am struck by her transformation from straight lines to womanly curves. The theme for the evening celebration is "Morgan's Studio 13." She lights the first of thirteen candles for Nana and Pop-Pop while an image of the two of them holding hands is shown on the big screen behind her. For me it is one of those sentimental moments (resplendent with sadness and joy) that let me feel my soul. As I look over at Debbie and Helaine I see that they, too, are teary-eyed as each returns my gaze. My thoughts drift back to the inexplicable séances in Bill Daut's living room, and I want so much to believe that the spirit world exists all around us and that Mom and Dad are here sharing this moment with us.

On December 27th Mom and Dad celebrate their first wedding anniversary in Heaven.

CHAPTER 35

The More Things Change....

In 2008 our lovely ballerina Stephanie will be going to college, but first she must apply. Unlike Eric before her, she has no interest in Duke nor does she want to remain in-state. Perhaps a bit adventurous (like her dad) she looks forward to getting away. Despite playing the "middle child syndrome" card when convenient, my accomplished daughter possesses all of the qualities (Morgan's cuteness and Eric's brains) she claims we attribute to her siblings. When I see her dance I am dazzled by her poise and confidence. A strong ballet program and a high percentage of hunks (good looking boys) are her main criteria for school selection. Too bad; UNC (a state university without a dance program) would be a huge savings even though it would create civil war in our family.

Her first choice is NYU, a hotbed for the performing arts and city life. We, of course, refuse to let her go to the Big Bad City (where a few short years ago one of Eric's old girlfriends was brutally murdered in the early morning hours after bar hopping). Fortunately, Stephanie hates the cold so she puts up little fight. Knowing nothing about the West Coast, she concentrates on the South despite being a Jersey girl at heart. End result? UGA (University of Georgia): the ultimate "Rah! Rah! experience" in the quintessential college town of Athens.

The first two months of college life makes her terminally homesick (maybe I jumped too soon at comparing her to my adventurous youth); necessitating a visit from Mom and Dad the five hour drive isn't bad, especially with Debbie driving; seems she doesn't trust me at the wheel for some reason. Miraculously, the trip does Debbie and me the most good: not only do we find Stephanie thrilled to see us, she proudly parades us around and enthusiastically introduces us to her friends! Deb pinches me and I pinch her back; it is not a dream. Before long our ballerina is plugged in with three close friends and a membership in SDT sorority.

While Eric loves Duke, he realizes that he is already half-way through his college career and fears that the end will soon be in sight. The recognition of having to make a living in a couple of years motivates him to start talking about graduate school. Many of his golf buddies have graduated and gone on to Wall Street; an idea that fit in nicely with Eric's plan of becoming stinking rich...until the economic crisis strikes. In many ways I am glad "The Street" is no longer an appealing option for him because I don't see my son playing the money brokering game. His love of sports and his writing ability make him a great fit in the sports industry. "Go to law school; become an agent or sports journalist," I tell him. "You love that stuff. It will make you happy and successful." He promises to take my advice "into consideration." The good news is he just turned twenty. Plenty of time to decide (and explore); I envy his youth and this special time in his life.

This ramped-up election year provides Debbie and me with more political fervor than I can ever recall feeling in the past. Despite both of us voting for my old pal Al Gore in 2000, we are again united in the belief that government should remain small and that the war on terrorism is the most important issue. Somehow we discover Fox News and The O'Reilly Factor. At 8:00 PM each night we snuggle up and watch *The Factor*. The guy is a gutsy traditionalist who stirs up the wholesomeness of our childhood years. Debbie has always had a conservative bent, but I have never thought of myself as anything but adventurous and ready to experiment. To my surprise I find myself extremely comfortable with tried and true American values: family first, respect for others (including their points of view), and pride in being an American. Despite its crooked politicians and despicable CEO/Wall Street narcissism, I love this country and am annoyed by those that find only fault with it and relentlessly damn its name.

The housing collapse and subsequent economic crisis is a dramatic wake-up call and hopefully will not lead to the abandonment of the free-enterprise system from which our country has become great. Panic leads to rash decisions and the loss of sound perspective. The country rightly wants to escape the corruption and greed that is responsible for our present economic recession, but change must come through correctly understanding our mistakes and making adjustments rather than a wholesale metamorphosis. We must not throw the baby out with the bath water.

Although both Debbie and I, thank God, are on the same page (voting for McCain because we feel sure that American security will be maintained) we are supportive of the new President-elect, Obama. He is, after all, to be our leader and we believe that once he takes office and sees what our country is truly up against he will be more centrist in his views and avoid radical change in the war on terrorism and our free-enterprise system. We want him to succeed for the sake of our nation.

The extended primary campaign and Presidential election triggers many discussions about where our country is heading and where we have been. I see much similarity between the divisiveness today and forty years ago with the unpopular wars and close-minded snobbery of the '60s. As I discuss the past with Debbie, I realize that although she is technically a Baby Boomer (born between 1946 and 1957 when the birth rate precipitously rose and maintained its rise until a very definitive downswing in 1958) we are from two different generations. Nearly eleven years younger than I she knows not of *Hopalong Cassidy* or *The Life of Riley*. Being only in grade school during the '60s she missed most of the first-hand counterculture revolution. More importantly, she was forced to act as protector of her two younger siblings during her early teenage years when her disturbed father selfishly abused the family and beat up her mother. Having to grow up too fast caused her to miss much of the "all-about-me" era that we more privileged punks enjoyed.

As I write *Autobiography of a Baby Boomer* and discuss memories with Debbie, the disparity between our generations becomes more evident. To a lesser degree I see generational differences with my sister Helaine who is not quite five years my senior (born in '42 before the postwar baby boom)

Despite the recession and some poorly timed real-estate investments that hopefully will recover with time, my retirement is not in jeopardy. I am still able to afford the family's annual "trip-to-someplace-warm" during the winter holidays. Debbie does her usual exhaustive due diligence and finds a prodigious resort on the Mayan Riviera in Mexico. Azul Five is brand new and our accommodations include a three-bedroom penthouse suite with a spacious balcony (important because we are six, including Eric's girlfriend). We anticipate spectacular service because the place is just opening and they should be eager to please. Our only concern is whether the place will be finished by mid December as billed. We are told repeatedly: "everything is on schedule" and the project manager himself assures us that they will suffer far more than we if Azul Five cannot accommodate their holiday guests.

For the past nineteen years we have had a wonderful Hanukah/Christmas/New Year's vacation. It has become more memorable as the family has grown and we explore more delicious warm places (Boca, Caribbean cruise, Atlantis, Scottsdale, Cancun, etc.). Debbie and I don't want it to end, but we know that our family sabbaticals are numbered because the kids grow up and, well you know, they head in different directions. So anticipation of this trip is cherished until the phone call (ten days before departure) comes telling us, "Sorry, the resort is finished, but the furniture is held up in customs so we will not be opening in time for the holidays."

Right! So much for due diligence! Frazzled and deeply

disappointed Debbie gets on the phone, online, and on the travel agent to find some place else warm that can accommodate six a week before the busiest vacation season of the year.

The outcome: Eric goes to San Diego with his girlfriend (who is from Southern California), Stephanie goes to Jersey to visit friends; and Morgan goes with a girlfriend and her parents to their timeshare in Aruba, while Debbie and I practice empty nesting down in Raleigh.

I have plenty of time to finish writing *ABB* and then allow two of my literary friends to have at it. Carl thinks it has worth and offers to submit it to his literary agent. Ben Younger (of *Boiler Room* and *Prime* fame) is complimentary of my writing style, but thinks the almanac-like references to world events have got to go. Since Ben is younger (*sorry*) and not of the Baby Boomer generation I don't fully buy his criticism. So I take a deep breath and send it off to a series of book agents who, as it turns out, are also of a more recent vintage and could care less about dates and events from the '50s and '60s. Those willing to offer more than the standard "this-work-does-not-fit-our-present-needs-good-luck" reply, like Ben, suggest canning the almanac stuff. So I figure that if I am ever going to reach the eighty million Baby Boomers for whom this book is written, I must go through a younger generation to get it in print. So the editing...no, rewrite (let's call it what it is) begins.

During the next year of refashioning *ABB* I have come to realize exactly what Ben had tried to convince me of after his first read—my story can stand on its own. It is everyone's story—or at least parts of it. Those who have lived in the Baby Boom era will relate to the ethos and language of the times, and those who did not, but are curious about it will get a taste of "those wild and crazy" days. Maybe Mark Twain was right: "The truth is stranger than fiction." After all, "you can't make this stuff up."

Following the high of what I see as a creative accomplishment comes the stroke and the terrifying news of my heart disease. Suddenly I'm old. My gait changes. My agility leaves me. I have daily medication to take and face open-heart surgery.

CHAPTER 36

A Not So Gentle Stroke

On Father's Day 2010 at 3:00 AM I get up to take a leak. Suddenly my left leg feels funny. Not "ha ha" "funny," but more like "uh-oh" "funny." I limp back to bed and become troubled by the numbness in my left arm.

Must be coming from my neck—a pinched nerve or something.

I do have cervical spondylosis (some degenerative arthritis of the upper spine) so I position myself as flat and straight as possible to elongate my neck and relieve nerve compression. Within seconds I become horrified by the numbness on the left side of my face. Immediately, I frown and smile; lift my left leg then my left arm checking for motor weakness as the nauseating word STROKE shoots through my brain!

No way! I'm Mister Healthy. Everyone says I look and move like I'm in my forties. Chris, more than a year younger than me, is often mistaken for my father. My blood pressure is 118/70. My resting heart rate is sixty; a testimony to my aerobic fitness. My cholesterol is 178 with a high HDL. *No way!*

My left arm and leg, though numb, move with power. I feel no drooping of my face. I wait. *This will pass.* But just in case I get up to take an aspirin. *Nope. I can't make it to the bathroom by myself.*

"Deb?"… "Deb!" "Get me an aspirin, please. I'm having a problem." Seemingly stupefied, Debbie gets me the medicine and remains speechless. Her angst begins when I suggest we head for the emergency room.

Unable to walk without maximum assistance I descend the stairs on my butt. Debbie calms down Stephanie (back from college) and tells her not to awaken Morgan. The drive to the ER is pure anxiety immersed in disbelief. The motor function is there, but the numbness is profound. My mind and speech are clear. I can swallow without difficulty. If this is a stroke, what part of the right side of my brain is affected? I review my neuroanatomy from thirty-five years ago.

By the time I am wheeled into a cubicle and an intravenous line is established Debbie is pale but stoic. Our eyes say *don't panic* as the E.R. doc begins his exam: full strength, but loss of fine touch and proprioception (position sense) on my entire left side. A CAT scan of my brain shows no hemorrhage, thank God (because the aspirin I took earlier would likely have made it worse).

Ambulance transfer to Raleigh Duke Hospital and a subsequent MRI, echocardiogram, carotid ultrasound, telemetry, and blood work reveal a small thalamic infarct (stroke). The neurologist believes I will recover, but the cardiologist wants further work-up for aortic valve insufficiency and a small patent foramen ovale (congenital hole between the atria in my heart). I am discharged the next day on aspirin. I can walk independently, but with caution and concentration.

Stroke and heart disease....

But I take such great care of myself. I even drink green tea, damn it!

The healthy-looks-so-young-Bob bubble is burst! Let the reverie begin—the perfect impetus to catch a glimpse of reality outside the frantic theater of racing toward another goal. Image building is profoundly tedious work and those of us who thrive on success fall hard when revealed to be just as frail as those over whom we supposedly triumph. How sad to be embarrassed by falling ill, especially with an old man's disease. The young attractive girl who outlives her beauty by middle age is the perfect metaphor. Where is the inner substance that supersedes such trivial vanity? I have weeks of recuperation to figure this one out.

As I muddle through the ensuing days (doing my damndest to act normal) I find myself, for the first time in my life, identifying with the infirmed. Sure I had been ill before: born with erythroblastosis fetalis, hospitalized with concussion and facial trauma in '67, knee arthroscopy in'81 and '87, shoulder surgery/arthroscopy in '90, '92 and 2001; but the temporary nature of these setbacks were always soothingly omniscient. Even my chronic back pain from degenerative spondylosis did not tip me over into the dispirited abyss of feeling like an invalid.

The cardiovascular system is different. Stroke and heart disease are different. This is a life changer!

There is not a day that I don't open my eyes in the morning hopeful that the E.R. visit, the terrorizing numbness, the difficulty walking, the stroke was just a bad dream. But as yet I have not awakened.

I deal with the reality of a numb left side that is less than coordinated and pray that it will get better. I fight off self-pity by doing my best to act normal. I walk at the most rapid (though hardly fast) pace possible without stumbling. I am able to drive, go to the hospital and operate with the residents (though my knot tying is tedious), and even work-out (swim laps, stepper, and some weight lifting). Golf is out of the question until I regain balance on my left side. I am better off than many (even if this gets no better) I know, but I still want to awaken from this damn dream.

The day I am scheduled for another heart MRI to further evaluate the degree of my aortic insufficiency I park in the staff lot (where I always park on the days I go into Duke to teach) anticipating leaving no later than 1:00 PM thus easily avoiding the traffic that comes with afternoon hospital change of shift. The exam takes about an hour longer than planned. Not unusual. But the imaging doc appears unsettled and motions for me to look at the images on the monitor explaining that he has unexpectedly picked up a clot in my lung. I urgently need a chest CAT scan with contrast to be certain and to evaluate the extent of the pulmonary embolism.

Super! Great! I'm not going to beat the traffic. In fact, I'm not going anywhere! If the scan is positive I need to be anticoagulated STAT! I could die from this!

Readmitted to the hospital (second time in less than two weeks) I begin blood thinners because my lungs (both sides) are filled with clots. No one can believe that I was not severely short of breath and could actually walk eight flights of stairs (as I did often in the hospital, always avoiding the elevators) and exercise without distress.

While in hospital more tests and consultations are performed. My aortic valve and arch are worse than previously thought. Once the lungs are clear and that immediate danger resolved I will be facing open heart surgery! Not a brain tumor or terminal cancer, but a real life changer, nevertheless!

The day I get out of the hospital I write a letter to my family, just in case.

Letter To My Dear Family
July 7, 2010

Dearest Deb, Eric, Stephanie and Morgan,

I love you guys so much. I will say this again in different ways. It can't be said too much.

Having just gotten out of the hospital for the second time in two weeks I feel particularly vulnerable physically and am facing unexpected heart surgery to preserve my life and our family as we have known it.

In the past I have used others' illness and misfortune to better appreciate what a wonderful, fortunate life we have had together: rich with prosperity, good health, and dreams. Now as I face my own mortality I appreciate it even more. Hopefully, I will survive the upcoming medical challenges and this letter need not be read. But if this is not the case, I want each of you to know how very happy you have made me even if I did not always show it.

Kids, your mother and I have worked hard to raise you to care about each other; to strive to be the best you can be; to be loyal to your future spouse; to respect others and be fair in your dealings with them. Eric, I know that getting a law degree and perhaps working in the sports industry will bring you great joy and success. Stephanie, I believe that pursuing a law or business degree will give you the independence to not have to rely on some dude to provide for you (listen closely Morgan). Morgie, you know how much joy your golf accomplishments have given me, but you have many other talents and special qualities to explore. Learn what they are and cultivate them.

Debbie, it was some ride. Thanks for sharing it with me. Now you can read the book (*Autobiography of a Baby Boomer*) and know that there was nothing sweeter in my life than our years together.

Stay united as family even though you may be apart with new families of your own. If you feud remember I am watching and that stuff pisses me off. Remind each other of my wishes for harmony between us *no matter what*. Let's never forget how much we mean to each other and how our love gives us strength to tackle the world.

Think of me when you can because when you do I am alive and want so much to be with you all.

XOB/XOD

Yeah, a bit emotional, but that's how I feel and make no excuses for it. Is there a future for me? And how long is it?

I kind of find myself living haircut to haircut. *Is this my last ocean swim? My last summer? My last Yankee game? My last supper with the family? My last full moon?*

CHAPTER 37

My Bonus Chapter

Take me home," I scribble; each letter superimposed on the first, preventing my kids from actually understanding my pleas.

The tube keeps my neck awkwardly straight, further frustrating my attempt to communicate. *I don't want people to see me like this! Out here in bed on the first fairway with a tube down my throat. Take me home. This should be private.*

Sensing my children squirming to calm me down, I somehow know that my circumstance cannot be as it appears. My hypoxic reverie is too far out there to be real.

Not having seen my parents or a bright white light, I must still be alive and delusional. *Go with it. The family would not leave you exposed like this to the world.*

***

A star! That's what I thought I would be post-op. The coronary angiogram was normal so all I needed was an aortic root and possible valve replacement. Out of bed and walking on the day of surgery confirmed my will to leave the hospital in four, not five days like Dr. Hughes, my surgeon, thought. Then, the damn peumothorax later that night put a damper on things. The emergency chest tube insertion knocked the crap out of me. Just moving or taking a breath was agony. *Not so tough, Robert, after all.*

"No. Don't let her come up and see me like this," I told the nurse when Debbie phoned into the ICU.

The next day, my transfer out of The Unit to step-down seemed like progress, but the chest tube still hurt like hell. And, again, I told the nurses not to let my wife see me like this.

Hours later, something was wrong. No longer with one-on-one nursing, I pressed my call button. Nothing. Pressed it again. Nothing—still. The damn chest tube and previous intubation left my voice ineffective. A prisoner in bed with an ominous feeling gave me new respect for POWs. John McCain came to mind. Then the stupidity of not letting my wife visit with me.

But somehow, miraculously, Debbie was right there in my face telling me to "Fight!" "Be strong!" I whispered about my letter to the family in the safe. Dr. Gritchnick replaced Debbie and explained the necessity of awake intubation.

"Hang the Dopamine," I heard. A vasopressor that maintains blood pressure and increases kidney flow is the cry of a last ditch effort to save a fading life. Like hanging crepe.

But my parents or the White Light never appeared— only my embarrassment of being in bed on the first fairway.

Back in the ICU, having survived a large pulmonary embolus, I hallucinate for days. The white walls of the hospital burst forth with intricate patterns, as do the simple blue scrubs worn by the staff. Harry Potter pictures dance before my eyes leading me to wonder if I will have any squash left once my brain is sufficiently oxygenated. LSD was understandable: a game; an adventure; a trip. This is pure insult. Not asked for, not anticipated, not good.

At times the double vision from my 1967 automobile accident comes back. And the numbness on my left side becomes profound. The neurologist suggests that the physiologic insult I have suffered allows previous weaknesses to recur. There is no new stroke. Without any better explanation, I accept this as temporary; and hope for the best.

My inability to be coherent (despite thinking that I am making sense during conversations) and my confinement to bed lead to rapid musculoskeletal deconditioning. This becomes terribly apparent once I am given the go-ahead to resume walking. The dependent edema in my legs from some right-sided heart failure and lack of exercise is shocking. The occupational therapist (barely older than my daughter Stephanie) suggests a scrotal wrap for my junk that is "big as a grapefruit." *Ugh, I'll pass on that, I am presently as emasculated as I can be, thank you very much.*

Each day a well wishing visitor or two from the orthopaedic department drops by. When I mention to Dr. Jennette that I had a nice conversation with two of our residents he says, "Yeah, they told me they stopped in and said you were really out of it." Ah, reinforcement of my delusional state. Will my mind ever be whole?

On post-op day ten I take a HIT. That's Heparin Induced Thrombocytopenia. My platelets are rapidly dropping in response to an autoimmune reaction I am having to the blood thinner heparin (used to keep me from having another pulmonary embolus). If the platelet count goes down too low I will not clot sufficiently to prevent uncontrollable bleeding. So bivalverudin, a different anticoagulation drip, is instituted. It has its own risks and does not always work. I am not to leave the hospital until my coagulation system is properly regulated on oral medication, which can easily take another week to achieve.

The next week in the ICU, a jungle of beeps and bells and blood drawing, leaves me totally sleep deprived. Again, I imagine what POWs must go through, but with intended harm, not help. I try to be tough, but am amazed at my frailty. The twelve-hour nursing shifts melt into a revolving door of dedicated caretakers each calling me "Buddy" or "Bud."

"I know how you feel, Buddy." "Hang in there, Bud. Tomorrow will be better." "Just have to get some more blood to check your platelet count, Buddy."

And then there is David. A male nurse with years of ICU experience and a hell of a story to boot! A native of St. Louis, and long time diabetic, he made the trip to Duke for a kidney *and* pancreas transplant in hope of saving his life. "No place does more transplants than Duke," he declares. "Post-op I was right here in this ICU. Just like you, but I was on immunosuppressive precautions."

Home in about two weeks, David suffered a severe setback when the transplants failed. Back again for another try, he thought about just letting his disease take its course rather than submitting to the horrific struggle a second time. But his wife and boy made the decision clear. The second time was a charm. No more chronic renal failure. No more diabetes. A new man who now dedicated himself to taking care of others in this very same ICU.

When David says, "I know how you feel, friend," it is the truth. Empathy—not sympathetic compassion. He is full of tough love and I am sad to see him change shifts.

Once allowed to eat solid food and encouraged to get up and walk, my spirits soar. The food has flavor and consistency. The chest tubes and A-lines are gone and now it is up to me to revive my humanness. The only rule when getting up is not to use my arms, for fear of pulling apart my sternotomy (the repair of the breast bone through which the open heart surgery was performed).

"Use your legs and core to stand up. Don't lean on the Swedish Walker. It is there for balance and reassurance only," the PT Ashley advises. At first I am worried about covering my ass (so freely exposed by the shrunken hospital gown), but I am soon consumed with my profound feebleness and physiologic decrepitude. *Walk? I can't even stand up!* I watch the orderlies and food service people outside my door push mops and carry trays, thinking *how blessed and amazing they are to be able to stand and walk so easily.* My sadness borders on self-pity, which I fight with all my might.

The long road back to leaving the hospital sixteen days post-op is symbolic for it being Thanksgiving Day. Not one to make speeches before holiday dinners, I give thanks to God and my parents for letting me share a real meal with my wife, kids, my sister (who drove down from Maryland), and Grandma Betty.

Part Three

CHAPTER 38

Reflections

Life's journey is not to arrive at the grave safely in a
well-preserved body, but rather to skid in sideways,
totally worn out, shouting 'holy shit...what a ride!'
(George Carlin)

I am the same self-reliant, cerebral guy who ran off to India forty years ago, so when my wife asks me on the ride back from UGA (after visiting Stephanie for "Daddy-Daughter Day"), "How do you discuss politics with Carl and Elliott and manage to reconcile your liberal hippy days with your conservative views now?" I respond by saying that I *don't* discuss politics with them. Out of mutual respect for one another we have declared a moratorium on political discourse, especially during this past incendiary election year.

With regards to my own seemingly incongruous cultural beliefs of yesteryear and today, I do not feel at all hypocritical. The very same familiar voice of reason and perspective that was with me on the island of Formentera is still with me right here in Raleigh, North Carolina. The difference is hair length, skin turgor, and forty years of living. The latter means a lot, of course, when it comes to dealing with today's challenges including marriage, parenthood, retirement, illness, and world events.

I, like many of you, am flirting with my sixth decade on earth; an adventure that always seemed isolated to my parents' generation. But here we are! Is it the beginning of "old age," an extension of middle age, or just some existential BS that is better left alone for fear of getting totally bummed-out? Well I have no intention of defining the state we are in or heading into. My only desire is to continue sharing the joy I get reflecting on our very special Baby Boom era and all it has given us. Even my teenage kids (sorry Eric and Stephanie, I know you are now in your twenties) find our era (its music, "Age of Aquarius" style, and bravado) awesome (or as we used to say "groovy"). Tom McGuane said it best, "We were the last generation to be cooler than our kids."

When I started writing this book I thought, *who am I to write an autobiography? After all, autobiographies are written by famous people.* Even my local fame up in New Jersey, when I was at the peak of my medical practice, wouldn't be enough to sell many books. But my voice of reason told me that I am not alone. I am one of eighty million Baby Boomers who, as a generation, have true celebrity. We are fascinated with ourselves and each other. We love watching *Leave it to Beaver* and *I Love Lucy*, listening to the Beatles and Eagles on classic vinyl, and revel in the ageless Rolling Stones on tour (still *painting it black*) as much as our kids do. That is *our* stuff and it is so solid it has survived to become classic. How different it is from our parents' big band era that pretty much died when Rock and Roll took over. Not even hip hop or rap can squeeze out the Baby Boom culture; nothing can. And we lived through it! How special is that?!

So I, Bob Schultz, may not be famous, but my story is your story. It is a story about growing up in the '50s when a haircut cost 50 cents and a super jumbo banana split at the F.W. Woolworth Co. soda fountain set you back 39 cents. When penny candy reigned and a Three Musketeers Bar had two grooves so you could break it into three parts and share it with two friends or save some for later. When the sound of the Good Humor Man's bell started the race to see who could get to the ice-cream truck first. (Mr. Frosty had a different sounding bell that I never answered because Mom made it very clear that Mr. Frosty was inferior to the Good Humor brand. The Mr. Frosty truck wasn't as clean or white either and all the stickers on the outside made it look cheap.) When black and white World War II movies and Westerns were shown at the local drive-in and Roller Derby on TV proved that women were just as tough as men (with or without the feminist movement).

Back in the day, our parents didn't lock the house or car doors and we didn't chain our bikes to the bicycle rack because nobody thought about taking things that didn't belong to them. People worked, cared for their families, looked out for their neighbors, obeyed the law, and respected their country. It was a simpler time; maybe because we were young; maybe because there were fewer people; maybe because traditional family values were sacred; maybe because we didn't have the internet to rape us of our innocence. We thought of our service men and women as heroes (not political puppets or "baby killers") and most of us wanted to be policemen or firemen or teachers when we grew up (instead of hating authority and finding fault with anyone telling us what to do).

Christmas was a special time for good cheer, peace on earth, and giving. Being Jewish didn't ruin that spirit for me one bit. Scrooge, the original Grinch, represented the nasty, self-absorbed side of people none of us ever wanted to be. The "warmth" of the holiday season made us all feel like kids at Christmas time with magic filling the air and our dreams. The divorce rate (2.2 per 1000 population in 1957) was low (as compared to 5.3 per 1000 in 1981) and there was no glorification of criminals (the good guy wore a white hat and the bad guy wore the black hat).

Now somewhere along the line, it became wrong to have the bad guy wear a black hat and I do get that argument when it comes down to skin color and personal experience with prejudice. My "brother" Elliott proved that to me first-hand when we were trying to catch a cab in NYC back in '05 and the drivers wouldn't stop since he was black. But totally flipping things so that "bad" means "good" and the "gangsta" life is cool, well, that's just way too much spin for this Boomer. I can hear my mother up in heaven shrieking with laughter at this comment. "See Bobby, now you know how we felt when you grew your hair long, ran off to India, and told us we were crazy for not understanding." *Hmmm...*

So I am writing my autobiography, but it is really *our* autobiography. This story covers our era nearly year by year. And although I relate everything from my point of view, I hope it will tickle the nostalgic center in every Boomer's brain. I also believe that if your children or grandchildren (careful) read *Autobiography of a Baby Boomer,* they will be stimulated to ask you questions about what that time was like for you. Why? Because it is about our era, a special time when we all lived our separate lives but were miraculously bonded by profound and unprecedented experiences and events: the assassination of a beloved President, the landing of a man on the moon, the psychedelic experience, the belief that love and peace could conquer all.

We've all been around the block (even if it's your very own block). Some sixty years of living can be an awfully good teacher. The greaser who road a 650 Triumph, smoked outside of shop class and made out with his girl under the bleachers is now a banker. The Vietnam vet who survived the terrifying jungles of Southeast Asia fighting for democracy (not to mention life itself), and found himself called a "baby killer" when he returned home is now a financial planner. The hippy who dropped out of medical school to find Nirvana in India is now an orthopaedic surgeon. The *Yippy* (member of the Youth International Party, a la Jerry Rubin) in the '60s becomes a *Yuppie* (young upwardly mobile professional) in the '80s and then a hedge fund CEO. This work is meant for you guys because I know you can relate. So if one of my kids is reading this **put it down right now**! I may sound hypocritical, but this book is not an excuse to run off to India. Honestly, I think my kids are way too smart and secure (without the drugs and '60s stuff) to feel that they must find answers to life from a little old yogi sitting under a Banyan tree, anyway.

I have written *Autobiography of a Baby Boomer* primarily in the present, using the patois of the time in order to best capture the ethos we may have forgotten, but desperately long to remember. Sure, there was a lot of crap back then that no one wants to rehash, but we call them the "good old days" because the good stuff rises to the top of our consciousness along with the strength and excitement of our youth. Few can deny that we Baby Boomers have impacted the world like no other generation before. And we are far from done, if only by our sheer numbers alone. We are eighty million strong and this is our story. It is why I have confidence that what is contained in these pages will be entertaining to many and deeply touching to others who, like me, find fascination in "the good old days."

Although four years younger than I,and claiming never to have tried drugs, including weed, I find Bill O'Reilly's book *A Bold Fresh Piece of Humanity* to be recommended reading for Baby Boomers. If, for some reason, you can't stand the guy or his views, then just read Chapter 14 "Mysteries of the Universe." From the outset he tells you not to read this chapter; apologizes for writing it, and then goes on with a sardonic romp through the not so distant past. When you are done with that one, get *Boom!* by Tom Brokaw. Though not a BB himself since he was born in 1940, his book about the '60s is well researched and includes many interviews with authentic Boomers who look back on those years. Rereading Tom Wolfe's *The Electric Kool-aid Acid Test* and Robert M. Pirsig's *Zen and the Art of Motorcycle Maintenance* will make you wonder, "Where the hell was my head at back then?"

The '60s, I am sure most of you will agree, is the first decade that comes to mind when our era is referenced. Although it represents just one sixth of our time here on earth it is clearly the flagship of our epoch and certainly the period that most fascinates my kids and me. "Turn on, tune in, drop out." "Sex, drugs, and Rock and Roll." "If it feels good, do it." "God is dead." "If you remember the '60s, you weren't there." "America, love it or leave it." "We shall overcome." "Burn, baby, burn." "Don't trust anyone over thirty." "Power to the people." "Generation gap." "We thought we could change the world with words like 'love' and 'freedom'" (*The Sad Café* by the Eagles, 1979). It has pizzazz because it was a time of dramatic, rapid change that came at us like a runaway freight train. Civil rights, the feminist movement, the Vietnam War, the drug culture, and divisive politics smacked us in the face with unrelenting passion. Even without the information boom of the IT era, few escaped its revolutionary whirlwind. There was simply no place to hide. While some men walked on the moon, others were dying in Vietnam and at Kent State. Our new, huge generation is the product of assassination, war, racial upheaval, sexual revolution, and recreational drugs.

The decade of revolution really started in 1963 with the assassination of JFK and ended, for the most part, in 1974 when Nixon resigned. Both political dramas serve as historical bookends framing a time of fantasy (the end of Camelot) with an outrageous culture war over civil rights and Vietnam so intermingled with psychedelic drug use that smarter people than I are still trying to figure it out. 1968 alone (sometimes referred to as "The Year that Hope Died") brought us the Tet offensive in Vietnam, LBJ's declaration that he would not seek reelection, the assassinations of MLK, Jr. and RFK, and riots at the DNC in Chicago. Police were called "pigs" and returning Vietnam vets called "baby killers."

With the loss of inspirational leaders and the frustration

that young people feel when they do not get what they want quickly enough, the civil rights and anti-war movements got ugly. Reverend King's dream of a peaceful emergence from white dominance became dominated by Black Nationalism and the Black Panthers. Like the unabashed racism of white supremacy, black power mongers like Stokely Carmichael, Bobby Seale, and Huey Newton turned to anarchy as did SDS Weathermen Mark Rudd, John Jacobs, Terry Robbins, and Bill Ayers. Abbie Hoffman's *Steal this Book* and *Fuck the System* were books with catchy titles, that I must admit, seemed very "far-out" and "right-on" to me at first, but I eventually recognized them to be exactly what they were: destructive.

I credit Elliott for helping me to feel comfortable being "color blind." At this high-pitched time he allowed me to forget he was black; not because he acted white, but because he didn't allow race to divide us. It was about the important stuff: chicks, music, and having a good time.

I kind of missed some of the aggressive, caustic nature of the counterrevolution because Hamilton College was a small, isolated all-men's school that was relatively radical-free. Oh we had the drugs and long hair all right, but *sans* sit-ins and administrative building take-overs. The lack of women on campus until my senior year, I believe, had a lot to do with the low-keyed nature of the student body and the lack of heroics. There were no cute chicks for whom to show off. We were more about partying ("rolls" to Skidmore, Cazenovia, and Syracuse), education (all I wanted to be to that point was a doctor like my dad), and moving on. When I left medical school in 1970 to go on the road in the Eastern Hemisphere I missed all of the American turbulence for the next four years. Sure, I read about it, but my mind was on chicks, partying, having a good time, and, oh yes, finding Nirvana. I certainly did not miss out on the self-indulgence part of the '60s; dropping out and becoming one of the road people was the epitome of self-absorption masked in the form of a quest that would make Don Quixote blush.

Of course, young people must find themselves. It is part of growing up. My son chose law school and my oldest daughter, who just finished college is job hunting while contemplating graduate school. My youngest is filling out college applications So far, academic choices head their list of important decisions (although I am sure they have other concerns of some magnitude about which I am unaware, and, honestly I am not sure I really want to know those details). I want to think that they are fortunate not to be on the college campuses in the '60s with so much distraction and guys like Timothy Leary and Richard Alpert around glorifying LSD and mind expansion. My son doesn't have to worry about the draft despite our country being at war. My daughter doesn't have to feel pressured into having sex with the guy she's with just because the prevailing creed is "free love" and Crosby, Stills and Nash are singing, "If you can't be with the one you love, love the one you're with." As a "cat" back then, that whole open-minded free love thing was the supreme tool (along with drugs) used for getting into chicks' pants.

A twenty year old has enough hormonal confusion going on as it is without the extraneous blasting from his peers that "you can't trust anyone over thirty" and "*1984* is just around the corner so watch out!" Still, the new millennium has tremendous similarity to the '60s. Forty years has brought us once again to a divided country and an unpopular war in a land where we do not speak the language and cannot often distinguish civilians (whom we are there to liberate) from the enemy. Drugs have not gone away nor has peer pressure. Despite electing an African-American President of the United States we are still being torn apart for not being "progressive" enough for some. Secularists declare that those of us who believe in God are fools and work hard at shaming retailers and government into dropping the words "Christmas" and "God" from use. The friction is made worse by two simple facts: the rapidly rising population and the communication explosion. The world has gotten smaller without getting friendlier. This is not good.

CHAPTER 39

Freedom

Being incarcerated really got my attention. Sure, Germany and the Philippines were one-night stands where the level of fear was so low it bordered on inconvenience. But Turkey, let me tell you, though just one night, put the fear of God in me because it was Turkey! It was one of those guess-my-folks-were-right moments that knocked me down a notch (*believe me, an oversimplification now that I'm not scared shitless*) and made me face my own mortality. But even that experience was relatively brief, like being scared out of your hiccups, in relation to the span of one's life. The impact of that mental trauma was quickly forgotten (and even looked back upon as an exciting adventure).

My Afghanistan internment was different. Not only was I confined to a dank 9'x12' dungeon filled with slime and four Afghan eyes consuming my privacy; the place reeked of human waste so vile that its memory viscerally upsets me to this day. Beyond the disgust and humiliation were twelve days of Hell that burned the ordeal into my soul. Time matters. It permits reactions to develop and take hold. It allows each cell to fully absorb the essence of the milieu, however noxious. I cannot imagine how a longtime POW or hostage to terrorists manages to maintain the faith, but I can relate on more than an intellectual level. With each passing day the anticipation of freedom becomes more obscured. Hope becomes a struggle and the voice of madness begins to whisper.

Nearly forty years later I can still taste the anguish and smell that cell. The other day, on a pit stop heading to Georgia with Debbie and Morgan, I hit the head at a gas station out- house and got my socks knocked off by the stench waiting for me behind the door. Vapors of stale urine momentarily transported me back to that Kabul jail. I nearly dropped to my knees, simultaneously thinking how funny it was that a scent could trigger the brain's memory neurons to fire, revealing thoughts not accessed in decades.

"Freedom" is an interesting word: *The quality or state of being free.* The dictionary says nothing about being out of prison or physical confinement. It does provide the synonym "independence" which makes me think of a state of mind as much as a physical state of being. Make no mistake, getting out of jail initially brought on a profound sense of freedom and relief, but that gift was fleeting…especially after the one-nighters in Germany and Manila. The liberation experience after a night in the Turkish jail was longer lasting because the fear factor was greater. I am perplexed, however, that my jubilancy after emancipation from the devastating Afghan incarceration also had a time limit.

Whether lasting days, weeks or months the ecstasy of

physical liberation (or surviving a near death experience, for that matter) is finite because normal life resumes and in that normalcy the gratefulness is lost. What takes its place is an all-consuming refocus on life's countless games (many of which are absolutely necessary and solemn) that leave little time for simple appreciation of one's autonomy.

As hard as I try, I cannot consistently hold on to the paradigm of gratefulness combined with relief and satisfaction that I found so easily upon getting out of the hoosegow. I am angered by my inability to remain in the embrace of freedom, to cherish and adore it because, when I did, it felt so damn good. Instead I lock myself up in a mental prison of recurring pettiness and dissatisfaction. All those years of travel, the internments, the times I thought that I might die, six decades of experience...certainly by now I should own the message. But there I go, digressing, finding fault with the process and becoming impatient.

Maybe freedom can't be appreciated without bookends of imprisonment?

CHAPTER 40

Growing Up and Parenthood

We Baby Boomer parents tend to coddle and over manage our children, possibly because we had so little structure ourselves, outside of school, and perhaps because of overpopulation, the internet, and our awareness of child predators. We do their homework, pay for SAT tutoring, set up play dates, organize their sports (often acting like children ourselves, right before their eyes), take them on elaborate strategically planned vacations, regularly update their personal computers and cell phones, and hypocritically denounce the wildness of our youth. No more knocking on neighbors' doors asking if Johnny can "come out and play" (in part because we don't even know our neighbors anymore). No more riding a bike without a helmet or sitting in the back of a moving pick-up truck. Now that our generation is in charge we are a bit freaked out by the awesome responsibilities that we routinely rebelled against forty years ago.

But have we taken away our own children's freedom?

It's kind of like the wild, footloose, and fancy-free guy who becomes a strict father because he is so well versed in all of the temptations and ways to screw up out there. The once promiscuous mom sets the earliest curfews and the parents who wound up with menial jobs because they blew school off are anal about their kids' grades. We want the best for our children and recognize disaster in our own past transgressions.

The feminist who had a child "late" and went through the scare of perhaps not experiencing biological parenthood at all, encourages her daughter to be aware of her own biologic clock and not feel forced into competing with men in the work force just because it is a "noble" cause. As Anne Taylor Fleming says in *Motherhood Deferred*, "It was absolutely joyous to be a young woman in the early '70s... I put contraception—and ambition—between my womb and pregnancy." (Enovid, the newly available birth control pill produced by Searle in the early '60s was the pharmacologic gateway to the sexual revolution.) She warns women, "You're making choices if you are not making them. So pay attention." It reminds me of a high school classmate of mine whom I saw at a recent reunion—she became so dependent on her striking beauty (and recreational drugs) that she chose being a Mafioso trophy rather than finding the right guy, marrying and having children. Now in her sixties, without her youthful beauty, she appeared lonely. I don't know about the drugs.

For some, parenthood came before growing up. It was one of those harsh reality checks that leave little wiggle room for copping out. Some grew up quickly in the jungles of Vietnam while many of us found the road to responsibility to be a much longer route. The egocentricity of youth is a strong driving force made even more powerful by the "feel good, everything else be damned" ethos of '60s and '70s. The single-minded task of getting high or getting laid or finding Nirvana was far less stressful than the multitasking needed to become successful in business or in raising a family (much less, both at the same time).

By the '80s we Boomer flower children and radicals had to finally face the fear of not having money. The real world will do that to you. Delivering the "message" works for just so long, when you are young and healthy despite what you throw into your body. As Lawrence Kasdan, writer and director of *The Big Chill* once said, "College gave us a false sense of power and entitlement, and then we hit the real world"… giving us that "big chill."

Fortunately, IT technologies provided fertile ground for financial success for many of us. Our generation is particularly good at playing games, and the money making game is no exception. Long hair and tie-died shirts gave way to razor cuts and three-piece suits; Afros to shaved heads; beads to Rolexes; meditation to due diligence. We have produced more billionaires than other generations have produced millionaires. While I am certainly not one of the lucky stinkin' rich, I did (as you have seen) turn in my hippy gear for a white coat and surgeon's gloves. More than two decades of that vocational change allowed me to explore the realms of retirement.

As you have noted I have "young" children (24, 22, and 18) because I did not marry until age 39 to a woman more than a decade my junior and had my first child at 41. Many of my peers are grandparents and tell me, "It's fabulous!" They've gone through empty nesting, their kids' weddings and watching their children have children of their own. I have not yet done those things and am grateful (God willing) that they are still to come.

I want to stretch this whole life experience out as long as possible and fill my book with as many chapters as the binding will hold. It keeps me young and looking forward. But I am interested in your story if you are a BB on the grandparent side of things. I encourage everyone to write your story; if not to be published, then at least to share with your children. I assure you that they will be fascinated to hear about your take on our history. Write it down. Help tell our story. Not being female, black, or a Vietnam vet I cannot scribe from these perspectives. There are eighty million points of view on our era and I can't wait to read some of them.

CHAPTER 41

Two Generations of Baby Boomers

I have already mentioned that although my wife Debbie qualifies as a post-war Baby Boomer because she was born in 1957 (just prior to the sudden decline in the new birth population) she is actually of a different generation than I. She does not remember *Charlie Chan* (nor his number one or two sons), *Hopalong Cassidy*, *Life of Riley*, *Amos N' Andy*, *Topper*, *Cisco Kid*, *Broken Arrow*, *Burns and Allen*, *Dobie Gilles*, *Car 54 Where Are You?*, *Highway Patrol*, *Howdy Doody*, *Rin Tin Tin*, *Death Valley Days*, *Queen for a Day*, *Sky King*, *Wanted Dead or Alive*, *Wagon Train*, *Gene Autry*, *Your Show of Shows*, *This is Your Life*, *The George Gobel Show*, *People Are Funny*, *I Remember Mama*, *The Phil Silvers Show (Sergeant Bilko)*, *The Tonight Show with Jack Paar*, *Arthur Godfrey and Friends*, or *Your Hit Parade*. Shows like *Our Gang* (which she calls The Little Rascals) and *The Honeymooners* she knows from watching *Nickelodeon* with the kids.

While I was at the Hamilton College pub in 1968 having a beer in celebration of nightfall, she was studying for an arithmetic test she had coming up the next day at Hubbs Elementary School in East North Port, Long Island. She may have watched the Beatles morph from clean-cut guys into Sergeant Pepper's Lonely Hearts Club Band, but she was too young to recognize them as champions of the guru circuit and drug culture. By the time she got to Penn State University in '75 the Vietnam War was over so she didn't rub elbows with antiwar protestors. Streaking had taken the place of sit-ins and mod replaced the hippy/bohemian look. The only politics Debbie recalls on campus had to do with securing football seats on the fifty-yard line in Happy Valley.

So by missing the whole psychedelic scene with its "mind-opening" recreational drug using counterculture, she can only shake her head when asked to reflect on the '60s. What she really knows of it she has gotten second hand from books and movies and my nonsensical bloviating. So we have a bit of a dilemma: you are technically a bona fide Baby Boomer if born between the end of WW II and 1957 (based on the post war population explosion and the rapid birth rate decline after '57), but those born in the later part of that fornication frenzy, for the most part, missed an essential part of our era (the '60s) because they were too young. After much thought and some nonscientific research (talking with younger friends) I have come to reconcile this conundrum with the belief that we all still have at least four decades of similar memories to share even if they are not quite as sexy as the '60s.

My sister, Helaine, born during WW II and nearly

five years earlier than I, graduated college in 1964 and was busy raising a family while the Vietnam War and the counterculture started heating up. So while she certainly remembers the beginning of Rock and Roll and the old TV shows and movies of the '50s, she was tucked away in a conservative household while the rest of us slightly younger chicks and cats were grooving on the incense trip. She, of course, doesn't qualify as a BB anyway because most Americans were far more consumed with fighting the Big War than making babies in 1942. Her tiny generation was okay with simply growing up and turning into their parents (raising kids and keeping house was just fine with her). Contrast our huge generation that believes it has the power to do anything, even break the mold.

I am sure there are some out there who were born outside of the years that define the post war baby boom era, but who experienced and contributed to the ethos of our time. As well, there must be those who did not get swept up in the turbulence and drama of the '60s, but will nevertheless find much in this book over which to reminisce. For the most part, I am always skeptical when I hear someone my age saying that they never tried pot or that they took a hit but did not inhale. For all those Bill Clintons out there, "it's okay; we all did it. It was a time of experimentation and letting your (long) hair down. As long as you're not still hitting the Kool-Aid and looking for a nickel bag you are probably successfully plugged into mainstream America and a fine example for your kids.

CHAPTER 42

The Hiatus

There are some of us who took an alternate route. Call it a leave of absence, sabbatical, or hiatus from the straight and narrow; most of us had a detour along the way. It likely came during the '60s and early '70s; mine certainly did. The times called for turning on and dropping out. Some were more dedicated to the hippy approach than others. There was certainly a hierarchy of freaks based on commitment to the lifestyle. The longer your hair, the thinner you were, the more rings and beads you wore, and the more Far Eastern your rags (no underwear, of course), the more you looked the part. Bumming around the country, getting on the bus (*a la* Ken Kesey's Merry Pranksters) or, better still, leaving the country to bum around the world and follow the sun scored big points!

The road people, as I call them, were truly hard core. These Westerners (mostly Europeans) spent year after year on the hippy trail, from Ibiza, Formentera, and Morocco in the spring and summer to Kabul, Kashmir, and Goa in the fall and winter. Among the spiritual seekers and dabbling psychedelic enthusiasts were the forlorn junkies who found their daily fixes abundant in the Far East where pharmacies (believe it or not) sell cocaine and heroin with complete deference. Opium dens are abundant and thrive by supporting, and profiting from, dope habits. As ridiculous as it may sound, back in the day, there was such a fascination with drugs that even the hard stuff like smack (heroin) had a mystique and allure about it for many. The naive and foolish included John Lennon and Yoko Ono who spent upwards of a year in their New York apartment (the famous "bed-in") strung out on dope. For the disbelievers, just listen to the song *Happiness Is a Warm Gun* written by J.L. (though credited to Lennon/McCartney).

Now, the world has dramatically changed since the early '70s when I and thousands of other freaks rambled through the Middle East. No more Shah of Iran at the helm to make the trek through Persia to the Orient not only doable but fun. And those damn Taliban have surely eliminated Siggy's restaurant in Kabul where we used to hang, smoke chillums and listen to Cat Stevens. Being jailed in Afghanistan today, no doubt, would be far more stressful than it was for me back in '71 (and as I mentioned, that was horrific). Driving a Volkswagen bus through the Khyber Pass in 2013 would likely be an adventure you would not live to tell about.

So I am extremely grateful that being in my early twenties at the right time in history gave me the opportunity to journey unharmed overland from Europe through Turkey and the Middle East to India and beyond. Although my four-year junket was torture for my parents (particularly Mom) I will play the spoiled child and admit that I would not trade it for Warren Buffet's wealth. The thrill of solo navigation through the wild frontier (proving time and again that I was resourceful and self-reliant) and meeting the most far-out people imaginable was absolutely priceless.

Having related tales of my travels to many, I have been encouraged over the years to write a book about them. Not until recently, however, did I view my story as noteworthy or interesting enough to commit to print. My excuse has always been that my globetrotting days were nothing unusual for back then. It seemed that everyone was doing something way out there. But now that things have settled down and *so many* years have passed, I see that many of us BBs share a fascination with those glory years when we had our youth and free spirit. So my interest in what happened to me has resurfaced and I sincerely hope that I have delivered the ethos of our era successfully through my story. You guys have come a long way through your own hiatuses and deserve a jolt to your memory so you can temporarily recapture the flavor of those "glory" years.

Whether you took a spiritual trip to the Island of Eleuthera like my buddy Peter, or lived on a kibbutz like Beth's sister Judy, or hung out in Haight Ashbury like my pal Cakes, the time to do it was back then, when we were young, uncommitted and adventurous. As long as you survived with your faculties intact, you are no doubt richer for it. I know I came back with a much deeper appreciation and respect for myself, my parents, and my country. Often I met those who had no safety net; no loving parents to return to or a land of real opportunity that awaited them once they got the travel bug out of their systems. And those pitiful junkies who sacrificed their birthright for that elusive high; how sad it was then and how profoundly sad it seems now.

CHAPTER 43

Politics

Discussing politics today seems more than ever to be a sure-fire way to disrupt a good dinner or end a long friendship. "Politics" in its purest definition means *"the art or science of government."* It has, however, come to mean *"competition between groups or individuals for power and leadership."* Instead of a collection of minds working diligently and honestly towards the goal of staying on the course our brilliant Founding Fathers designed, and adapting to the ever increasing American population and its challenges, we have a shameful bastardization of a magnificent system.

I am not deriding the concept of differing opinions or the two party system; I am simply upset with the motivation behind those that come to political office. Greed and avarice unfortunately go hand in hand with capitalism and free enterprise. Like Michael Douglas said in *Wall Street* (1987), "Greed, for a lack of a better word, is good." It is the supreme motivator in the money game. It makes pigs like Bernard

Madoff and Enron's Andrew Fastow possible. Hey, I see it in my own profession of medicine where rogue surgeons sell surgery to trusting patients just for a buck (despite taking the Hippocratic Oath, swearing "above all to do no harm").

Greed and self-indulgence are not going away. John Lennon can "imagine" all day long, here on earth or in heaven, but the reality is that some people simply cannot control themselves. They certainly should not be allowed to become doctors or government representatives of the people. Unfortunately, unscrupulous people hide their greed and selfishness well and attain positions of power. Do I have a solution? No. There are simply too many people desirous of becoming lawmakers or doctors (although Obamacare may well take care of this) to adequately weed out the bad guys and girls before they can wreak havoc.

So, that's it? We are stuck with corruption?

Well, we have been for years and it has gotten worse because, although the percentage of evildoers may not have changed, the total number has no doubt increased with the population rise. It is like an infection: the body gets contaminated with bacteria and if left unchecked the bugs multiply rapidly, feeding off its host until it dies. As doctors we must make the diagnosis of infection (fever, redness, elevated white blood cell count) and fight it with antibiotics. As citizens we must recognize that our country is contaminated with power hungry bastards and carefully elect officials who have demonstrated proper public service and intolerance for corruption (like Rudy Giuliani did in New York City).

I for one am amazed that we have allowed the patient to get so sick. The ombudsmen (on both sides of the political aisle) were negligent. They were too wrapped up in their own agendas ("Everyone should own a house" and "How can I get reelected?") to step back, take stock, and defend our country from crooks and bad policy. Now that we are in economic crisis, and we know exactly who most of the bad guys are, we must get them out of positions of power and prosecute those who have broken laws in order to send a message to other upcoming scumbags not to try it. As slow as the medical profession has been over the years to police its own, after being pretty much taken over by "managed care," it is now implementing strong measures to help assure that the rats are kept in check. We voters must do the same.

Although I have always fancied myself an independent thinker, voting for the quality of the candidate rather than along party lines, I have, over the years, definitely developed strong opinions about our country and how it should be governed. My travels tell me that the United States of America is the very best country I have seen—by a mile! We have the rule of law, state of the art technology and, above all, we value human life and freedom (explicitly proven by the fact that, as distasteful as she is, the mindless Chelsea Handler can get on the air and call our President a "rat bastard.")

History tells us that nondemocratic forms of government do not do well. The Communist Block in our "short" lifetime has fallen. There is little to envy in the Arab world and its lack of respect for human life, women, and diversity is egregious. Our free enterprise system has produced more knowledge about our earth and beyond (leading to inventions that benefit all mankind) than anywhere. Israel is a close second despite existing as a nation no longer than most of us Baby Boomers have been alive and having a population of just over seven million.

America is an easy place to live because we its citizens value freedom. This is what binds us together and makes us great. And we must cherish what we have fought and died for over the last two and a half centuries, keeping in mind that the enemy to our freedom may not simply be Islamic terrorists from the Middle East, but can come from within. The Civil War almost destroyed us one hundred sixty years ago and our own present divisiveness keeps that threat alive.

What I see today reminds me of the '60s and the hardheaded conflict (young against old, distain for the establishment and disgust with the counterculture) that nearly tore us apart. We are waist deep in a culture war between traditionalists and secular ideologues who want to change America into a government controlled welfare state devoid of religious guidance.

While I am by no means a religious zealot I can't help but remember how upset and confused my sixth grade girlfriend Joan was because her Jewish father and Catholic mother chose not to give her a religion at all. She simply had no faith to relate to (or fall back on) like the rest of us. Our nation was founded by Pilgrims pursuing religious freedom. Over the centuries we have grown strong as a melting pot of religious and ethnic tolerance. Slavery and racial discrimination was a profoundly dark side of our evolution as a nation and although there will always be bigotry in this world we have come a long way. We are finally getting it right with regards to race, but the pendulum may be swinging too far left where intolerance of religion and pursuit of the American Dream is defiled.

CHAPTER 44

Retirement and Old Age

I pulled the trigger on retirement on August 10, 2004 at age fifty-seven. It is over eight years now and fortunately I have adjusted well. Much has to do with perspective and planning. My attitude has always been that my chosen vocation is a means of making a living and accumulating wealth so that one day I would no longer *have* to work. That is not to say that I would not have continued to practice medicine for longer if the thrill remained, but it did not (managed care and ruthless government scrutiny saw to that).

The people who stick with their career work until someone or thing forces them out to pasture I call "lifers." My dad was one. As I have mentioned, were you to ask him "Irv, who are you?" he would answer without hesitation, "I am a doctor." Only after further questioning would he reveal that he is married with two children. That is not to say that he did not love and enjoy his family, but rather that he identified his persona with being a physician. Understandable; he dedicated most of his life to the profession. Dad was secure in his role, did it very well, and was highly respected for it. When he finally retired at age eighty-one it was because he had outlived the hospital age limit (eighty) to operate and shortly after that his patient base rapidly dwindled (not to mention that Mom had been on his case to retire for more than a decade). He managed to live for four more years: playing cards, some golf, and following my mother around. But clearly, the *joie de vivre* was sapped from him.

It is terribly important to know who you are, as early on in your life as possible. That way you have more time to prepare for the inevitable. Certainly, attaining financial independence (aka, "F-U money") makes things easier, but does not completely address the emotional part of no longer having your customary work routine (and for us guys, the manly role of hunter, i.e. bread winner).

I, for one, was never comfortable standing pat for very long. Although I practiced orthopaedic surgery for nearly quarter of a century, I experienced great change during those years (getting married, raising a family, and moving several times). My desire for new experiences (or fear of boredom) has always been with me. My meta-cognition gives me the overview that life is short and I want desperately to fill it with as many chapters as reasonably possible (without hurting anyone, too much, along the way…sorry Mom). Retirement is not the final chapter.

I retired on my own terms—not because I was fired, too old, or stricken with illness. The decision was easy because I had no fear of wondering what I would do with myself. Firstly, I did not want to continue missing my kids' activities and watching them grow up—as much for me as for them.

Hearing about how they played or performed (even when watching video of the performance) is a quantum drop beneath the real experience. Secondly, I still had my health so the things I love to do like exercise training, golf, and travel would be more accessible. Thirdly, I strategically set up a part-time gig at Duke University teaching orthopaedic residents in and outside of the operating room. This helped curb the guilt factor of letting my hard earned skills go to waste, and gave me a sense of purpose. Fourthly, I had always been enamored with writing and looked forward to having the time to see what I could produce.

What has been difficult, though not surprising, is the sudden loss of stardom that I enjoyed for many years as founder and senior doc of Garden State Orthopaedic Associates. While prepared for no longer being "The Man" (live long enough and the ego stroking, I guess, becomes less important) I am a bit bothered by the lack of clout I have in my new community. I left New Jersey because I was convinced that I would constantly be barraged with medical questions by all who knew me and, not wanting to be rude, I would answer them. In that case, I'd still be practicing medicine and might as well get paid for it. So we moved to North Carolina, but saddly found that we left our home network and the luxury of VIP treatment up North. Just like everyone else, we now have to wait (sometimes weeks) for a doctor's appointment. No more being squeezed in at our convenience. Welcome to the real world, Schultz!

Truth be known, I have had only one bad dream: where I went back up to Jersey to visit the old office. It was being renovated and looked entirely different; in fact, it was huge; the size of a football field. As I entered, not sure which way to go, I became painfully aware that no one knew me and just about everyone was new. When I did see faces that I recognized (like Irene and Ken) they had no time to talk to me. I tried to act like I had a purpose for being there, and accept my fate graciously, *but*...and then I woke up. This nightmare happened only once, surprisingly on August 10, 2009, the fifth anniversary of my retirement.

Clearly, my powerful ego lives! It's been with me all the way, and it is no doubt the glue that holds me together. But even though I may be starved a bit for recognition, I find solace and joy in owning each day, as I did during only one other period in my life—when I bummed around the world free of timetables, alarm clocks, and hourly commitments.

Now, I can resume the search again without rushing. While I know that happiness (the Holy Grail/Nirvana) is the combination of being satisfied and grateful, I also know that, within the game of life, it is often fleeting and elusive—a riddle yet to be solved.

Retirement, as I am sure many of you are finding out, requires motivation and discipline (just like back in the working days) so you don't become a bloated, fat, blob on the couch who your spouse wishes would get out of the house. It is a period when you have time to commit to your dreams of lowering your golf handicap, taking a masters course in fine arts, or volunteering at the Ronald MacDonald's House. A sense of purpose at this stage is absolutely essential because the advancing years hold the supreme challenge ahead: an aging body! This brings us to the final category...

Blah! Nobody likes it. That "grow old gracefully" stuff is BS. It is said by young people or those who are old and lying through their teeth. If you disagree with me I will get sixty-six year old Sylvester Stallone to pay you a visit and straighten you out on this. But arthritis happens and it hurts. Memory loss happens and it's scary. Heart disease happens and it's frightening. Lack of respect as a senior happens and it's insulting. This latter problem is one of the few things I have found that Eastern cultures have all over us. They revere their elders because they see life as a continuum of spiritual evolution; just because the body deteriorates doesn't mean that the soul is not growing.

With 26% of the American population in or approaching their sixth decade it just may be that there is a new demand for respect of the "older generation." Certainly Madison Avenue recognizes the power of our numbers and shows only active, attractive men and women in their fifties and sixties using products that shrink the prostate, protect against osteoporosis, overcome erectile dysfunction, and lead you joyfully down the path to retirement. Our old friends Robert Wagner (pitching mortgages for the Senior Lending Network) and (until his passing in 2010) Dennis Hopper (talking about retirement for Ameriprise Financial) were used to help us relate to a new (old) stage of life. I can still see Bob romancing Natalie Wood, and Dennis riding on the back of Peter Fonda's chopper in *Easy Rider*.

Sayings like "sixty is the new fifty" and "reinventing aging" reverberate the theme that we will fight to stay "Forever Young" (performed originally by the German rock group Alphaville in 1984 and later sung by Laura Branigan, Rod Stewart, and others). Cher and Sly Stallone are certainly not the only ones stretching their skin or turning to chemicals to preserve that youthful appearance. The American Academy of Orthopaedic Surgeons claim that

80% of people taking PEDs (performance enhancing drugs) are non-elite athletes and many of them are Baby Boomers attempting to supplement for supposed hormonal deficiency (*AAOS Now,* Vol. 2, No. 10, October 2008).

Books like Natural Hormone Balance for Women by Uzzi Reiss, M.D. and, more recently, Testosterone for Life by Abraham Morgentaler, M.D. from Harvard provide compelling research that declining hormone levels, an inevitable process of aging, may well render us to a state of ill-health. Thus, it is argued, one suffers from fatigue, frailty, loss of mental acuity and libido, and other commonly accepted maladies of the elderly. With properly guided hormonal replacement and monitoring perhaps we will find more joy in the golden years.

The other side of the coin is seeing Jerry Mathers ("The Beaver") on the cover of the magazine *Diabetes* (Vol. 13, No. 4, August/September 2008) or running into an old classmate (one of those who never comes to reunions) and being stricken by how terribly old he/she looks, or the shock of looking in the mirror and seeing your dad (or mother, as the case may be).

The moribund side of aging is difficult to discuss. Unfortunately, it affects us all (if we are lucky enough to get there). The degree of decay, of course, is determined by our age, genetics, and how we take care of ourselves. All the sun exposure we got before we knew about the damaging effects of UV rays (ladies, remember lying out with reflectors, slapping on baby oil mixed with iodine?); cigarette smoke everywhere (even in the womb from Mom); recreational drugs; salami and eggs for breakfast and a big steak each night for dinner; it all adds up to damaged skin and arteries.

We had only Jack Lalanne (working out for two hours every morning until his recent demise at age ninety-six) there to give us fitness guidance ("if man made it, don't eat it;" "if it tastes good, spit it out").

Unlike the "road people" I knew and traveled with for years in the early '70s, I was hooked on running, doing push-ups, and standing on my head. So I maintained a certain level of fitness even back in the undisciplined, pleasure seeking, drug days. When I finally returned to medical school in New York City, I turned to skipping rope and running stairs; occasionally running along the FDR Highway despite the putrid smog. When I met Debbie in 1983 we immediately found that we had daily (often twice daily) exercise training routines in common. When I noticed that I was losing flexibility and balance in my fifties, I began taking Pilates instruction (despite mistakenly thinking it a joke for years). And, of course, I never smoked cigarettes.

Despite all of this and having good longevity genetics (Dad lived to eighty-five and Mom to ninety-four) I have some degree of daily back pain, generalized stiffness due to age related arthritic changes, and stroke/cardiac issues. Pilates and a sensible fitness routine have helped, but there are days when I must take NSAIDs (nonsteroidal anti-inflammatory drugs) to feel well. Every so often I have such a bad day that I can't help but think that aging gradually prepares one for death. As the body fails and hurts it becomes easier to give it up. A morose thought, no doubt, but I share it with you not to bring you down, but to tell you that you are not alone in these difficult moments.

Most recently, a longtime friend of mine from New Jersey, who used to coach my son in basketball during Eric's middle school years, called me about some hip problems he was having. Chuck, though two years my junior, retired (from his prestigious job as head of human recourses for Pfizer) about the same time as my retirement.. As an avid runner, golfer and weekend warrior, his hip pain was unacceptable. I arranged for him to see Sam, one of my partners at Garden State Orthopaedic Associates in Jersey. Sam called me after the office visit mentioning that he did not like the skin bruising he saw and advised Chuck to see his family doctor for blood work. Chuck's voicemail to me a few days later was chilling despite his calm, even upbeat delivery: "I am calling from Hackensack Medical Center, with a picc-line in my arm. They tell me I have acute leukemia and may be a candidate for their treatment protocol. I hope everyone is well at home. Thanks for referring me to Dr. Snyder; he was terrific. Talk soon."

Though his message was left more than a year ago, I continue to save Chuck's voicemail and play it for myself often. There is not a day that goes by where I don't think of the hell my friend is going through. As I walk sundrenched golf fairways, I know that I am blessed with cancer-free health and prosperity. When my back hurts I think of the painful bone marrow biopsies Chuck goes through. When I bit my tongue the other day lifting weights, I thought of the mucosal slough from chemotherapy that keeps Chuck from being able to eat, defecate, or simply swallow without excruciating pain. It is my reality check now that I am retired and no longer have the daily reminder of my patients' suffering to keep me appreciative of my own good fortune.

The fight goes on to keep things in balance. If not so much to look younger then certainly to feel younger—or at least not to feel old. I wish it really were all just a state of mind, but reaching my sixties tells me otherwise.

And after all these years—all these experiences—it comes to mind that the search goes on. With so many obstacles, answers are not easy to come by. One wonders if the discovery is really the journey itself.

Author's Note

This is the section I have been looking forward to. It is my chance to throw some random thoughts and memories out there without having to link them purposefully together. I will simply let them stand on their own as fun things representing the years of change we have all gone through. So here we go. It's free association time. `

In the '50s thirty-five percent of college students were women; today it is 60%.

In the '60s hippy counterculture many that were disdainful of material goods and free enterprise are now among the wealthiest people in the world.

Today the "American Dream" still means something (unlike a Soviet, or European dream). Let's keep it that way.

"When you're in your twenties, you make mistakes. When you're in your sixties, what's your excuse?" (Paul Simon; *Boom!* by Tom Brokaw).

Gone are the days of waiting anxiously for the *White Album* to come out. Today everything is instantly available online 24/7/365.

Do public libraries still exist? (Let me Google/Bing that question.)

The Whole Earth Catalog (the '60s search engine) is now *Google.*

Encyclopedia is now *Wikipedia.*

"Sock it to me" is now "my bad."

"Groovy" or "it's a gas" is now "awesome."

"Far-out" or "spaced out" is now "crazy" or "sick."

Let's "split" or "boogie" is now let's "peace out."

"Cat" is now "dude."

"Chick" is now "babe."

"Dynamite" is now "hot."

"Later" is now "hit me back."

"Make out" is now "hook up."

Going "steady" is now "together."

The "tube" is now the "flat screen."

"Crew cut" is now "buzz cut."

Rotary phone? Party line? Typewriter? Record player? Records? Pay phone? Soda fountain? Egg cream? Penny candy? Drive-in? Milk man? Barber pole? Gimbels? Bamberger's? Korvette's? Penny loafers? Saddle shoes? Poodle skirt? Petty coat? Neckerchief? Flash bulb? Street skates and skate keys? Doo wop? Tang? Slide rule?

The fascination with Dick Tracey's wrist radio has morphed into an obsession with pocket electronics (God help our kids and their creativity).

"When you see Earth from the moon, you realize how fragile it is and just how limited the resources are. We're all astronauts on this spaceship Earth—about six or seven billion of us—and we have to work and live together." (Captain James Lovell).

For the first half of my life I just could not understand why Jack Benny kept turning 39; now I get it.

On February 19th it will be Presidents' Day. Remember when we celebrated Abraham Lincoln's birthday on the 12th and George Washington's on the 22nd (regardless of the day of the week)?

"Youth is wasted on the young" (George Bernard Shaw).

People used to smoke on planes; now it's a federal offense to carry a lighter on one.

"The thing the '60s did was to show us the possibilities and the responsibility that we all had. It wasn't the answer. It just gave us a glimpse of the possibility." (John Lennon).

Our parents knew nothing of bicycle helmets, seat belts (much less air bags), infant car seats, tamper resistant caps on medicine and food products, and child proofing .

We drank from garden hoses and could not conceive of bottled water (much less having to pay for it).

We were out all day playing (without cell phones) and no one could reach us.

Remember hitchhiking? Everyone did it back then.

As kids we had no electronics; we had friends and we went outside and found them.

When we had Little League tryouts, not everyone made the team; if we screwed up our parents actually sided with the authority. You dealt with disappointment and no lawsuits were filed.

The lap seat belt was first offered as an option in 1955 by Ford (thanks to its executive Robert McNamara). The Saab GT 750 was the first to have seat belts as standard equipment for the front passengers. The three-point harness type was introduced by Volvo in 1959. By 1964 most US automobiles had standard front seat belts; rear belts were made standard in 1968. In 1985 New York made use of seat belts mandatory. New York became the first state to require seat belts in large school buses.

The Twist, the Stroll, the Mash Potato, the Monster Mash, the Monkey, the Swim, the Bop, the Lindy Hop, the Shag, the Jitterbug/Swing, the Hand Jive, the Cha Cha, the Madison, the Slide, the Jerk, the Slop, the Funky Chicken, the Fly, the Camel Walk, the Shimmy, the Applejack, the Quiver, the Pony, the Bump, the Hustle, the Locomotion, the Hully Gully, the Freddy, the Bird, the Duck, the Watusi, the Hitch Hike, the Hanky Panky, the Tighten Up, and the Pop Corn.

Shelley Fabares (of the Donna Reed Show) singing *Johnny Angel*.